LET THE

Rivers Clap Their Hands

MARTHA JORDAN

First printing

Let the Rivers Clap Their Hands
ISBN: 978-1-936521-01-2
Copyright ©2016 by Martha Jordan

Published by Barefoot Publishing
Tulsa, Oklahoma
www.barefootpublishing.com

Table of Contents

I dedicate this book with love to the memory of my precious granddaughter Emmalee Rose Halstead 2009-2013. I miss you.

"Let the rivers clap their hands; Let the hills sing for joy together"

Psalm 98:8 (ESV)

Prologue

1838

The Cherokees

- Trust Me, I'm From the Government -

"They're coming!" The early morning light filtered through the window, casting a faint glow on his face. His piercing black eyes were fixed upon his father. He had just flung those two words stubbornly in the air. He was Cherokee; he was thirteen; and he was afraid.

The Cherokee people had been deceived. On May 23, 1836, the United States Senate ratified a treaty. In spite of petitions with 15,656 Cherokee signatures denouncing the treaty as fraud, it was ratified. Under the provisions of the treaty, the Cherokees had been given two years to voluntarily leave their homes. Two years to leave of their own volition or they would be snatched away from the sacred grounds of their ancestors. Throughout Georgia, Tennessee, and the Carolinas, Cherokee families had been told that they would have two years to either leave peacefully or be evicted from the lands of their forefathers. They soon realized that unless they could persuade President Andrew Jackson to stop this madness, the eviction notice would be hand delivered. One hand would hold the notice, and the other hand would hold a gun. At the end of the trigger would be the strong arm of the government of the United

:s of America.

When the Europeans began landing on the eastern shores of the country, the Native Americans were already thriving, especially in the great mountains. They had made their homes among thousands of acres teeming with abundance. The land had been theirs for centuries. Contrary to what many had come to believe as fact, the Cherokee people were not troublesome savages, but rather, they operated a very sophisticated society flourishing amid order and laws.

As it is in most societies, some of the Cherokee families were in fact wealthier than others. Some of the more prominent families owned sprawling plantations. The ingenious businessmen and honorable statesmen lived quite opulent lifestyles and employed a multitude of household servants and laborers. However, most noticeable in the Cherokee villages was the thriving middle class. The Cherokees were excellent craftsmen and most of the families lived in sound and cozy log homes with outbuildings ranging from smokehouses and barns to root cellars and chicken coops.

The Cherokees living in the great mountains had also managed to successfully farm the fertile soil. Surplus corn was sold, and traded to provide cash and goods for the families. Crops grown by the Cherokees included not only corn, beans, squash and pumpkins, but also collards, English peas, lettuce, watermelons, cabbage, turnips, cucumbers, peanuts, and onions. Although the main crop grown was corn, by far the crop that was to change the history of the Cherokee people was the simple and fluffy cotton boll. The annals of history did not justly address the significance of the meager cotton boll to the demise of any honor-struck treaty binding the U.S. Government to the Cherokee tribe. Why cotton? Cotton was one crop that could not be grown in Europe. Therefore, as vast numbers of settlers sailed back and forth from Europe to America, the Europeans were quickly introduced to bolts and bolts of crisp Sea Island, cotton fabric. The small cotton farms along the eastern coast of the United States could not produce enough to satiate the distant continents desires for more of this wonderful fabric. Moreover, it was soon discovered that through mass plantings of cotton crops, the distinctive downside to the production of cotton was that in a very short time, it depleted the soil of all nutrients, leaving the once fertile ground quite useless. Hence, the newly wealthy cotton magnates, anxious to add to their coffers, soon turned their eyes upon the vast fertile farmland in the possession of the Indian tribes living in the mountains of what was then Georgia, the Carolinas, and Tennessee. Simply put, the cotton kings wanted that land, and they swiftly went to work to acquire it.

Chief John Ross and a delegation of Cherokees went to Washington, vowing to fight to the finish against the forced removal of the Cherokee people. They were the rightful owners of the land. How could the government just come in and forcibly remove them from their homes? The homes they had built with their own hands. It wasn't right and they fought the good fight, but in the end it was to no avail. President Jackson had sold them down the river. The removal was to commence in two short years. The fight was over.

The two years passed quickly, and only two thousand Cherokees voluntarily complied with the treaty and left their lives behind in the eastern United States to travel to the land that would later become known as Oklahoma, "Land of the Redman." The new land was around one thousand miles to the west of the lush mountainous areas of the great Smokey Mountains. Two years from that fateful day, on May 23, 1838, by orders of the United States government, the remainder of the Cherokee people were to be forcibly removed from their homes. They were to be gathered by the military like cattle. By force. So it was this crisp spring morning of May 26, 1838, that young John Lowry stood in the only home he had ever known, fearful yet defiant, searching for an answer from his father. "Father, the soldiers are coming. I saw them with my own eyes."

The silence in that home was deafening. Young John had always looked at his father as the bravest man he had ever known. Wise and brave, that was his father, John Lowry. He was the head of his household and respected by many in his community as a man true to his word and loyal to his clan. He stood in front of the hearth, his back to his family, hands to his sides, hands opening and closing, gripping as if he were holding everything he owned in them, fearful that if he released the hold, his life and every meaningful morsel in them would slide right off the tips of his calloused fingers. Strong hands, which had worked to bring forth crops to feed his family. Loving hands, which had tenderly cupped each of his newborn children as he welcomed them into the world. The elder John Lowry knew without a doubt that his home, his wife, and his children were all precious gifts to him from the Sacred Spirit, and it was in these hands that their trust had been placed.

He was a praying man, but at this particular moment in his life, he was at a complete standstill with God. Many times as he walked through the forests hunting for meat for the evening meal, he had felt His presence. He often looked into the clouds and felt comforted knowing he was not alone. Many times he stopped at the end of a long day to give thanks for all that had been bestowed upon his family and himself. John Lowry knew how to pray. He often prayed for wisdom, safety, and security for his loved ones, a good hunt, a bountiful harvest, even a refreshing nap. Today, however, nothing formed at the end of his lips. There were no pleas for help or cries of despair. He could not bring himself to pray. It was as if everything that lay at the bottom of his gut had suddenly been sucked right out of the top of his head.

He was an empty vessel that held the weight of the world upon his shoulders. The proud Cherokee man had the eyes of every member of his family fixed directly upon him. At that moment in time, however, he felt vastly alone. Had God chosen this moment to abandon him? Had he unknowingly angered his Great Comforter? Was this a test of faith? Releasing the grip to clear his mind, the smell of smoke began to enter the home. It was not the smoke from their chimney. The acrid smell was coming from outside. In an instant, they all clamored to the windows, and with a swift gathering of the curtains, the Lowry family stared wide-eyed as they could see the home of their neighbors engulfed in flames!

They instinctively knew that their neighbors, the Walkingstick family, had told the soldiers they would not leave. With his chest out and jutted chin, Mr. Walkingstick stood just outside his cabin door and bluntly told the soldiers that they would not walk away from their home peacefully. Therefore, without a moment's hesitation, the soldiers proceeded to kick open the door and cast ignited torches into the midst of the Walkingstick's cabin. Immediately, the rug on the wooden floor burst into an all-encompassing inferno. The United States government's soldiers had set the neighbors' home on fire, and now they were headed to the home of the Lowrys. Big John Lowry, his wife Awinita, and their three children, Young John, Tsula, and Salali stood inside their home and watched from their windows as the Walkingstick family bolted from the blazing structure, coughing and gasping for air.

In denial until the end, the Walkingsticks had not packed any of their belongings. They hastily scurried from their home with nothing but the clothing on their backs. Defiant to the last moment, now homeless, with nothing but each other.

The Lowry family saw them coming. Staring out the windows, they saw the group of people in the distance, but more profoundly, they heard the cries. Wails of despair! Young John's eyes didn't change the direction of their gaze. His thoughts were racing!

"Father, say something! Can this really be happening? What will you do, Father? Will you stand and fight these soldiers? If so, I will stand with you! I will fight!" The thoughts were spinning around in his young mind. "These soldiers will never take our home!" The vow was whispered with clenched teeth, clenched teeth of a teenaged boy, vowing to fight like a man beside his brave father!

Young John glanced at his mother, his beautiful mother, standing in the early morning light with his two little sisters, their arms wrapped tightly around her waist. His strong- willed mother, awaiting the birth of another child, stood staring out the window, taking in all of the commotion that was coming from the path outside her home. Her jaw was set as her coal-black eyes fixated upon the despair in the faces of the Walkingsticks as they headed toward her family's home.

The unborn child inside his mother's belly would arrive soon, and Young John couldn't help but think of the little baby being brought into all of the sorrow and confusion. His mother clasped her hands in front of her apron. The dishcloth she held hung in her fingers as limp as she felt at this very moment.

Amidst the confusion, they saw them coming. The soldiers, followed by the families. The Cherokee families. Women, holding their babies, tears rolling down their faces. They were trudging slowly toward the Lowry's house. They saw all of them coming, some walking, some pushing carts, some atop wagons filled with all of the earthly possessions that they could squeeze aboard in just a moment's notice.

"Quickly grab what you can! They are lighting the torches!" The torches with flames that would consume everything they touched! "Hurry, get the food and blankets!"

Young children looked at their crying mothers, all with the same question. "What is happening, Mother?"

As he peered out the window of his home in disbelief, Young John saw them coming. It was a sight he would hold in his memories as long as he would be here upon this earth. His gaze was fixed upon them. There among the weeping and wailing women and children, Young John saw them coming. He had a sickened feeling deep inside his stomach as his mind took in the sight. Once proud with shoulders erect, he could see them in the crowd, the Cherokee men. Deceived and defeated.

They were coming.

There were no words to express his anger. Young John was seething. Father did not even attempt to stop the soldiers from burning their home! Just minutes after they destroyed the home of the Walking-stick family, down the lane from the Lowry farm, the government troops trounced up to the porch stoop and hollered for the door of their home to be opened. Even though the words were spoken around a generous chaw of tobacco stuffed abundantly in his jaw, the family understood clearly what the soldier said. After quickly wiping the excess juice from his mouth onto his sleeve, the soldier bellowed, "By order of the United States government we are here to remove you from this property! You and your entire family are to abandon this place immediately. You have ten minutes to remove yourselves and any belongings you desire to bring with you. Ten minutes!" Young John's father had been the one to open the door and was practically bowled over as the group of soldiers forced their way into their home. "Ten minutes, and we won't wait one second longer!" the soldier barked. Another soldier pushed Young John's father up against the wall. This soldier did not wear the uniform of the United States army. He was with the contingency of volunteer citizen soldiers of whom the Cherokee people had been warned. The volunteer soldiers were rumored to be an irreverent and bellicose lot. They were serving their country simply for the promise of payment upon delivery with no expectation of compliance to any of the rules or regulations spoken or implied by the swift execution of the oath. The oath that was sworn with a wink as they were gathered from every saloon and street corner throughout the countryside.

The barrel of a gun against his ribcage quickly convinced John Lowry that those rumors were in fact truths, and he, therefore, chose not to resist. He did nothing but look toward his wife, Awinita. "We will go. Gather what we have prepared. Young John. Young John! Help your sisters. We must go."

Their home went up in flames as they fell into line with the other families, and Young John Lowry could not take his eyes off of the blazing structure. Hot tears streaked down his cheeks. He looked at his parents and noticed that they did not, or would not, look back.

"They are treating us like cattle!" Young John barked toward his father.

What had happened to his father? Why didn't he stand and fight those soldiers? his thoughts screamed back at him. Nothing made sense. Just yesterday he had gone to the stream with his father, and they had caught enough fish for his mother to fix for supper. He had played games with his friends in the forest, the same forest that they were slowly leaving behind. Nothing made sense to him.

They trudged on for miles that first day. More families were gathered; more homes were burned. Young John witnessed some of the men trying to resist and fight the soldiers. The ones that resisted were beaten. Many of them were introduced to the "business end" of a rifle, as the bayonet was pointed between their eyes. As much as a young boy could, he was beginning to understand why his father chose not to fight. It still made him angry to think about it, but somewhere in his mind, he was beginning to see that there were only two choices: go peacefully like sheep or attempt to fight and be treated like dogs. There were only two choices.

Futility and frustration set in quickly as the Lowry family realized their quandary. They barely understood the seriousness of their present situation. Simply put, they did not bring a wagon. Young John's father had been repairing the wheel the night before when Samuel Longknife and Jasper Walkingstick had run up to John and told him of the emergency gathering of the council at the meeting lodge. Upon hearing the unsettling news, John Lowry threw down his tool, and the three men left hurriedly to attend the meeting. It was there in the village council house that they were told the soldiers were on their way. Long into the wee hours of the morning the group gathered in the meeting lodge. Hollow voices. Some rang loud. Some were inaudible whispers of disbelief. Fists rose, and heads shook. Hats were pulled from Cherokee heads then slapped along the sides of their legs in a futile exercise of defiance. The hours crept by as the Cherokee men finally realized the inevitable. All hopes of defeating this travesty were lost. They would be forcibly removed from the Great Mountains and escorted by the soldiers to a place many miles to the west. They had heard rumors that Cherokee scouts had traveled to this new land and had come back with news that this place was "like a desert, with sticks for trees."

The fact was they were not an organized army of Indian men. They were reluctantly and painfully absorbing that plain reality. They knew then and there that they had to leave the land of their ancestors. Mountains green with lush forests. Cool, clear streams brimming with fish. Spring had just come to the mountains, and they were alive with wildlife.

At daybreak, they would leave paradise to go to the desert.

Each Cherokee man walked slowly back to his home to break the devastating news to his waiting family. The sun was slowly rising on the fateful nightmare that was to ensue. John Lowry's steps were slow and methodical. His thoughts were centered on Awinita and the children. How would he tell them? He was exhausted from the long night meeting. The closer he got to his home, he sensed an awful dread surrounding his entire being. Everything he had been taught by his own father was grounded in Cherokee pride with a strong emphasis on bravery and honor.

John Lowry had arrived home empty handed as he placed his foot on the stoop of his home. He had nothing for his family but sorrow. He turned to gaze at his beautiful mountains, trying his best to soak in their vastness. Could they reach out and tuck his family into a secret hiding place amongst the dark crevices in the rocks and trees? Run! Hide! Escape! They were his mountains. The Cherokee people had owned these mountains for centuries.

No more. It was over.

As he took one last look before entering his home, he knew it could not be denied. From his porch, he could see that about a mile from his home the soldiers were coming toward the village. It was over. He didn't wonder what he would say to his family as he realized the soldiers were preparing their own announcement in just a matter of time.

Awinita and the children were already gathered in the living room. The two young sisters had slept off and on, but Awinita and Young John had kept their own vigil throughout the night, waiting for some news of their plight. They had prayed for good news from the village meeting. They could do nothing but pace the floor all night long. Young John and Awinita had the same sense of dread that had enveloped the entire community. Sadly, their fears were confirmed as John Lowry entered the house with a stoic silence. He could not look them in the eye as he strode toward the hearth. Young John bolted toward the door and ran out and down the path toward the neighbor's house. It wasn't long before he was confronted with the same sight that had taken his father's breath away just moments before. The soldiers were indeed coming. It was over. Ten minutes. They had ten minutes to gather their life here in the Great Mountains. The soldiers were not giving an inch. Their scowls and rifles spoke volumes. With the broken wheel still lying beside the wagon there was no choice but to send Young John scurrying out behind the barn to fetch the two wheeled cart. His mother hastily gathered as much as she could scoop into her arms. She heaped it full of dishes, pots, pans, blankets, clothing, and food. Young John's two little sisters, Tsula and Salali, had made sure that their cornhusk dolls found a prominent place to ride in the cart, little handmade faces peeking out from between Young John's hand hewn bow and a soot covered coffee pot.

Profoundly, there had simply not been enough time to do a thorough checklist of their belongings. No last minute chances to grab precious heirlooms. Heirlooms, which had been tenderly guarded through the years, were now being reduced to a smoldering pile of ashes. Gone forever.

Mile after mile, they pushed the cart filled with all of their earthly belongings. The soldiers did not allow them to stop and rest very often this first long day of their journey. Mother was exhausted. She had grown heavy with the unborn child that she carried in her womb. Tears ran down her cheeks as she held her hands to her lower back. Young John knew that his mother was in pain. The only consolation was the sight of the sun going down behind the mountain. It brought hope that they would all be able to stop and rest for the evening.

They were soon glad to see that up ahead, the families were beginning to stop walking. They would be stopping for the night. Young John was tired and hungry and emotionally drained. It would be nice to rest.

Their meal would consist of bean bread that his mother had made fresh that morning. It tasted so good. He thought he would be able to eat more than his share, but he realized that he was too tired to eat more than one piece. He wanted to sleep. He clung to the hope that this was a bad dream and that when he awoke, he would be back in his house, snuggled in his bed, with mother fixing breakfast.

Sleep came quickly, and he was soon dreaming that he was in the forest playing with his friends, carefree and laughing, loving life in the forest.

Unfortunately, however, his dream didn't last long. He woke with a start and saw the soldiers' torches bobbing in the distance and heard their angry voices. He wasn't sure what they were saying, but many of the conversations ended with a cry from one of the members of the other families. He was afraid, but he would never admit it. He was a proud Cherokee and would not let those cries break him. He would be brave. He kept telling himself he would be brave. He continued repeating those words quietly to himself as he cried himself back to sleep. The morning came much too quickly and with it the realization that the nightmare was real. They would have just a short time to eat some more of the bean bread before they would start walking again. Long days, short nights. Tears and sorrow. That was the new world of the families that made their way west. Soldiers barking orders. The heartbreaking saga seemed to have no end in sight. The stick that Young John had picked up alongside the trail left a small furrow in the dirt as he let it dangle loosely in his hand. His mind wandered back to the Great Mountains. He imagined himself swimming naked in the cool waters of the stream. In his vision he and his friends were laughing as they each took turns pretending to be a stalking bear. His friends. He realized he had not seen his friends since they left their village for this tortuous journey. Would he ever play again? Would he ever laugh again? He could not muster the gumption it took to even go to that place in his mind.

The days turned to weeks of sadness, hunger, and sickness.

The sickness.

There was a horrible sickness with bony fingers winding its way throughout the Cherokee families. Fingers that seemed to point at random and steal the life from one after another, sickness then death. Young and old would be surrounded by the sickness akin to a fog settling on the mountain. The Cherokee medicine elders had relied on herbs from the woods as remedies to cure their tribesmen of various illnesses. Unfortunately their supplies of such herbs were quickly depleted and they were not allowed to forage for more along the trail. They watched as their friends and relatives lay dying. They had no remedies at hand, as many fellow Cherokees fell to the sickness. Adding further torment to their pain, the soldiers would not allow the Cherokee people the time to administer the proper funerary rites to their dead. They were forced to leave them where they took their last hollow breath. Dead bodies lined the trail. Anguished mothers were seen clinging to their tiny, lifeless babies, refusing to leave them to be torn apart by the coyotes, which taunted in the distance.

Young John was startled back to reality by a loud cry. It was his mother! She sank to her knees grabbing her belly as she slid to the ground.

Was it the sickness? Was his mother going to die? He was immediately stricken with fear. No, not Mother! Several women hastily surrounded Awinita. They quickly covered her with blankets and wheeled around on their knees to shoo the onlookers away. She was in labor, and it was obvious that the time was very near. Father sent Young John and the other children scurrying over to the Walkingstick family.

It wasn't long before they heard the faint cry of an infant. Young John could not stay put. He ran to his mother's side just in time to see his new brother. The women were wrapping him in a cloth and scolded Young John for peeking in on the activity. He felt so relieved! His mother seemed fine, and his brother had arrived. That was about as much as a young boy could absorb at the moment.

Lamentably, it wasn't long before the soldiers made their way back to the group to see what, or who, was making all of the commotion. One soldier barked toward the women huddled around Awinita and her newborn son.

"Git her up! You're a'wastin' daylight! Move on now!" It hadn't taken the Cherokee people long into their journey to realize that any order coming from the soldiers should be followed with haste. "Hell to pay" was an understatement. Father hastened over to Awinita and tenderly helped her up from the ground. He placed his strong arm around her waist and started to slowly guide her in the direction of the trail. He held her up for hours as they walked the dusty road. She was weak and in pain but managed to keep a steady pace. Awinita's sheer will and determination helped her put one foot in front of the other. The long day had stretched into early evening as the weary band of travelers made their way along the path.

Young John could see that it was a struggle, but he knew if anyone could muster the strength it would be his mother. His sisters took turns carrying their little brother. Young John and another young Cherokee boy pushed the family cart.

John Lowry never released his grip on Awinita. As the sun was setting on the western horizon, he could be seen gently lowering his brave and beautiful wife to the blanket on the ground. Finally, she could rest.

The little family gathered around their mother and father as Young John took the tiny infant from his sister and tenderly laid him into the crook in Awinita's arm. "He will be called, Degotega" Awinita whispered, meaning standing together. It fit. Father stood and placed his arms around his family as they stood looking down at Mother and Degotega. They felt safe that night. They were always comforted when their father wrapped his arms tightly around them. They felt loved and safe. And so, on that night, they felt safe.

It wasn't long before word reached back to their assemblage that the soldiers had received orders from the government that they were to make sure the Cherokee families reached the ferry in no later than three weeks' time. The Indian scouts calculated, and three weeks to travel that distance was not good news for the Cherokees. If they felt they had been prodded like cattle up to this point, they knew that it was going to be even worse with such an unrealistic demand being placed upon this weary band of displaced souls.

Compounding their misery, many of the new mothers found that due to the lack of food and water and the toll that the many miles of walking had placed on their bodies, their breasts were unable to produce enough milk to feed their newborn babies. Such was also the case for Young John's mother, Awinita. His little baby brother, Degotega, was beginning to cry harder and harder as Awinita's breasts went dry. Young John saw fear for the first time in his mother's eyes.

The contingency of Cherokees traipsing down the road had encountered many different people along the way. More often than not they were met with signs displayed in the yards of the settlers, "Go away savages" or "Don't come here. We have nuthin for you." In lieu of signage, some farmers sat quietly on their stoops holding their rifles. The Cherokees didn't need anything posted in their yards to understand the meaning of these displays, but every so often, they came upon a kind soul willing to share a scrap or two with one of the daring tribesmen, baring the fortitude to sneak up to the back door to ask for a handout for his starving family. Even if it was slop meant for their farm animals, the Cherokees would consider it a blessing to receive any kind of nourishment offered. Valiantly, Young John vowed to not stand idly by and watch his little brother starve to death. Against prior admonishments from his parents, Young John decided that the very next farm they came to, sign or no sign, gun or no gun, day or night, he would go. He would go to save his brother.

As luck would have it, the very next farm did not bode well for Young John's plan. In bold letters, the sign said, "Go away injuns." The sun was beginning to set, and there was the silhouette of a man standing on the porch. A faint smoke ring circled from his pipe as he caressed the long rifle in his hands.

The Cherokee families passed by in silence, trudging step by step toward their destination. Young John felt a hollowness in his stomach as he was momentarily stung with doubt. Was this going to be the end for his little brother? The hopelessness of the situation was starting to swallow him when suddenly he saw her! Out of the back door of the farmhouse came a woman. She was standing with something in her hand. Was that a pail? Young John sprang into action! In and out of the moonlight he weaved toward the back of the house. Stopping abruptly, wide-eyed in the darkness, he heard her voice.

"Who is there?" she whispered.

Silence.

"I know you are there. Come over here." She had a kindness in her voice that made Young John let down his guard. His trembling knees were knocking together as he carefully stepped into the yard.

"What are you doing here, youngun?" the woman spoke with a tinge of fear in her voice.

Young John slowly moved toward the woman with his head down. "Ma'am, can you please spare some milk for my little brother?" The lady looked down into the pail that hung in her hand. "There's nothing in this pail but some curdled milk that I was gonna give my hog."

She looked up at Young John and knew by the pained expression in the young man's eyes that the pail of spoiled milk meant life or death for his little brother. "Here, feller, take it, and run fast, son! My husband will shoot you dead if he sees you on our land!"

Young John had never run so fast or so hard in all of his young life. The contents of the bucket sloshed and swirled, but he did not spill one single drop. Running back to the campsite toward his family, in and out of the moonlight, he glanced toward the house. From the corner of his eye he saw the man come lumbering down the steps, rifle in his hand!

"Who's out there? Dag-nabbit! I'll shoot!"

Young John was like a deer as he made his way back. Long, quick strides. He kept the bucket handle firmly in his grasp. The man stopped a few feet from the porch looking out into the darkness.

"Must have been a varmint," he muttered to himself as he turned to head back up the steps.

Young John kept up his pace and didn't look back. His heart was pounding right out of his chest when he reached his mother. "This is for my brother." He could barely catch his breath.

His mother grabbed the pail from Young John and began to feed the baby the sour, lumpy milk. The small mouth pursed open to receive the nourishment, just as a baby bird would beg for a worm.

Awinita turned to Young John and cupped his sweaty face in her hands. She peered deep into his sad black eyes and whispered, "You saved him. God will smile on you. Now go get some sleep."

The word of the forced removal of the Cherokee people spread like a wildfire throughout the mountains of southern Tennessee. Many of the tribesmen held secret meetings in caves hidden amidst the piney woods. Their people were being herded westward like sheep, and they had no clue to how to fight this futile battle. Would they just give in and give up their land and homes?

The Cherokee people were not without allies among the few white settlers in the mountains. Sprinkled throughout the faces in the meetings would be a loyal friend or two. They had formed the bonds of friendship, and the white people were there to see if they could think of anything to help. There is an old saying, "two great minds on one great channel," and the scheme, which was hatched in those caves, was phenomenal. It would take courage and loyalty to pull it off, as well as a lot of theatrics, but pull it off they did, on a grand scale!

The intricately concocted plan called for those that decided to try to stay to hide in the caves as long as they could. Friends would sneak them food and supplies. When they received word that it was safe, they would slowly and methodically begin to reintroduce themselves to the community as immigrants from a foreign land. In some areas, they were known as "Black Irish." In most of the mountainous areas, they would call themselves "Black Dutch." They even changed their names to match their new nationalities.

They didn't necessarily always pick Dutch sounding names. Quite often, they would simply choose an English name such as Miller, Johnson, Brown, Butler or Tiffin. "Miss Sarah, I would like to introduce you to my cousin Sally. Sally Johnson. Coffee or tea, Mrs. Johnson? Why, Mrs. Johnson you are going to have to share with us what it was like to live in... now where is it you are from? Oh, yes, yes, maybe I have heard of that place. Here have another cookie, Mrs. Johnson. Welcome to Tennessee."

To put it simply, it worked. Whether it was because the government of the United States was so embroiled in the fiasco that was playing out farther west with the Cherokee people freezing to death and dropping like flies along the trail or perhaps it was that the Cherokee people had a flair for the stage, all that mattered was that it worked.

As time went by, the Black Dutch "immigrants" soon began to intermarry with the white settlers. When asked, they would deny their Indian heritage and cling to their stories of traveling from some far off land. It was a tremendous price to pay, but they did it for the love of their native land. Life wasn't always easy from that point on, and it was often a dangerous time for the Indian people in those Great Mountains. Therefore some of them did stay and continued to farm the lands, hunt the forests, and fish the streams.

Joseph Calls the Wind chose for his family the Dutch surname of Vann. He and his wife, Mary, reintroduced themselves and settled back into existence on their family farm, which had been in their possession for many generations. They soon added seven children to their clan. Farming was in their blood. The children joined in as soon as they were old enough to carry a bucket or pull a rake. The Vann family loved farming. However, there was one exception: the one son with the wanderlust they named Amos.

Amos was a day dreamer. He was mesmerized by the tales he heard about the West. Several of the Indian families that had been able to remain in Tennessee were beginning to get word back from other family members that had survived the trail westward. Quite surprisingly, sprinkled within the tales of woe, there began to be tales of excitement.

What about those sticks for trees they had heard about? Wasn't the land to the west nothing but a dry, barren desert? Apparently after the winter had stripped the trees of their leaves, springtime in Oklahoma soon brought those sticks to life with an abundance of green leaves! Farms in the new land were producing quite a variety of crops. Many of the Indian families were finding new wealth after their trek westward. Oil had been struck on the Indian lands! Black gold made many Indians instant millionaires! The railroads were winding their ways westward and the news from the West was front-page news in the East! "Go West, Young Man" was the current slogan that beckoned to those who had a taste for travel and adventure!

Amos Vann could taste the west as if it sat smack dab on a plate in front of his face! He spent countless hours daydreaming of living in the land of oil, money, women, and song! Farm chores were like a dim bulb in comparison to the way he felt lit up every time he would sit and listen to travelers spin him around and around with the stories of the new land of the Cherokees, Oklahoma! His bag was packed, his family was in shock, and Amos Vann was headed west!

The Englishmen

- Setting Sail For America -

Yorkshire, England in the spring of 1838 was conflicted indeed. The Industrial Revolution had commenced in England before it hit Europe and the United States. What was considered a boon for some in the cities, only brought about misery and poverty for the rural farm-

31

ing communities scattered throughout the English countrysides and the poor working-class citizens in the factory villages. Charles Dickens had just published his novel, Oliver Twist, which graphically portrayed the dismal conditions surrounding these unfortunate families. Workhouses were becoming commonplace, and no hope for a better life was anywhere in sight.

Even though word would trickle in that life was better across the ocean, mass emigration to Australia, North America, or South America was actively discouraged by the English government. It was felt that England needed men to serve in the American and European wars of the late eighteenth and early nineteenth centuries plus the loss of manpower in the factories would not benefit the goals of the Empire. Victoria had been on the throne for only a year, and she had visions of grandeur for her reign.

Henry Thomas Devon had grown weary of the effects of the downturn in the economy in his beloved England. A silversmith by trade, times were hard and money was tight. He saw nothing but a dismal future for his family. His only son, Thomas Henry, was just a young lad, but his father could already see his brilliant mind. Henry could not sit idly by and watch his son's future squandered merely because Queen Victoria wanted a legacy. Henry had gotten reports from other friends and family members who had taken the plunge by loading all of their earthly belongings aboard an ocean liner to sail to the new country across the Atlantic. America was the land of opportunity. Dreams were becoming reality, and Henry realized that he'd have but one chance in this life to give his family a shot at a better future.

Ellis Island was in the distance. He had to pinch himself as the ship neared the harbor. He had done it. Henry Devon had uprooted his family from the only country they had ever called home and set sail for America.

They pulled their trunks behind them as they disembarked the ship, going through the proper checkpoints on Ellis Island, and from there, the Devon family boarded a train that took them to a city called Franklin, Tennessee, joining awaiting extended family members who were already well on their way to success in America.

He was a foreigner in this new land, and Henry wanted nothing more than to have his family assimilate as quickly as they could, to join the ranks of other immigrants from all over the world who desired to become Americans. He wanted nothing better for his son, Thomas, than to be a proud American.

Chapter 1

Pickford and Kate

Pickford Watie's family had come to Oklahoma in 1838 by way of the Cherokee Trail of Tears. Forcefully removed from their home in North Carolina, his family suffered greatly along the way. However, his staunchly proud Cherokee parents never spoke of the tragedy except for the one kind United States Army soldier who had a huge heart for the band of travelers in his keep. His name was Pickford Aloysius Sullivan. The Watie family owed their lives to Pickford Sullivan, so in his honor, their son was given the name Pickford. Pickford Aloysius Watie.

When Pickford Watie first laid eyes upon Kate Lowry, he could have sworn that a celestial choir hit their highest notes in celebration of that second glance, which almost put a crick in his twisted neck! "Ain't she a purty one!" Pickford sighed under his breath, as he jumped off the wagon and headed immediately to scoop up the wayward ball of yarn that had rolled out of Kate's satchel.

"Here you go, Miss. I'm thinkin' that you might need this here ball of yarn. The weather's changin' and no tellin' what comfort you could bring to a pair of cold feet when you twirl this yarn into a set of cozy socks!"

Kate had no idea that the yarn had taken a mind of its own and jumped right out of her satchel and rolled conspicuously toward Pickford's wagon. Could it be that a helper from above picked that exact moment in time to stroll by and flick an angelic wing tip to the ball of yarn in Miss Kate's satchel? Mountains have been moved, so why not yarn? Furthermore, that celestial choir had probably been tuning up, knowing that they would soon be witnessing a divinely orchestrated miracle right in front of Parker's General Store!

The sudden appearance of the charming Cherokee man, grinning from ear to ear with a familiar looking ball of yarn in his hand, sent a red hot flush to the cheeks of the startled Kate Lowry.

"Why, thank you, I don't know how that ended up in your possession, but I am certainly grateful that you saved it from sinking into that big mud puddle. Washing a ball of yarn wasn't on my schedule of things to do today," she said with a coy grin.

Pickford couldn't contain himself and jumped right in with the presumptuous notion that perhaps Kate's schedule for the day's activities could be altered to include more than just polite introductions and a bit of small talk. He slid his hat off his head and with both hands held it tight to his chest.

"My name is Pickford Watie. I recognize you as John Lowry's daughter, Kate, and since, thanks to me, you won't be havin' to wash that ball of yarn today, maybe you could fill that open space of time with some porch time with me, say, in about an hour?" His grin was infectious.

Kate was so taken by surprise at the boldness of this handsome man that she couldn't believe her ears when she heard herself actually agreeing to hurry home to get the approval of her father for welcoming Mr. Pickford Watie to her front porch. She also couldn't believe her own eyes when she witnessed, first hand, herself being lifted back up into her buggy by his strong arms, barely stopping to tell him goodbye, grabbing the reins, and sending her mule an urgent message by the fiery slap of the leather,

"Hurry, old Hank! Get me home fast!" That trip home couldn't have been counted by a stopwatch. Kate had Old Hank at breakneck speed as she turned her buggy into the lane and headed toward the house.

"Mother! Mother!" she was breathless as she flew through the front door. The old screen door slammed behind her as she raced through the house and was quickly planted right in front of her mother, who was dutifully busying herself in the kitchen.

"Kate! My goodness! What in the world has you so worked up? Are you okay?" Kate's mother stuffed the dishtowel in the front of her apron. Her mother quickly started to chuckle as she smoothed her daughter's windblown hair. "Well, well, and just who is he? It is written all over your face."

Kate hurriedly and breathlessly relayed the chance encounter in front of Parker's as her mother stood with her two feet planted in front of Kate. Mother's arms were crossed, cautious and inquisitive.

"Is it all right, Mother? Can he come visit just out on the porch? Please?" When her mother realized that twenty minutes of the awaited hour had just been swallowed up in explanations, she jumped into gear.

"Go freshen up, I'll run out in the garden and warn, I mean, inform your father," she said with a wink.

Kate's father, John Lowry, loved his family beyond measure. As a young boy, he had made the horrendous trip across the country on the Trail of Tears. The memories of the travesty that had befallen his family would be forever etched in his heart and mind. His own father, Big John, had become ill in the extreme winter conditions, collapsed, and froze to death along the trail before they reached their destination. Young John, his mother Awinita, siblings Tsula, Salali, and tiny Degotega, were all completely devastated by the loss of such a great man. However, Young John had not hesitated to step up as man of the house, and he and his mother, Awinita, forged ahead, making their way in the new land.

To say that John Lowry was protective of his precious daughter, Kate, was an understatement. John Lowry would definitely be front and center when it came to picking a worthy suitor for his only daughter.

Kate looked down at her gingham print dress and turned a few circles in front of the mirror in the hallway and declared herself suitor ready. Apparently her father didn't feel the need to bring the machete that he was using to chop weeds in the garden into the house, and to Kate and her mother that was a very good sign. Mother scurried about to make a fresh pot of tea from the roots of the sassafras trees, which grew haphazardly throughout the woods behind their house. The smell of a good pot of sassafras permeated the air, butter cookies were placed neatly on a lace edged platter, all in good time.

Almost to the second, as the hour approached, there was a light tap on the screen door. John Lowry opened the front door and welcomed Pickford into his home. Mr. Lowry was well acquainted with Pickford's father, John. John Watie had a good reputation, and John Lowry was more than willing to show hospitality to a good neighbor's boy.

True to her nature and good sense of timing, her mother came forth with the tea and cookies. Pickford went through the motions of sipping the tea and taking small bites of the sweet treats, but his attention could not be moved from the sheer beauty that he saw as Kate entered the living room and hurriedly ushered everyone out to the front porch. Kate loved the smell of lilacs growing by the house. In fact, her favorite pastime was sitting on the porch, enjoying good company, and smelling the sweet aroma of the lilacs.

It seemed that no topic was left unturned as the afternoon was filled with tidbits of news, weather, crops, and the soon to be completed schoolhouse. On and on the group of four chatted. It wasn't long into the afternoon that Pickford displayed his knack for turning Kate into a giggling schoolgirl.

The hours passed quickly, and the sun began to dip slowly into the west. Reluctantly, Pickford stood to stretch his legs and bid the Lowry family a fond farewell. Their kindness had made him feel at home, and he sure did want to stay longer. But after a heartfelt invitation to stay for supper, Pickford knew he had various farm animals that needed his attention. He told them he was much obliged, but he needed to go home and do his evening chores and get ready to help his father plant corn the next morning.

Pickford removed his hat and shook Mr. and Mrs. Lowry's hands and turned to leave. He sauntered down the steps, paused just a moment, and slowly turned back to Kate.

"Miss Lowry, I sure am glad that ole ball of yarn rolled my way. It just wouldn't have been right for you to have had to spend your time over a bucket of soapy water, and well, I don't know how your schedule might be looking for tomorrow evening about this same time, but mine sure does have an open spot."

Kate was swooning over the mile-wide grin of this handsome young man standing not even two feet from her when Mother spoke up, "Pickford, you just bring yourself right back over here tomorrow evening, and Kate and I will have a nice meal set out. "

"You're sure to be worn out after a hard day of plowing and seeding that corn!" Kate excitedly echoed her mother's invitation and giggled as her suitor agreed to their next meeting.

All three Lowrys stood and watched as Pickford Watie jumped up in his wagon, clicked the reins, and headed off into the evening sun toward his parents' farm.

"He's as twitterpated as an old hound dog, Kate!" Mother joked as the last sight of Pickford's wagon turned the bend in the road. Kate blushed and as far as her mother and father were concerned, Kate shared equally in the twitterpation.

The courtship was brief, and before a small crowd of family and friends, the feisty and playful Kate Lowry said her wedding vows, and they were answered heartily by her Cherokee prince.

Pickford scooped Kate up into his arms, loaded her onto his wagon and headed down the road to follow their dreams and begin their lives together.

Their love nest was a cute dog-trot cottage nestled on the edge of the Lowry's acreage. Pickford farmed from sunup to sundown while Kate busied herself around the house counting the seconds until her handsome husband would bound up the steps of their home and scoop her up in his brawny embrace, planting sweet kisses on her forehead. He was tender, playful, strong, and wholly smitten with his beautiful Kate.

Nine months to the day after their wedding, Kate gave birth to a strong baby boy. Kate's instructions were that he was to be named Columbus. She loved reading about the history of her country and thought it fitting that her first born would carry the name of the explorer from Spain that discovered America.

Columbus Watie. Pickford gently held the little child in his strong hands and kissed the forehead of his son. Tears ran down his face onto the head of his newborn infant. On this very day, he witnessed the arrival of his son, and on the day following, he would be burying the baby's mother.

Two hours into her labor, it was obvious to Kate's mother that her only child was in serious trouble. She fought valiantly to live. She had looked forward to many days ahead where she could raise her baby and be a good wife to her beloved husband. As her mother and several of the neighboring women did the best that they could to help, the struggle was in vain. The baby came as Kate took her last breath. She held on as long as she could, and the loud cry of the infant seemed to be the signal that it was okay for her to go.

Kate was dead.

Pickford handed little Columbus to Nellie Fortner as he knelt beside the bed. He took Kate's lifeless hand and intertwined his fingers around hers. He kissed her gently on the lips and whispered into her ear, "Please know that you were the light of my life. I will always love you, my precious."

As he stood and turned to take back his baby, the floodgates were opened, and an endless river of tears streamed steadily down his face. The kind and gentle farmer was with his love as the angels came and took her home. Standing there beside her bed, Pickford stared at her lifeless body. She looked so peaceful. She had clung to life with everything in her. He wondered, did her soul tarry awhile to see her husband hold their child? He imagined that she stood before him and took his face in her hands and bid him goodbye with a tender kiss upon his lips. He could almost feel her presence in the room as he held their child. He prayed that she had placed a kiss upon the pink and heart shaped lips of little Columbus. Her body had given up her beautiful soul to be with her Lord and Savior. He knew that to be a fact. He held their son tight and promised God that he would be a good father and strive to be a good man.

He also had to remind himself to breathe.

Kate's mother walked silently toward the window beside her daughter's bed and slowly raised the sash to let some fresh air into the stuffy room. As if by a special order sent from above, a sudden breeze billowed the curtains and a familiar aroma filled the room. Lilacs.

"Goodbye, our precious one! We will see you one fine day as we join together on the distant shore!" Kate's mother shouted. She too felt the fading presence of her daughter's spirit. Kate Lowry Watie was now safe in the arms of Jesus.

Chapter 2

The Sun Rises and
Sets Like Clockwork

Pickford took to calling his little boy Kip. He was proud of the name Columbus, but every time he would see his young son peek around the corner of the kitchen table, the child would beckon to his father to play a game of hide and seek by trying to say the name Pickford. It always came out "Kipper," a kind of backwards version of Pickford. Kipper became Kip, and the name stuck. Little Kip was ornery and playful, just like his mother.

With Kate's death, Pickford was determined to make a good life for his son. No matter how exhausted he would be from a day in the field, he always took the time to play with Kip. Kate's mother cared for her grandson during the day but as soon as Pickford came home from farming, Kip knew whose lap to find. Kip went everywhere with Pickford.

They were inseparable.

Pickford's love for his son was often overshadowed by his profound grief. He missed his beautiful wife, and it wasn't hard to realize that he was lonely. One look at his son, who was the spitting image of his mother coupled with the waves of heartache that fell over him on a regular basis, made the days somewhat unbearable. Pickford knew that he needed to go on with his life. He was still a very young man, and even though he was an excellent father, Pickford knew that Kip was in need of a mother.

He prayed that God would send him a virtuous woman with a good heart. He asked God to make her a good momma to Kip, and while he was at it, he figured he might as well fill in the rest of the blanks—a good cook and mighty "purty."

God and his infinite wisdom didn't tarry, and before long, through mutual friends, Pickford was introduced to a short, sweet, and "purty" Cherokee woman who had recently lost her husband, Chester Barnes, in a freak accident while working on the construction of the railroad. The St. Louis and San Francisco Railroad (The Frisco) was winding its way through southeastern Oklahoma by hook or by crook, and it seemed that Chester Barnes learned the hard and tragic way that constructing a trestle passage for the railway over a lazy river could be a deadly undertaking. His fall was swift and his death was instant as his head landed squarely on a sharp river rock. News of the accident traveled fast, and Simmy Squirrel Barnes found herself widowed and heartbroken. Chester had fathered two sons with Simmy. Two youngsters, Ernest and Howard Barnes, were fatherless and grief-stricken after suffering such a profound loss.

As was common in their culture, Simmy's tight knit circle of family and friends pitched in to help her in any way they could. The neighboring towns were small and news was passed around in bits and pieces by chance encounters over fence posts, in front of stores, and between two passing buggies on a well-worn dirt road.

It wasn't long before the two families traded their stories of the mutual losses suffered by Pickford and Simmy, and the matchmaking was quickly set in place.

In a whirlwind courtship, Pickford and Simmy fell in love and were married in Sallisaw, Oklahoma in a ceremony that intermingled Cherokee customs and Christian vows. Their two broken hearts came together as one, and it didn't take long for young Kip Watie to settle into life with his ready-made family.

Pickford and Kip had found a happy home when Simmy took the reins. She had the merriest eyes that twinkled above her chiseled, Cherokee cheekbones. Short in stature but tall in the kitchen, Simmy Watie could whip up a meal that was "larrupin' good!" The children quickly bonded, and Ernest and Howard Barnes soon took Kip, their new step-brother, under their wings.

Pickford continued to farm the land that the Lowrys had made available to Kate and Pickford. The Lowrys were happy for Pickford and Kip, and they soon fell in love with Simmy and her two sons and welcomed them with open arms as their extended family.

Pickford and Simmy increased the size of their family with the addition of a baby brother, Edgar. Then came daughter, Nellie and two years after that another baby girl, Ophelia. They had a bustling life on the farm. The older boys helped Pickford with the plantings and the smaller children stayed under Simmy's feet as she busied around the house, keeping the cupboard filled with food and making sure Old Bossy the cow gave wholesome milk, enough to satisfy her hungry brood.

Life on the farm with Pickford and Simmy Watie was never dull. With Pickford's sense of humor and Simmy's giggles, the Waties and their six children found life, love, and laughter abounding in the modest house. Surrounded by music on the Watie side of the family, Pickford soon mastered the fiddle and often the house was not only filled with the wonderful smells coming from Simmy's kitchen, but also toe-tapping music echoing from the rafters. It was not uncommon, after the farm chores were done for the week, to find a gathering of family and friends at the Watie's house on a Saturday evening. Simmy and the other Cherokee women would fill the long wooden tables with food as Pickford and the other men tuned up their instruments for a long evening of fellowship and music. Hymns in the Cherokee language, accompanied by the beat of a distant drum were intermingled with the newer sounding melodies sang in English. The slow cadence of the Cherokee dance steps was often overshadowed by the introduction of the foot stomping and twirling of the Irish jigs. The railroad certainly brought change to the Cherokee people who had settled in Oklahoma!

Change was evident. However, interwoven within the excitement and uncertainty of change came hardships. The hardships were many for the families in the country, and the Waties had their share.

One sunny afternoon, Pickford was plowing the fields preparing for the next crop of peanuts, when his old mule, Lester, spooked by a rattlesnake, bucked and twisted in his harness. Pickford was walking closely behind his trusted animal and never knew what hit him when the frightened animal's hind hoof was planted directly into Pickford's fore-head. His neck was broken in an instant, and death came quickly to the kind and gentle Oklahoma farmer.

Simmy was in the chicken coop gathering eggs when she heard Lester braying uncontrollably. She shoved her egg basket on the shelf and went running toward the field. All six children heard the commotion and fell in line behind Simmy. Instinctively, Simmy knew before she reached her husband that he was dead. As she ran, she began to loosen her apron so that she could quickly place it over Pickford's twisted and bleeding head, shielding the horrid sight from the children. "Pickford! No!" she screamed as she fell down beside him. She cradled his head in her lap, rocking back and forth, as one by one, the four boys and two girls made their way to the field.

Their father was gone.

Lester the mule had stomped the rattlesnake to death and had calmed down enough to turn and face the crowd. When Ernest Barnes had heard the commotion outside, he had grabbed his shotgun on his way out of the door. By the time he reached the field and saw his beloved step-father lying dead in the neatly plowed row of dirt, he didn't hesitate to raise the gun and pull the trigger, planting a bullet smack dab into Lester's forehead. The old mule fell with a thud right where he stood. With mother's face still buried deep into Pickford's chest and the other children standing motionless beside her, it seemed the right thing to do. The old mule had to carry their pain to his demise.

The early afternoon sun was beating down upon their necks and standing there in a stair-step row beside their mother, Ernest, Howard, Kip, Edgar, Nellie, and Ophelia burst into a simultaneous eruption of tears and sobs. Along with Simmy, they were totally inconsolable. Pickford was gone, and they were heartbroken beyond measure.

It seemed like an eternity. The seven of them huddled around Pickford as he lay lifeless in the patch of turned up earth. What a contrast. The gentleman farmer lay dead in the field that was to have offered up new crops to sustain life for his family. Old Lester was dead too. Simmy knew before she allowed the boys to give her a hand up from the ground that she had never known hard times like the wave that was to surely come knocking on their door. No matter the grief that was coming over her like a storm, she knew she had to get a grip.

The burial took place in a thunderstorm. Sheets of rain washed over the group of mourners who gathered to say their goodbyes to Pickford Aloysius Watie. Some whispered that he was with Kate again. Others gathered around Simmy and the children as they tried to convey their condolences to the grieving widow and the six traumatized children.

There just didn't seem to be words to express the utter sadness that hung in the air. "Ashes to ashes and dust to dust" was followed by a loud clap of thunder. The crowd hurriedly took off toward the church for the customary funeral dinner. Simmy made the children go with Aunt Birdie, but Simmy herself refused to leave the graveside. The simple wooden coffin was lowered into the muddy hole as Pickford's remains were left in their final resting place. Simmy's place was there with him. Her goodbye was the last to be spoken. The gravediggers thought she was crazy to be standing sopping wet in the cold rain. The man was dead. What good was it to be tempting fate to catch a cold standing, looking down on a coffin in this kind of weather? They had seen it all they supposed.

Even though it wasn't easy burying another husband, she did what any other strong woman would do. She picked up the pieces and went on to raise the six children by herself. She certainly wasn't the only widow in these parts. Just like the sun would rise and set, death came to the plains of Oklahoma. The hole in her heart would never close, as she missed Pickford quite fiercely, but she never gave up and Simmy Squirrel Barnes Watie saw her children to adulthood before she passed away. Chester Barnes and Pickford Watie would have been proud of the children that Simmy had raised. Good solid citizens every single one.

Chapter 3

Now Ain't That
Skippin' and A'Flyin'?

Shortly after the death of her husband, Pickford, Simmy Watie gathered up her children and moved to be close to her sisters in the nearby town of Sallisaw. It was a bustling little community and quite the melting pot as more and more families immigrated from Europe to Ellis Island in New York. Like arteries, the lines of new immigrants left New York and went every which way to search for the American dream.

The railroad was snaking its way to Oklahoma, and with the promise of jobs to all takers, the mantra continued to be "Westward ho!" and off they went to follow the railroad and their dreams for a better way of life.

Even though times were very tough in the southeastern parts of Oklahoma, good people knew how to have a good time. The third Saturday night of each month, a social event in Sallisaw, Oklahoma was held in the rear structure of the local Minton's Dry Goods. All families in the community were welcomed. The price of admission was simply "come happy, or don't come at all." There just might be a pie or two and, more often than not, a big heaping pot of stew. Rabbit, squirrel, or possum, it didn't matter as long as Miss Fanny brought enough of her corn pone bread to soak up the juice! The main event of the evening, without a doubt, was the co-mingling of local musicians. Fiddles, guitars, and mandolins. Foot stompin' and girl twirlin'!

When the door to Minton's would swing open wide and Simmy's boys, Ernest, Howard, Kip, and Edgar, would saunter inside and take a gander around the room, handsome and eligible. Simmy had raised them to be true gentlemen, and their good manners were only surpassed by their charm. Over in the corner, like a bouquet of sweet peas, they spotted the cluster of smiling women, each one hoping to be the next one picked for a promenade across the dance floor.

Minton's Dry Goods on any Saturday night held the promise for each of the girls that the man of her dreams was just a waltz, or a jig, away. The storeroom of Minton's Dry Goods made the perfect dance hall. The ladies would huddle like little chickens by the crates of flour and sugar, while the eligible bachelors stood like tin soldiers underneath the rafters. Several times during the evening Mr. Minton would sprinkle generous amounts of corn meal upon the wooden floor to make it easier to glide to and fro as the group of musicians provided the perfect selection of melodies.

Each time the door would swing open, curious eyes would cut toward the entrance to Minton's. As usual, the standout was always Kip Watie. Incredibly handsome, with a combination of the best features of his parents, Pickford and Kate, Kip's athletic good looks put him in the "head turner" category. The more outgoing of the boys, Kip absolutely loved to tease the girls. He had his father Pickford's mile wide grin and irresistible coal black eyes, all swoon worthy attributes. The tittering and tattering elevated to a fevered pitch whenever Kip would sidle over to the sea of giggles and fluttering eyelashes. With his hat cocked on the back of his head, a shiny black curl sliding down his forehead, Kip couldn't wait to offer his hand for a dance.

Pearl Winston caught his eye. "May I have this dance, Miss Pearl?" He snatched his hat from his head and went low for a bow as he extended his hand to the twinkling-eyed girl.

"Certainly, Kip!" she replied. As she reached forward to take the hand of her next dance partner, Kip suddenly spun around backwards, slowly returning his hat to his head, his hand would go behind his back and with a wiggle of his finger he would beckon the girl to grab ahold, then off to the dance floor they would go!

This little ritual was Kip's hallmark, and he performed it time and again without fail. No matter how many girls he would twirl each evening, they all acted surprised and delighted when they would be enticed to the dance floor by Kip Watie.

One particular night however, they decided to play a trick on the unsuspecting Kip. On this certain Saturday evening, Flora Peacemore, had brought her new friend, Addie Scott, to the dance. Addie had recently moved to Sallisaw with her mother, father, and five siblings. Moving from Arkansas, her father had gotten a job with the railroad and now they made this little town their home.

Flora and Addie became fast friends, and it didn't take Flora long to see that Addie's home life was hard, and she was thankful to be invited to come with Flora to Minton's. Addie was a bit shy, so she hung toward the back of the gaggle of girls that were all waiting anxiously to be asked out on the dance floor. When Kip headed toward Flora to ask for a dance, she smiled and accepted. However, upon Kip's famous backward twirl, Flora pulled Addie toward his crooked finger and planted Addie's hand into Kip's. As they went toward the dance floor, Kip turned to take his dance partner into his arms, and there stood Addie!

"Why, who do I have here in my arms? An angel?" Kip grinned from ear to ear.

Who was this pretty little thing that appeared as if a miracle had taken place right here in the storeroom of Minton's Dry Goods? The red-faced Addie could not even muster a single word. She lowered her chin to her chest. Kip gently placed his finger under her chin and tenderly raised her face to his. They stood for what seemed like an entire song just gazing into each other's eyes.

"You just have to have a name, don't ya?" Kip teased.

Addie looked at the handsome Cherokee man and slowly said, "My name is Addie."

"Well then, Addie, I came here tonight to dance. How about you? You wanna dance?" he grinned, and so did she.

He knew that was a yes, so off they went! The feisty Kip and the timid Addie danced the night away. He felt like he was in a dream, and she felt like she had just met the sweetest, kindest, and most handsome fellow in the whole world.

Chapter 4

It Ain't All Good

Kip continued to call on Addie and seemed to be falling in love with her more and more with each rap on the screen door of Angus and Ella Scott's house. As much as he cared for Addie, Kip knew things weren't good inside her home. Kip sensed it the minute he first laid eyes on Addie's mother, Ella. She was stormy. That was how he put his finger on it. One look in her eyes and he could see one brewing, like a tempest. Kip had read about the tempest storms in his Bible. The one that came to mind when he looked at Ella Scott was the storm that caused the shipwreck carrying the apostle Paul to Melita.

Can a soul be shipwrecked? Kip wondered to himself as he crossed the threshold to enter the Scott's house.

Angus and Ella Scott met in a small town in Arkansas where they attended the little one room schoolhouse that had been built by the Benevolent Brothers of the Holy Cross out of Kansas City, Missouri.

So many of the Indian children that survived the Trail of Tears found their new home in Arkansas, and Ella Vann was one of them. Ella's family had been one of several of the local families surrounded in mystery. By their skin color and facial features they were obviously of Cherokee descent, but they carried the surname of Vann. They called themselves Black Dutch.

In 1838, when President Andrew Jackson signed the order to forcefully move the Indian families westward, not every Cherokee family had complied. Ella's family had been one that had scurried into the Smokey Mountains to hide from the long arm of the government. That long arm usually had a gun with a sharp bayonet attached to it, and defiant pockets of Cherokee men decided to mount a defensive to the mandated removal of their families from the only homes they had known. It wasn't a military defensive. It was a cunning, strategic, and very dangerous plan.

The Calls The Wind family hid up in the mountains for a good while and eventually reintroduced themselves as the Vanns. They said they were Black Dutch to explain the color of their skin.

Unfortunately Ella's family, like some of the others in hiding, were flushed out. Just a few steps ahead of the soldiers, they scurried down the mountain to join up with relocated family members in Arkansas.

Another group in the little schoolhouse was the children of immigrants that had crossed over the Great Pond and found themselves searching for the American dream. Angus Scott's descendants came from Scotland. He was a Scot through and through. His skin had a reddish tint, especially when he laughed. His family came through Ellis Island in New York City and headed west to seek their fortune. Arkansas was about as far west as they got at that time, and their fortunes, per se, never ever panned out.

Years passed and after a brief courtship, Angus and Ella got married by a justice of the peace in Fort Smith, Arkansas. Angus was hired to be a federal marshal for the Arkansas Northeast Region, and the couple settled in to married life.

Angus Scott was a good marshal with an exemplary record. His duties included transporting criminals to federal prisons throughout the country. Angus could be counted on to complete the task at hand, and he was known to be honorable and trustworthy. Things seemed to be rocking along quite nicely for the two until one fateful day, Angus was walking home from work when he was attacked from behind. His assailant was armed with a singletree, a crossbar pivoted at the middle to which the traces of a harness could be fastened to pull a plow. Angus Scott, being a tall and lanky man, was caught off guard by the pummeling he was taking from the stranger wielding the leather and metal makeshift weapon. Dazed and bleeding, Angus was able to reach into the front pocket of his trousers and grab his pocketknife. He mustered up enough strength to spin around and take a furious swipe at the neck of his attacker with the sharp blade. The crazed man stopped in his tracks, blood gushing out the gaping wound in his neck. Time seemed to stand still as the two stood looking at each other for a brief second before Angus's attacker, holding the singletree in both of his hands, crumpled to the ground in a heap, dead.

Angus Scott had just taken the life of another human being, and he had no idea what had provoked the attack. He crouched down beside the lifeless body and looked him over. His thoughts were racing.

Was this a bitter family member of one of the prisoners he had transported to spend time breaking rocks at the federal pen? Was the man deranged and happened to take his fury out on Angus Scott just by happenstance? Angus knew for sure that he had no recollection of ever laying eyes on this person before.

As he gazed upon the face of the stranger, the sound of footsteps and gasps broke into his train of thought. A crowd had begun to gather in the alleyway behind Angus Scott. His head was throbbing, and he felt the stinging on his back where the leather of the singletree had made its mark. As he pulled himself up to stand in the brick alleyway, he turned to face the gathering crowd. Angus had a slowly sinking feeling in his stomach. Something told him that these people knew the dead man. Hands were covering gaping mouths as the onlookers stared in disbelief at the federal marshal that had just sent the only son of Judge Bewley O'dell to meet his maker. Sonny O'dell was dead, and Angus Scott stood holding the knife that had slashed his throat.

It made not one iota of a difference if Sonny O'dell had been a public nuisance, town drunkard, and persistant troublemaker. Angus Scott, bloody and beaten, was led away in handcuffs to the county jail. He was tossed into a cell close to the deputies, and it didn't take him long to realize, after overhearing conversations between the deputies far into the night, that his goose was cooked. Judge Bewley O'dell owned this town and Angus Scott had just taken the life of his only son.

The next morning a grief stricken Judge Bewley O'dell, refused to recuse himself from the hearing and handedAngus Scott back over to the sheriff to await trial for murder. Murder in the first degree. The singletree had mysteriously been removed from the clutches of Sonny O'dell's dead hands. There was not one witness to the scene in the alleyway that was willing to come forward and attest to the fact that Angus Scott was bleeding from injuries to his back and the back of his head. No one "saw" a singletree. No one.

One after the other, so-called eye-witnesses testified in a very theatrical fashion that they saw Angus Scott, two heads taller than Sonny, wrestle the innocent and unarmed Sonny O'dell to the ground and slash his throat. In succession, as each right hand was placed on the Holy Bible, they swore to tell the truth, the whole truth, and nothing but the truth. Their tale never faltered as one by one they recounted that, watching from a distance, Angus Scott proceeded to crouch down beside the helpless and dying Sonny O'dell and rummage through the poor man's pants looking for money. In their testimony, they made sure that Judge O'dell heard them loud and clear that Angus Scott murdered Sonny O'dell with plans to rob him.

Poor Sonny O'dell. He was just a solid citizen minding his own business, and now he was dead. No one in the courtroom that day mentioned the blatant coincidence that every single eye-witness had a family member awaiting trial in the near future in Judge Bewley O'dell's court.

Angus Scott sat in disbelief as one testimony after the other painted him to be a cold-blooded killer. Even his own court appointed lawyer refused to allow him to testify in his own defense.

Railroaded.

The trial was swift, and Angus Scott was given a sentence of life in prison to be served in a federal penitentiary in New York City. His attorney's watered down plea of self defense fell on ears that had been subject to the iron fisted rulings of Judge Bewley O'dell for decades. Not one person was willing to stick his neck out to speak up for the quiet federal marshal with a new bride at home.

Summarily, Angus found himself shackled and placed on a train to the east coast the following week. He had made this trek many times, but the roles were certainly reversed as he was now the prisoner and his co-worker, Roy Haddock, accompanied him as the newly appointed federal marshal. Roy, once Angus's good friend, sat next to him on the train, silent and aloof. Life had taken a cruel twist for Angus Scott, and as for Ella, she did not attend the trial, nor did Angus see her in the crowd as the train pulled away from the depot. He was forlorn, confused and in complete despair. Everything that he lived for was gone. Just like that.

Being a man of little means, Angus Scott accepted the cold hard fact that he had no money to hire a fancy lawyer to appeal his case. This was what life had stuck in his face, and he saw no way out. He settled into the daily grind of prison life. In his despair and confusion, he never failed to stand in line for mail call. He waited daily for mail from Ella, but it never came. Month after month there were no letters from her.

Back in the south, unbeknownst to Angus, there were some clouds of change blowing his way. Seven months after the old judge banged his gavel and pronounced a life sentence for Angus, Judge Bewley O'dell succumbed to the deadly effects of years of hard drinking. The newly elected judge, at the persistent bequests of Angus's brothers, took a look at Angus's case and one year, and one day after being incarcerated, Angus Scott walked out of the New York federal prison a free man. Angus was ecstatic as he boarded the same train that had deposited him in New York. He was headed home, and the nightmare was over. Somewhat, that was.

Upon arriving back in Arkansas, Angus was greeted by Ella and her three-month-old son, Jessie. Angus could count and he knew that this boy was not his child. For what seemed like an eternity, Ella and Angus stood looking at each other. Angus knew that things would never be the same between him and his wife. Ella had no explanations, and Angus had no inquiries. He was glad to be home and free. They left it at that.

Angus was also aware that his desire of working for the government was over. Even though he had been declared innocent by reason of self-defense, he would never be able to stomach being a federal marshal again. He decided to take a job with the railroad in Oklahoma.

As Ella's mental state was deteriorating, Angus's burning love for his wife never waned. He would never abandon her. Angus could not keep himself from trying to coax the clock to go back into the time when she welcomed him into her embrace. He never stopped trying. They would have intimate moments, passionate moments when she seemed to remember how much he meant to her. Fleeting moments.

Afterwards, she would immediately push him away with disgust. "I'm hungry," she would say as she crawled over him to abandon the bed, grab her robe, and go into the kitchen, leaving him there with a tremendous ache in his heart for the old Ella. He could hear her slinging around pots and pans as if pounding them on the stove could tamper her rage. He couldn't make out exactly what she was mumbling, but it definitely wasn't soft and tender thoughts about him. That he knew without a doubt. He longed for his sweet, happy go lucky, Ella. Now she was hollow-eyed, distant and as far removed from her former self as she could be.

Time marched on at a steady pace. Reluctantly, Ella bore him seven children. She was not the same woman he had left when he was led away to prison, but they stayed together. Something had happened while he was gone. Something dark.

She refused to elaborate and he could tell by her lack of warmth toward her son, Jessie, that she had no intention of discussing the boy's heritage. Rumors swirled around the community that the late Sonny O'dell had developed a secret crush on the beautiful young wife of Angus Scott. Apparently Sonny had followed her home earlier on that fateful day and forced his way into her home. They concluded that Sonny had raped Ella and in the process had beaten her to a pulp. He left her bleeding and battered, sprawled across the bed as he headed to the wash pump to clean his bloodied hands. The spoiled and ungrateful son of the corrupt judge, Sonny, stood in Angus and Ella's kitchen, slowly drying his hands, concocting a plan to get rid of Angus so he could have Ella to himself.

Sonny's eyes went directly to a box on the back porch just off

Ella's kitchen. His mission was to kill Angus Scott, and the singletree he spotted in that box was just the weapon to do the trick. He grabbed his hat from the kitchen counter, stooped over and picked up the singletree and headed out the back door, down the sidewalk and toward town.

Sonny never thought for one moment that he would be punished for the crime he was about to commit. His father had gotten him out of every pickle he had ever been in before, so why should he be worried now? Sonny always got what he wanted. For once, however, Sonny O'dell got what he deserved.

Sonny O'dell had been seen leaving Angus and Ella's house on the day that he was killed in the alleyway. The neighbors were pretty sure that Sonny had harmed Ella in some way, but not one single soul went to her house to check on her. As he sat in jail waiting for his trial, Angus pleaded with anyone that would show up at his cell to allow him or someone to go check on his wife. His pleas fell on deaf and uncaring ears. Her absence told him something horrible was wrong. They loved each other and she would never abandon him in his time of need.

A few weeks after the trial was over and Angus had been loaded on the train and sent to New York, Ella was seen carefully stepping out the front door and off her front porch. Wobbly and unsure of her steps, she looked up toward the sun, covering her eyes from the bright rays. Weeks in the dark house, all alone and trying to take care of her wounds, Ella's eyes had to adjust to the light as she held onto the post that supported the porch roof. A nosy neighbor across the street had been peeking out her front window curtain on that day that Ella first appeared after all of those weeks. The neighbor recalled to her knitting circle a few days later that she would never forget the look on Ella's face as the young woman stood almost as in a trance in her yard. It was as if there was a face but there was not a soul. A hollow face that had been wiped clean of any expression at all. The knitting group muttered a few "tsk tsks" and "that's too bads" but that was all the effort they put forth toward the plight of Ella Scott.

Ella was on her own in that town. Her husband had been branded as a cold-blooded murderer and thief, and no one wanted to be involved with the likes of Ella Scott.   Ella had laid unconscious for three days. Sonny had banged her head against the metal bedpost many times and punched her up the side of her jaw too. It seemed that the more he punched and hit her, the more aroused he became. When she came to, the first thing Ella did was place the back of her hand on her swollen lips. Blood had clotted each area that had split open when he slapped her mouth. Her lips were huge and sore and crusted over. She could only open her eyes enough to see through the slits, and it took her a good ten minutes to figure out where she was. She recognized the pictures of her family on the wall, but her mind just didn't seem to register that she was in her own bedroom. Everything seemed foreign to her at first.   Then she remembered.

Every single second that Sonny had spent in her bedroom came smashing into her mind. Even the putrid smell of his breath as he hunkered over on top of her body was still lingering in her senses. The beating. His panting and grunting... and thrusting. She remembered it all.

At that moment, Ella Scott began to scream at the top of her lungs. She cried out for Angus. She called for her mother and father. She called out to God. It was a long, loud guttural scream that lasted until there was no sound left.

Then it stopped.

Just like that, the sweet and quiet woman that Angus Scott had taken as his bride was gone. Her mind had sent that Ella away. In the twisted emotional remains of the woman lying on that bed, it was as if the former Ella was a dying ember, slowly going out. If that Ella was gone, then the pain and memories would go away too.

She was replaced by the new Ella. Mad Ella. Cold and mean and mad Ella.

The day that Angus Scott stepped off the train platform and saw his wife in the crowd, holding the infant in her arms, he instantly knew that life as he had known it was over. What was once an innocent and abiding love between Ella and Angus slowly veered off course into more of an existence than a marriage. Ella was most often hateful and brooding. The eight children seemed to be a burden to her. She did not find much joy as she went about the daily chores that came with raising a family. Mental illness had wrapped its bony fingers around the essence of Ella. The real and invariable nature that was once Ella was now engulfed in misery, pain, and hatred. Hatred for the skin crawling effects of human touch. Deeper and deeper she spiraled into her brooding existence.

She had grit though. It was if the old Ella refused to be totally swallowed by this nasty creature that had taken roost in her body. The balance was easily tilted, but somehow, she seemed to hold it somewhat together every now and then.

After the railroad was completed, an offer to be a share-cropper came Angus's way, and he and Ella moved to the Oklahoma town of Sallisaw with their eight children, Jessie, Adair, Douglas, Duff, Logan, Esme, Maisie, and Addie.

In spite of their mother and her demons, Ella's children grew up as close to normal as they could. Angus Scott saw to it that they knew at least one loving and caring parent. He tried to stand in the gap as often as he could, but it was no small feat. Ella could be a bear.

Kip Watie noticed it immediately when he offered his hand for a handshake the first time he came to Sallisaw to call on Addie. He removed his hat with one hand and thrust the other hand toward Ella. With a snarl, she looked him up and down, hands stuffed in her apron pockets.

"Kip? Is that your name? Don't take one step into my house unless you wipe those muddy shoes. I ain't got all day to clean up after the likes of you."

No hello or howdy or welcome to my home. Without another word, she strolled off the porch and headed toward her vegetable garden. Kip had her number for sure. Ella was stormy.

With each visit to see Addie, Kip knew he was falling hard for her. He thought about her when he was not with her, and he couldn't take his eyes off her when they sat together watching the sun set slowly into the west from the front porch of her parent's house. He was like a love-sick pup.

Unfortunately for Kip, there was a nagging and glaring problem that kept him from sweeping Addie up into his arms and taking her with him to be his wife. She had never been to church.

Angus Scott believed that each time he stepped foot outside the door of his home to work in the fields that God was there. His church convened every day. He was a believer and prayed out loud before every meal (and with Ella's cooking that was definitely a necessity), but he had ten mouths to feed and ten bodies to clothe and saw no use in stopping for one day a week just to sit around in a clean pair of overalls in a stuffy church. He knew most of the people in that church, and if God was showing up there every Sunday they would be the last to notice. Ella's cooking was just as bad on Sundays as it was the other six days, so there was nothing to look forward to there. In his opinion, if God needed him, He knew where to find him.

Ella, on the other hand, never spoke of God or Jesus or church, for that matter. She never read her children Bible stories when they were little. As a matter of fact, if one of her children saw her headed toward them with a book, they knew they better high tail it out the door. She just might throw a fit and the book!

So with that in mind, Kip tried to talk to Addie about his faith. He was so strong in his beliefs and knew that the woman he chose to marry and have a family with needed to share in those beliefs too. Addie was clueless.

Addie told Kip that she knew she was a good person. She knew

69

that she would be a good mother and a good wife. She believed in the Golden Rule. Didn't that count?

No, to Kip that wasn't enough. He wanted a Godly woman— one that was saved by the blood of Jesus Christ.

So there they were. Sitting on the Scott's porch watching the sun go down. Kip seemed to be slipping away and Addie knew it. A chilly wind whipped some leaves off the old oak tree sending them crackling and fluttering by the two of them sitting there staring off into the distance. Kip made the first move.

He rose up and brushed off imaginary somethings from his pants. He held his hat in his right hand and stuck his left hand deep into his left front pants pocket. He turned toward Addie and with his voice barely above a whisper, told her he needed to go home.

The only thing she could think of to say was to tell him to watch out for the mud puddles. That was it. Kip jumped up on the wagon and clicked the reins a couple of times and said, "Gidyap!" He never looked back to wave like he usually did. He left and that was that.

Addie stood stoically on the front porch as Kip's wagon slowly pulled away into the distance. "What difference should it make if I go to church or not? Kip Watie, you think you are so high and mighty!" she shouted to the wind.

Kip was a long way out of hearing range, but Addie wanted to make sure she got the last word in, no matter if he heard her or not! She didn't care!

"I don't care!" she told herself. "I just don't care at all..."

Addie fell into a heap onto the porch and buried her face into her arms. She wept for what seemed to be an hour when her father, Angus, appeared around the corner of the house. He was wiping grease off his hands with an old rag. He had been working on some tools out in the barn when he thought he heard something and decided to come take a look.

"Addie, what in the world is wrong with you?"

"Oh, Poppa, I am so sad! Kip left, and I don't think he's ever coming back!"

Angus always had a deep fear that one of the eight children might show signs of being like Ella. He had seen bits of her in some of the others. Duff, for instance had shown signs of a temper, but seemed to be able to keep it in check. Maisie could be flighty at times, but he mostly attributed that to her free spirit.

Addie would be the very last one that he would think would provoke anyone to anger. Addie was tenderhearted and kind and never showed any outward signs of aggression.

"Why on earth would Kip ever be mad at you? I thought you were two peas in a pod?"

"Well, Poppa, he thinks he can't marry me because I don't go to church and am not saved!"

Angus stuffed the rag he was holding into the bib of his tattered overalls and reached into his pocket for his pipe. As he lit the tobacco pressed neatly into the bowl of the pipe and took a few deep puffs, he looked right at Addie and said, "Well, sister, seems like he's a man that

71

knows what he wants."

And with those few words, Angus Scott headed back out to the barn, leaving Addie sprawled out on the porch like a tuckered out, old hound dog.

Chapter 5

Knock and It Will
Be Opened to You

Fall turned to winter, and winter turned to spring, and Kip was still gone.

Addie was brokenhearted and miserable. Many days and nights she would sit on the porch and hope to see him coming around the bend, clicking the reins and hollering at the old mule pulling his wagon.

Addie was hoping against hope that he would come back to her, but so far, that hope hadn't stood up against Kip's desires. He was nowhere to be seen. Addie's mother, Ella, had a sister named Senda that lived over in Leflore. Word got to Angus and Ella that Senda was sick and needed someone to help take care of her. Senda's daughter, Tabitha, was trying her best, but Senda needed around-the-clock care, and Tabitha couldn't do it alone. Angus decided that it would be good for Addie to get away for a while and spend some time with her Aunt Senda and cousin Tabitha. Besides that, he needed some relief himself from seeing Addie mope around the house all day.

Addie welcomed the chance to go see her family members and packed her bag. By early that morning she was ready to go, and her brothers, Logan and Duff, drove the buckboard over to Leflore and Aunt Senda's house.

Aunt Senda was very ill and had taken to her bed three weeks earlier. Tabitha greeted Addie at the door and welcomed her in with a big hug. Tabitha waved to Logan and Duff as they drove away knowing that those two boys had no desire to come into a house with a sick old woman in it.

"Why, Addie! Don't you look so pretty! Come in here right away, and I will fix you some lunch. I hope you don't think I am meddling but you do seem to have lost some weight. We need to get some meat back on your bones, dear cousin! Is it Aunt Ella's cooking? Bless your heart, come right in!" Cousin Tabitha was going a mile a minute, not giving Addie a second to fill in the blanks.

Addie knew she would have plenty of time to give her cousin the lowdown, but at the moment, she spied a large pot of homemade stew simmering on the stove and the aroma itself seemed nourishing! Aunt Senda was sleeping, so Tabitha and Addie sat at the kitchen table, ate a hearty bowl of soup, and discussed life over in Sallisaw. Tabitha knew Kip and his family very well and when Addie came to the part as to why Kip left her, Tabitha placed her hand on top of Addie's.

"Addie, we can talk about the rest of this later. Give me some time to put my thoughts together. I would also like to talk to Mother about it when she gets to feeling better. If the two of us can get her over this hump and on the road to recovery, I know my Mother has a sound mind and a big heart, and I think she is just the person to get some good advice from when it comes to matters such as this."

The two cousins lovingly took turns giving care to Senda for the next several days. Her fever finally broke on Wednesday, and by Friday, she actually felt well enough to sit up in the bed and eat her dinner.

Addie always loved her Aunt Senda and had long ago accepted the fact that her mother, Ella, was not and would never be like Aunt Senda. She could fret about it all she wanted, but she figured out when she was just a little girl that Ella Scott was not "gifted with a maternal instinct."

On the other hand, Aunt Senda was gracious and kind and loving. Senda often told Tabitha and Addie that her sister Ella had lost her way and her mind many years ago. Senda took up for Ella most times and if she witnessed Ella being cruel to the children she would find a way later on, out of earshot of Ella, to give hugs to Ella's children and try to explain to them that some people have broken bones and some have broken minds. She pleaded with them to not hold a grudge against their mother. If anything, Aunt Senda was the glue that held Ella Scott's children on the straight and narrow path. She loved them all as if they were her own.

By Sunday, Aunt Senda was feeling perky and had even gotten out of bed long enough to sit on the front porch for a spell. The girls had helped her with her bath and had her back in bed before dusk.
Tabitha felt that the time was right to approach her mother about Addie's dilemma.

"Mother, Addie and I were wondering if you could give Addie

75

some advice."

"Most surely, I can, Tabitha. What seems to be the problem?" Senda spoke as she pulled herself up higher in the bed.

"Well, Mother, you remember that Kip Watie had been courting Addie, don't you?"

"I sure do, honey. I felt like he was a fitting suitor for our Addie. Has something happened to Kip?" Senda's eyes darted back and forth from Tabitha to Addie.

"Mother, Kip broke it off with Addie. He told her that he wanted to marry her, but that he couldn't because he had promised God he would marry a church going woman that has accepted Jesus as her savior." Tabitha laid it out for Senda as Addie sat in the rocker beside the bed. Her hands were clasped in her lap, and her head was down. She felt ashamed.

"Addie and Tabitha, my sister Ella told me in no uncertain terms many years ago to not stick my nose in her business when it came to anything about the raising of her children. As best as I could, I have always respected her wishes. However, I have prayed fervently for all of the Scott children that one day they would all come to know the Lord. I refuse to stay out of this one." With that said, Aunt Senda turned to Addie and said to the young woman, "Addie, do you know that Jesus loves you?"

Addie looked right at her Aunt Senda and said, "I have heard that, but I really don't understand why it is supposed to be important." That's all it took for Senda.

76

She jumped out of bed and went over to her niece, Addie. What happened next was nothing short of a miracle! Aunt Senda got the Holy Ghost! In between quoting scriptures and dancing up and down, Aunt Senda grabbed Addie's hands in hers and pulled her out of the chair. Addie listened intently as her beloved Aunt Senda spoke to her and told her that she would inherit an eternal home in paradise if she accepted Jesus as her savior! Furthermore, she explained to Addie the power of prayer!

"Addie, accept Jesus as your savior, and then we will begin to pray an earnest prayer that your Kip will be returned to you!"

Addie fully understood everything that her Aunt Senda shared with her, and before she knew it, she had invited Jesus into her heart. Then they all got on their knees and began to pray Kip home!

The three of them prayed and laughed and danced up and down on the wooden floor. There were times that they felt like the floor would fall in with all of the jumping up and down!

That night Addie had the best night's sleep that she had had in a long time, and the following afternoon, Logan and Duff came to fetch Addie and take her home. When they saw Aunt Senda standing at the doorway when they pulled up, they knew it was safe to go in the house. Logan and Duff enjoyed a piece of pie that Tabitha had made special for them and loaded Addie up for the trip back to Sallisaw.

"Well don't you look a whole lot happier than when we left you here last week!" Logan couldn't help but remark when he saw the glow shining on his sister's face.

Addie giggled and put her head down. Logan and Duff loved

to tease their younger sister, but today they left her alone to bask in her happiness. They turned their conversation to their last coon hunt and headed back home.

It seemed to take no time at all to get to the house and Addie was anxious to jump down from the buggy. She was giddy and excited, but she had no idea why she was feeling the way she did.

She was happy that she had become a Christian regardless of the fact that she knew it would have to be a private endeavor when she got back home. Aunt Senda had sent a lovely Bible home with her and had given her some scriptures to study until they got together again. Addie knew that she could tell her poppa and he would be happy, but she had no intentions of sharing her news with her momma.

Still there was something making her smile, and she decided to go with the feelings not knowing where they would lead. After a supper of corn bread and milk, Addie went to the bedroom that she shared with Maisie and Esme and began to unpack her bag. She placed the Bible on the table when she suddenly got the urge to open it up. The pages rolled about and landed on the book of Matthew.

"Matthew," Addie whispered aloud to herself. "What a nice name for a book of the Bible."

Her eyes went directly to Matthew 7:7. Addie began to recite the verse, "Ask, and it will be given to you; seek, and you will find; knock, and it will be opened to you." Addie read the verse again. Aunt Senda told her that she could talk to Jesus anytime she wanted and that He always listened.

"Jesus, I am new to this, but the only thing I am asking for right now is Kip. Can you open Kip up for me?"

Addie Scott stood in her bedroom holding her Bible open when she heard a knock on the door. Chill bumps went all over her body. Quietly she lay the Bible down on the table, and started slowly walking out of her bedroom toward the living room.

There, looking right at her through the screen door, stood Kip. He held a tiny bouquet of wildflowers in one hand and his hat in the other.

"Addie, do you mind if I come in?"

Chapter 6

Kip and Addie

When Kip Watie married the love of his life, Addie Scott, he struck out on his own to become a sharecropper in the foothills of Oklahoma, near the town of Leflore. Kip headed out to the fields each morning, and Addie stayed home to care for their rapidly growing family. Kip was never happier than when he held each of his children in his arms for the first time. He was a proud poppa, and Addie was a sweet and loving momma. They never ran out of kisses for any of their precious children, and it was always a joyous occasion to welcome each and every tiny child into their brood.

Their first-born child was daughter, Iris. Iris was pretty and quiet, just like her mother. She was tender hearted and never balked at helping with any of the household chores. Iris was followed by the twins, Augie and Alice. Alice was beautiful and more outgoing, like Kip. As for Augie, it seemed that he knew that his most important task at any given moment was to play whatever game Alice had cooked up. He adored his twin and obliged her every whim. Next came their son Joe. Sweet Joe was tall and handsome. He got his lanky good looks from Addie. Joe was the tease, just like Kip. He loved to make his sisters laugh. Pickford, Pick as he was called, was named after his late grandfather and could almost pass for Joe's twin. The two boys certainly favored their mother. They were kind-hearted boys and loved helping their mother whenever they could. Two years after Pick was born, they welcomed little Lionel, who soon became known as "Cubbie." Cubbie looked exactly like a young Kip but had a sensitive nature, like Addie.

Every one of the Watie children adored their parents. Kip was a loving and playful father that never hesitated to grab his fiddle and strike up a tune. It made his heart soar to see the laughing faces of his six children as they clapped their hands and stomped their feet and joined their father as he sang a song picked out special for them.

Momma would laugh and sing and blow kisses to Kip. He would pretend to catch the kisses and gather all of the children together and they would hold out their hands and Poppa would pinch off a bit of Momma's kiss and place it in their hands. On the count of three, they would bring their hands up and plant their share of Momma's kisses on their lips. Momma would clap and little Cubbie, who was snuggled in her lap, would clap and say that he wanted his very own kiss directly from Momma's lips to his.

As the evening would wear on, Addie would stand beside Kip as he played the first chords of an old hymn. Addie's face would look like an angel as she looked into the heavens and the most treasured songs would fill the room. At just the perfect time Kip would join in, and the blending of their voices was so hauntingly beautiful. Their children huddled on the floor beside the old stove with their eyes glued on the two sweethearts as they worshipped the Lord in the best way they knew how. Six loving children were being serenaded by their precious parents, and they never wanted the songs to end.

Kip and Addie Watie worked hard to make a living in the sandy hills of Oklahoma. Sharecropping never paid all of the bills all of the time, but in spite of the hard times Kip and Addie had a fierce and un-dying love for each other and for their precious youngsters. They had a house filled with love.

Chapter 7

The Big Move

There was undeniably an unsettling fear of financial hardship on the horizon. The construction of the railroad had been completed. The last of the hiring had been settled to get the railroad line in operation, which left hundreds of displaced construction workers from all over the country out of work. Many of the families were leaving town to go back east for promised employment in some of the burgeoning factories popping up all along the eastern coast.

No doubt about it, the farmers in southeastern Oklahoma were in big trouble. No matter how much back breaking work the families would put into tilling and planting the soil, there had to be the promise of a waiting buyer or it would all be for naught. Each sharecropper had the obligation to give their landowners the first and best of the crops. The landowners in turn sold the crops for their payment. There was an abundance of crops but not a big enough market to support both landowners and farmers. Something had to give. Kip and Addie Watie were in the same boat as all of the other sharecroppers around Leflore. Since they were into the third year of the downturn in the economy, the land-owners were going belly up and losing their farms. That was bad news for the sharecroppers because when a piece of property went back to the bank, not only were the landowners booted off it so were the sharecroppers. They knew their days were numbered on the little farm in Leflore.

Angus came to Kip and Addie and told them that he was being offered a place to farm over in Dustin and that there was enough land for Kip and Addie too. The Dustin area had been weathering the downturn in the market a bit better than Leflore which gave them all a bit of hope.

Without a moment's hesitation, Kip and Addie packed up their belongings and their six children and headed over to Dustin. They were so thankful for the opportunity to stay in Oklahoma and the relief they felt was like a big stone being lifted off their shoulders.

Chapter 8

Up on the Mountain

The sun was setting low over the mountain just outside of Dustin, Oklahoma. Kip and Addie had settled in nicely on the little piece of property that sat atop the mountain and were delighted that it didn't take an act of congress to coax their crops out of the ground.

Kip was actually enjoying farming again. It didn't take too many seasons of crop failures to take the starch right out of a hard-working man like Kip and to see row after row of corn, beans, peas, squash, and melons flourishing in his garden gave him have a new kick to his steps. Iris, Augie, Alice, and Joe had easily made friends at their new school in Dustin, and Addie was enjoying her time with the two little ones.

Pick and Cubbie were inseparable. Pick loved his little brother, and they played games at Momma's feet as she prepared vegetables for canning or churned the sweet cow's milk into butter. The boys loved taking turns with the churn. Up and down the ladle would go. Momma would pour off the buttermilk, scrape the fresh butter into a bowl and pour more cream into the crock for another batch. They loved being with their momma during the day. They watched her do her morning chores, and in the afternoon, they would sit with her on the porch, listening to stories until they would fall asleep. She would gently pick her babies up and place them on their beds for a nice afternoon nap.

Lunch was always something warm and tasty right out off the stove. They loved Momma's soups with a piece of homemade bread all slathered with the fresh, soft butter.

Chores around the house were routine, and the days passed quickly. It wasn't long before it was time to wait for the older children to come up the lane from school. Momma would put a blanket on the ground and sit with Pick and Cubbie as they watched for the first sign of their returning brothers and sisters. When they would catch a glimpse of them, Pick and Cubbie would jump up off the blanket and go running down the pathway into the waiting arms of Iris and Alice. Augie and Joe would pick them up and twirl them around like airplanes.

Life was good for the Watie family up on the mountain in Dustin.

Until the coughing started.

It started with just a little dry cough. A dry, hacking cough.

"Must be something in the air," Addie would say as she covered her mouth hoping to suppress another bout. Neighbors stopping by with recipes for home remedies became a normal occurrence. Awful smells from steaming pots on the old stove kept most everyone outside most of the time. Except Addie.

Addie grew weaker as the days went by, and the coughing turned into violent and wracking wheezing and near choking episodes. The old doctor made his way up the mountain in a fancy buggy with a couple of high stepping fillies. When they came to a stop in Kip and Addie's front yard, six sets of eyes peeked out of the curtains. The children had never seen a doctor at their house before, and they didn't want to miss a thing.

Aunt Maisie and Aunt Esme, Addie's sisters, had come to stay at their house about the time she could no longer sit up in a chair. She had been confined to her bed for five days when Poppa announced that he wasn't going to wait any longer for remedies or concoctions. He was going to town to fetch the doctor.

Doc Eddings made his way back to the bedroom where Addie was sleeping. He spent about 30 minutes with her and came down the hallway. He took Kip by the elbow and told him to step out on the front porch with him.

Addie had the consumption. There was no known cure, and her time on earth was almost at an end.

Kip was devastated

Chapter 9

Where's Momma?

Four-year-old Pick had seen his mother being doctored for many days. He would peek into the bedroom and see her as she lay limp and pale, her frail body just a speck amidst the blankets piled high upon the featherbed. The consumption wracked her body. The medical field at that time had not discovered the antibiotics needed to aid Momma in her fight against what later became known as tuberculosis.

His father, aunts, and neighbors took turns with the all-night vigils as they hovered around her bed. The wracking coughs grew weaker and weaker. The older children stayed close by their mother's bedside, and the babies, Pick and Cubbie, were taken into the bedroom on a few occasions. Momma would try hard to raise her head to plant a soft kiss on their foreheads.

"Oh, there's Momma's sweet baby boys," she would coo in a faint whisper.

Pick longed for the time where he would sit on Momma's lap and help her snap green beans, sneaking a few bites here and there. Cubbie would be napping on a blanket on the porch at Momma's feet as she and Pick shared quiet time together. Snapping beans and singing. Momma always sang old hymns, "In the Garden," "I Need Thee Every Hour,"

91

and "Love Lifted Me."

Pick longed to hear her sing again. Oh how he wanted to hear her sweet voice! More ladies coming and going from the bedroom with their heads hung low, boiling this and washing that. Constant commotion.

One day it all came to an end.

On that particular morning, there was a bustle of activity. Relatives, neighbors, and friends began to show up at the house. Whispers and crying.

In his four years of life on this earth, Pick Watie had never seen his father cry before this day. Oh, how his poppa looked so sad! He was always ready to dance a quick jig with daughter Iris standing on his feet and daughter Alice hanging on his back. Round and round he would go!

"Yee haw! Girls! Dosey doe!" Giggles and pig tails! Love and laughter had always filled their happy home.

Until that day.

Pick did not see that twinkle in his Poppa's eyes now. Pain and sorrow, hugs and tears. Poppa seemed inconsolable.

"My Addie, my Addie! Oh, Lordy, Lordy! My Addie is gone!" Little Pick looked all around. Where did Momma go? Why did Poppa say Momma was gone? He ran toward the bedroom where she had been attended to for so many weeks. The door was shut. He was quickly shooed away.

"Now, Pick, honey, go back into the living room with Iris. Go on now, baby. Go play with Alice and Iris." Aunts and uncles, friends and relatives would walk by, stoop down and pat him on the head. With each pat came a sigh and cursory, "Bless your little heart."

Iris, the twins, and his brother Joe huddled in a little pack in the corner of the living room holding each other and sobbing. Pick was confused. Where had Momma gone?

Later that evening several men carried in a long wooden box. Furniture from the living room had been taken out to the barn. Two straight back cane chairs were set facing each other about six feet apart. The long wooden box was placed on the seats of the chairs. Aunt Esme and Miss Belinda Barton scurried around and placed two coal oil lamps on tables at the backside of the box. Mr. Crittendon, who always wore a stovepipe hat and a jet-black suit, moved toward the container and gently lifted the lid.

There inside that wooden box and nestled atop a ticking covered pad, lay Momma. She wasn't moving. Her hands, one on top of the other, were crossed daintily on her chest. She looked white and frail.

"Momma!" the young voice came from the corner of the room. It was Iris, and she moved slowly toward the wooden box and looked at the lifeless body of her mother. "Oh, Momma!" she sobbed.

Iris lowered her head and cradled it into the crook of her arm that was resting on the side of the coffin. "Oh, Momma, please don't leave me."

There was more movement toward the coffin as next came Augie, Alice, and Joe peeking into the box and seeing their beautiful mother. No more suffering and no more pain.

His father came up from behind them, and as he knelt down, he placed an arm around the four children. He looked back and there stood the babies. He beckoned for Pick and Cubbie to come to him. Slowly they went toward their poppa. As evening fell, the oil lamps flickered, and there cuddled in the arms of Kip, were six children. Six children and their grieving father looking at the shell that once was momma.

"Why won't Momma open up her eyes, Poppa?" questioned little Pick.

"She is with Jesus, youngun." Poppa said.

"I don't want her to be with Jesus, Poppa. I want her to be with me!" Pick shot back.

All of the children turned to Poppa to see what he would say next. Somehow hoping that he could fix all of this mess right here and now. Kip hung his head to gather his thoughts.

Slowly he turned to face his six children and began, "Aw, now. I know you all want Momma to stay here with us. I sure do too. She was awful sick, and there was nothin' that we could do to make her better. Do you remember that song that we've all been singin' called, 'I'll Fly Away'?"

"Yes, Poppa, I love that beautiful song!" cried Alice.

"Well, Momma loved that song too, and I believe that when she got to hurtin' so awful bad, the good Lord in His mercy just told her, 'Addie, why don't you just fly away up here with me here in heaven? No more pain and tears.' And, children, your Momma is up there right now with Jesus! Now Momma is flyin' and singin' with the angels!" Poppa hugged them tighter and tighter and kissed them one by one.

Tears ran down Poppa's cheeks as he held his children. The hug was tight and they felt safe. They felt safe in Poppa's arms.

Chapter 10

Tell Mother I'll Be There

The evening passed quickly with neighbors and family stopping by to pay their respects. Aunt Esme came and gathered up the children and helped them get ready for bed. Tomorrow was going to be a long, hard day.

Morning came with a bustle of activity, the smell of coffee and bacon permeated the home as more and more people began to gather at the Watie house. Mr. Crittendon arrived again, this time riding a nice buckboard painted all in black, being pulled by four black horses. The lid was placed back on the wooden box where Momma lay and one of the men that accompanied Mr. Crittendon tapped nails all around the top. Mr. Crittendon, Poppa, Momma's brothers, Uncle Jessie, Uncle Duff, Uncle Douglas, Uncle Adair, and Uncle Logan, picked up the coffin and gently placed it on the back of the wagon.

It was time to go down the mountain. It was time to say a final goodbye to Momma.

The funeral procession was a quiet one.

All of the children had been dressed in their Sunday best. Iris and Alice had made sure that all of their brothers at least attempted to run a comb through their hair. After everyone had piled into their wagons, Mr. Crittendon said, "Hep!Hep!" to the horses and off they went down the mountain to the little Baptist church in Dustin. Poppa rode in the back beside the coffin. He hung his head in sorrow as he clutched a small bouquet picked fresh that morning from Addie's favorite lilac bush.

One by one they filed silently into the little wooden structure where Addie and her devoted family had often worshipped. The pastor stood in front of those that gathered there to celebrate Addie's life but found it hard to speak with the large lump hanging in his throat. He couldn't help but see Kip and those six devastated children staring up at him from the front pew. He knew they were consumed by their grief. The pastor had presided over many funerals in his long years as a servant of the Lord, but this was one of the hardest ones he had ever done. How could he console these children? How could he tell them that their precious mother was now in a much better place? How could he tell this devoted husband that life needed to go forth without his soul mate? "Their comfort must come from the Lord," he told himself as he garnered the wherewithal to begin.

He couldn't say enough sweet things about Addie Watie. She was so well known in those parts for her kindness, generosity, and sweet and gentle nature. With Mr. Short banging away on the old upright piano, Mrs. Short sang some of Momma's favorite hymns. The beautiful melodies filled the air. All with the uplifting promise that Momma was now in a real good place. "I Walk With The King," "Some Sweet Day By and By," and the one that brought so many tears from the entire congregation was "Tell Mother I'll Be There."

After the service, the family and friends of Addie Watie climbed back in the waiting wagons. The horses seemed to know the solemnity of their duty as they held their heads up high and carried Momma for the last time. Her final resting place there on earth would be the Dustin, Oklahoma's cemetery. A big hole had been freshly dug back by a fence-row. Wild, pink roses rambled along the barbed wire fence. It seemed fitting for such beauty to surround the place where they would leave her. The pastor said one last prayer over her remains and soon afterward the crowd slowly turned to leave. Poppa had motioned everyone to go ahead and let him stay with Momma for just a few more moments. There beside the grave he lowered to one knee and gently placed the sweet smelling lilacs atop the wooden box.

"Addie, you were one good woman. I don't even know for a second how I am gonna go on without you. I know that the sun is gonna come up and go down just like always. I know these children are gonna grow up and make you proud. I know the good Lord has His big ole' hand on all of this, but I just don't know about me. Breathin' don't even seem worth it without you. I'll do the best I can, but I just don't know about me, Addie."

Kip Watie stood up, brushed his knee off with his hat and pulled his handkerchief from his pocket. He lowered his face into the square of material that Addie had sewn for him. He swore that he could almost smell her as he wiped away the hot tears that streaked in an endless stream from his eyes to his chin. He sighed aloud to himself

"Please don't ever let me forget the sweet smell of that beautiful woman."

Before he turned to walk away he looked up into the billowing clouds and spoke to God. "Lord, you got her now. Take good care of this one. I know I don't have to tell you. You know she was special."

The arduous walk back to the waiting buggy was very painful for Kip. Leaving Addie there to be covered by that uncaring dirt seemed in itself to be the cruelest act of all. He wanted to hold her forever in his arms. He couldn't bear to leave her. He knew she always felt safe in his arms.

Chapter 11

In The Sweet By and By

The next six months flew by quickly. Kip Watie and his children had settled into a good schedule. Iris and Alice were old enough to help with the cooking and cleaning and looking after the two little ones. Augie and Joe were able hands to help Poppa with the farming. Poppa still wasn't able to smile much and his dust covered fiddle lay silent, but somehow they trudged on day after day.

Even though their strength to endure the heartbreak grew with each passing day, it was unspoken yet evident—Kip missed his wife something fierce. Not one of the children had mustered up the courage to bring up her name in front of their poppa. Their hearts ached for their mother and tears would fall on each and every pillow in the dark of the night, but talking to Poppa about Momma would just hurt way too much. Day in and day out life just went on for the Watie family, seven people with a huge hole in each one of their tender hearts.

One sunny fall day, like clock work, Poppa and the children rose early to perform the chores around the farm. Iris and Alice stood in the kitchen singing softly under their breath while they cooked and cleaned. They kept a constant eye on Pick and Cubbie as the two little boys played with marbles on the kitchen floor. It sure seemed like a regular day, but unbeknownst to them, just a brief six months after Momma went to heaven, there stood their Poppa out in the field wiping his sweaty brow on the back of his sleeve. Kip Watie was sick. He had tried to drink water, thinking that maybe he had just had too much sun the day before or something that he had eaten hadn't agreed with his stomach. All he knew was that he was nauseous and was beginning to feel wobbly in his legs.

Augie saw him collapse and high tailed it to his side. "Poppa! Poppa! What's wrong?"

All Kip could do was moan. He had been feeling a little under the weather for the last few days but wasn't about to let a little fever slow him down. He had too much work to do.

Living up on the mountain, raising six children, and utilizing every bit of daylight to get his crop planting done left him no time for worrying. He wasn't privy to much of the current events happening around that part of the state, and therefore, he didn't know that there had been reports of a nasty outbreak of typhoid fever with the death toll inching higher and higher. It hadn't affected anyone he knew, so Kip didn't think much about it when he started feeling poorly. Joe ran to tell the neighbors about Poppa lying out there in the field. They all helped him inside and immediately put him to bed.

Fear and uncertainty quickly settled in as there was an all too familiar flurry of activity in that little house. Six recently broken little hearts were too raw to even imagine what they would do if they lost

Poppa too. Poppa was their shield and their protector. He was the solid rock that was the foundation of what was left of their family. They felt safe when Poppa was with them. He often sat with them and held them all close in his arms.

As unfathomable as it may have seemed, two days later, they saw Mr. Crittendon drive up in his black buckboard. Iris immediately gathered up her brothers and sister and held them tight. Hot, stinging tears coursed slowly down their cheeks. A well-traveled pathway, the tears knew the routine. There was utter disbelief and not a dry eye in the house. Kip Watie was dead.

When the wooden box arrived, there was an unspoken yet painful recognition that Poppa wasn't broken hearted any more. They knew that God had said, "Kip, why don't you just fly on up here to heaven and be with Addie?"

Their poppa wouldn't have hesitated to accept such a gift. They knew he was with Momma again. Mr. Crittendon's team of horses knew the way to the little church in Dustin. Times had been hard in these parts, and so often, hard times are followed by sorrow and loss.

Sadly, the team of horses had become familiar with the ritual and their solemn duty. When the final prayer was said over the remains of Kip Watie, six orphaned children rose from the front pew and walked slowly toward the sleek wooden box. Mr. Crittendon walked toward them with a hammer in one hand and the top in the other as he prepared to seal the coffin for the final time.

Iris had her arms around Augie and Joe. Four-year-old Pick

held tight to the hand of his sister Alice. They seemed unable to move or think or even breathe. Wide-eyed and innocent, two-year old-Cubbie wiggled loose from the grip of Aunt Maisie and ran toward his siblings.

"I kiss Poppa! I kiss Poppa!" Without a moment's hesitation Iris scooped her baby brother up in her arms and held him up so he could place a tender kiss on the cheek of his father. Alice did the same for Pick. They gathered in front of the remains of their Poppa and held hands. Iris, with wisdom far beyond her young years spoke just above a whisper, " Dear, Jesus. We know Momma and Poppa loved each other so much. We want you to know that we understand that they need to be together. I know you will help me, Lord. I know you will help me keep us together. Tell Momma and Poppa that I will always see that we stay together. Amen."

Little did Iris know that the promise she had just made had already been circumvented. Before she was to climb aboard the buggy that would take her back home, Iris was pulled aside by her Aunt Maisie's husband, Uncle Jubal. As the conversation deepened, Iris gazed directly into Uncle Jubal's eyes. The words he spoke to the young girl sucked every ounce of breath right out of her body. The blow she took by every syllable tumbling from Uncle Jubal's lips was as if a building had collapsed right smack down on top of her head. Was it not bad enough that death had taken their loving parents away from them? All they had left was each other, and Iris could not believe what her ears were telling her brain.

The news that Uncle Jubal delivered to Iris that chilly fall day, as they stood face to face in the Dustin cemetery, was more than she could handle.

Just before she felt that she might crumple into a heap on the ground, Iris gathered herself up knowing that Kip and Addie wouldn't have wished this heartache on their children in a million years. They would have chosen to stay here longer. Heaven could wait and knowing that five children were now depending on their older sister, Iris took a deep breath, wiped the tears from her face and said a silent prayer. She needed strength and wisdom. At her young age, she wasn't sure what wisdom actually meant but she had heard her mother pray enough to know that when she really needed God's help, she could ask for strength and wisdom. Iris turned to walk toward the waiting wagon. She knew that she had to be the one to break this awful news to her brothers and sister. The babies, Pick and Cubbie, had already left to go back to the house with Uncle Carter and Aunt Esme. Augie, Joe, and Alice were waiting on the seat of the wagon, anxious to go back to the only home they had ever known. They were so very tired and they just wanted to go home.

It had been a long hard day. Iris looked up at her younger siblings sitting on the buckboard and heaved a big sigh. Knowing what she must do, Iris asked Uncle Carter if Augie, Alice, and Joe could sit with her in the back of the wagon for the ride home. It was a long, seven miles up that mountain trail, and Iris knew that it was about to get even longer.

After they nestled down in the back of the wagon Iris gave a hug and kiss to each of her brothers and her sister. She insisted that they hold hands as she began to fill them in on her conversation with their Uncle Jubal. Up the winding path toward home went the wagon. As Iris spoke, the little huddle of children seemed to grow tighter and tighter. The more Iris talked the farther down each little head would sink in despair. They couldn't believe their young ears. They couldn't understand for a minute how something so terrible could be happening to them. "Why?" was all they could muster as the wagon carried them up the mountain.

The ride up the mountain was bittersweet. They could see their home in the distance as the wagon rounded the last bend and their hearts sank to the pits of their stomachs as the reality of their dire situation loomed ahead of them. They loved that house. Augie and Joe first noticed the neatly plowed rows of the garden that they and Poppa had been working on for the last few weeks. The remainder of the withered plants from the summer vegetables had been piled up for composting and the soil had been turned under to prepare for the planting of the fall crops. They knew they would never forget the joy they had felt working alongside their father. In happier times, his eyes would sparkle as he told them stories from his childhood and they would burst out laughing as he broke into song and did a little jig for them as he guided the old mule along the neatly furrowed soil.

They would hold tight to the memories, Poppa in the garden and Momma in the house.

Momma loved having her daughters with her as she cooked and sewed and cleaned the house. Iris and Alice had treasured memories of spending so much precious time with their mother as she taught them skills they would need when they became homemakers.

Riding in the wagon up the mountain, Iris, Augie, Alice, and Joe felt a sudden urgency to try to soak in as much of their surroundings as they could. Time was slipping away from them, and life as they knew it here on this mountaintop was over. It was done.

The silence was broken as Uncle Jubal's voice boomed a hardy "whoa!" and the horses came to an abrupt stop in front of their home. Four broken-hearted children slowly began to climb down from the rear of the wagon and head toward the front porch of their home. They stopped long enough to look around the yard. A cool breeze seemed to have been summoned from above to release the sweet aroma from Momma's treasured lilac bush that Poppa planted for her at the corner of the porch.

They knew they would never forget this place. The Look, feel, and smell they would carry with them tucked in a special place deep inside their hearts where it would live forever!

Augie placed his hand on the door handle. How many times had he bounded up these steps and seen his mother standing in the doorway? Her smile, her hugs, her love. Poppa worked so hard to provide this home for them, and they never took it for granted. There was no place on earth they ever wanted to be but here, with Momma and Poppa.

It was over.

Once inside the house satchels and bags were being stuffed with clothing. Iris, the twins, Augie and Alice, and their brother Joe were scurrying around gathering their belongings and placing them in the containers.

Their four-year-old brother, Pick, had a sinking feeling in his stomach. He was just old enough to sense that he should be very afraid. Why were they packing all of their clothes? He knew that none of the things being placed in the bags were his. Was he supposed to go get his clothes? His brothers and sisters had tears running down their cheeks and they were busying around like he wasn't even there. Why wouldn't they look at him? What was happening? He overheard Aunt Maisie and Aunt Esme say the word Wyandotte. What was Wyandotte?

The commotion continued, and Pick felt helpless and alone as he watched them put on their coats and begin to gather up their baggage. All eyes soon turned toward the screen door. Pick Watie saw a black automobile come rattling up to the front of the house. A distinguished looking older man with plastered down white hair wearing a black suit got out and stuck his hand out as Uncle Jubal stepped off the porch and walked toward him. Pick didn't know what they were saying since they were speaking in low voices with their backs to the crowd.

"Come on, children. It's time to go" Uncle Jubal spoke as he turned to face the older children. Iris spun around and grabbed Pick and Cubbie with a fierce hug. Tears filled her eyes, and she could barely speak.

"I love you both with all of my heart!" Waves of tears streamed down her face. In a similar motion the others filed by and hugged their little brothers and headed slowly toward the waiting automobile.

When Kip and Addie Watie passed away, they were survived by six children. The four oldest orphans were transported on the day of their father's funeral to a government run boarding school called Seneca Indian School in Wyandotte, Oklahoma. There they would receive room and board and a good education. The two littlest orphans, Pick and Cubbie, at ages four and two were too young to be accepted at the school.

Therefore on that fateful afternoon, as dirt was being shoveled onto the coffin of their dead father, as he was buried beside the grave of their mother, the two little boys had not a clue that their clothing would be gathered and placed into satchels to be sent along with them to an orphanage in Ponca City, Oklahoma. They cried as they stood together on that porch. Two little brothers watching the last bit of their family being driven away in a cloud of dust. Their brothers and sisters were on their way to Wyandotte. Pick and Cubbie were not.

They stood hand in hand on the porch steps of their house, staring as the automobile that carried their brothers and sisters far away became just a speck amidst the rolling dust. Behind them was the house that used to be filled with laughter and music. An empty shell of a home that once sang with the deep love encircling Kip and Addie Watie and their six children.

The two littlest of the Watie orphans were so enveloped with sorrow that all they knew at that particular moment was that they longed for their mother. They searched for their father. They did not understand death and dying. They did not understand why their brothers and sisters were leaving them too.

It was 1929 and the country was on the eve of the Great Depression. As other extended family members were confronted with their own struggles, there were no takers for any of these children. There were no offers from anyone to come running up the front porch to scoop up these two littlest fellows. At four years old and two years old, Pick and Cubbie Watie had no one to rescue them. There was not one family member with a hand raised out there to pick up the pieces of these little broken hearts. They were orphans in the cruelest sense of the word.

Chapter 12

The Babies Had No Vote

Seneca Indian School was a very reputable boarding school under the auspices of the United States government. It sat perched among the scenic, rolling hilltops of the small northeast Oklahoma town of Wyandotte. The children were now in institutionalized care. The boarding school was clean and the food was good. They were old enough to be able to spend a considerable amount of time together. Iris and Alice were even allowed to be in the same room. Augie and Joe were on the same floor but had been placed in rooms with boys closer to their ages.

The environment was structured and orderly. They were clothed in the school uniforms, and the education was top notch. They were side by side with other displaced Native American children. They missed their mother and father immensely, but they were learning to adapt to their new environment.

Unfortunately for the babies, their fate was dismal.

The day after Kip Watie was buried beside his loving wife, Addie, their two young sons, Pick and Cubbie were driven to an orphanage in Ponca City, Oklahoma. The ride was long and both children slept most of the way. They were abruptly deposited at the orphanage like two packages. No arduous farewells and no promises of "we'll be back to get you soon." They didn't even know the name of the person that drove them to Ponca City. Two little babies all alone in an orphanage in Ponca City, Oklahoma.

The car had come to a stop in a circle drive just outside the front entryway to the orphanage. When Pick and Cubbie had been placed into the car they were each given a small sack. They did not remember who placed it in their hands, and they didn't know it was lunch. Neither boy had even looked into the sack to see that there was a chicken leg and an apple inside. The driver never spoke a single word to them the whole trip. Pick once asked if they could stop to pee and that was done quickly and silently. Upon their arrival, the car doors were opened and Pick and Cubbie were deposited on the steps to the orphanage.

"Go on in." the driver mumbled as he climbed back in the car and sped away.

Pick could barely reach the door knob. They soon found themselves inside a dark foyer. None of this made any sense to the two youngsters. Pick had a firm grasp on his little brother's hand as they walked toward the office of the orphanage. An older woman soon appeared, took the sack lunches from the boys' hands, tossed them in the garbage and unfastened the papers that were pinned to each child's shirt. She ordered the boys to come with her down a long hallway.

"Pickford, you will be in this room. This is your bed. Give me your satchel, and I will place it in this locker at the foot of your bed. Now stay here for a moment. I will take your brother, Lionel, to his room, and

I will be back."

"No! No! No!" cried Cubbie as the woman pulled his hand away from the grasp of his brother. Pick and Cubbie had never been apart. They slept together, ate together, and played together. They were inseparable.

Until now.

"Stop it! You have got to come with me now!" the woman snarled as she dragged Cubbie away from Pick. All Pick could do was fall on the floor on his knees with his face buried in his hands.

"Don't take my little brother! Please don't take my little brother!" wailed Pick. At that very moment, two little hearts broke again in a million little pieces and there was no one to comfort them. Cubbie was taken away and Pick was left in tears.

The rest of the afternoon the frightened and hungry Pick was taken on a tour of the home by another woman. He absorbed as much as a lonely little four-year-old boy could comprehend. He was led to the dining room where he was shown where his spot at the table would be and then he was taken back to his room. His head hurt, and he had a terrible stomachache. He flopped back on his bed and with long sobs cried himself into a deep sleep.

After a while, he felt a tapping on his leg as a boy about three years older than him said, "Come on. It's time for supper."

Rubbing his swollen eyes, he stumbled out of bed and followed the boy to the dining room. He sat down at his place and immediately began to search for Cubbie. He saw many children around the room. Some were little enough to be in high chairs. Where was his little brother? He had lost his appetite, and all he could think about was finding Cubbie. His little eyes scanned the crowd. He could not see him anywhere.

Reluctantly he ate a few bites of food and never took his eyes off the crowd of children, hoping to catch a glimpse of his baby brother.

With supper over, they were soon escorted to the bathhouse where he was scrubbed until his skin turned red. He really missed his mother now. When it was time for his bath at home she would sing sweet songs to him as she tenderly bathed his little body. This bath was not tender at all.

Lots of children to bathe and not any tenderness at all. Scrub and dry. Scrub and dry. One after the other the orphans were dipped and soaped and scrubbed and dried. Pick Watie was no exception. The nighttime bath was methodical and emotionless. He really missed his Momma.

Chapter 13

He's Got Ryzens on His Doopy!

After bath time, Pick was led back to his room. The room was filled with rows of little beds. Each one had a small boy huddled under the covers. Some were sleeping, but many were whimpering. Pick was only four years old, but he had experienced more sadness in his short life than many adults could imagine. The lights went out and he lay motionless in his bed. He had never slept without his baby brother. He was worried sick about Cubbie.

"Where is Cubbie?" he cried to himself. Then suddenly, off in the distance, he recognized his little brother's voice.

"I want Pick! I want my Pick!" Cubbie cried.

"You aren't leaving this bed, Lionel Watie!" the adult voice barked.

"My Pick!" he wailed.

Then, to Pick's horror, he heard the adult begin to spank his little brother! Over and over he could hear the slaps upon the little bare bottom. Pick sprang out of his bed and ran down the corridor toward the sounds of his little brother's cries. He knew that the wails coming from his baby brother were more than just the cries of a spanked child. They were cries of extreme pain!

Pick ran into the room, bawling and pleading, "Please, please ma'am. Please don't spank him! He has ryzens on his doopy!"

Cubbie had been running a temperature for several days before being taken to the orphanage. By the time he arrived at the home, he had several skin eruptions, called boils, covering his bottom, often referred to as "ryzens."

Pick knew that his little brother could not protect himself from the brutality of this woman. Of all the emotions swirling around in the mind of this four-year-old boy, the one that made its way to the top was seething anger. It was a blind rage. Two helpless children and one battle-ax. Pick could not stand to hear his brother cry in pain.

"Get back to bed now!" the woman gruffed as she twirled around and saw Pick standing by Cubbie's bed.

"Please, lady, you're hurting him! Please don't hit him again; he has ryzens!" The woman wasn't persuaded a bit by Pick's pleas.

"You have no business in here. Go back to your bed, and I will deal with you too!" She grabbed Pick by the arm and slung him toward the door.

Reluctantly he scurried back to his room. And my oh my, deal with him she did. He heard her shoes clomping down the hall as she headed back toward his room. He dove under the blankets but with a brisk sweep of her hand she found him fast and jerked him out from underneath the covers.

Wham! Wham! Her hand met the flesh on his bottom in several

swift strides.

"Now go to sleep and don't you ever think you can do as you please around here! There are rules and you will follow them all!"

Out the door she huffed. Oddly enough, the little four-year-old boy did not melt into a heap of tears. His jaw was set. He would not cry. He vowed that night that if he ever had any children he would never, ever spank them. He would save his little brother. It may take him awhile, but he would do whatever he could to protect his little helpless baby brother. Someday he would find a way to protect him.

Chapter 14

Aunt Nellie and Uncle Cade

Aunt Nellie and Uncle Cade hadn't been married but a few months when Nellie approached her husband about rescuing her dead brother Kip's two babies from the orphanage. Aunt Nellie, just nineteen years old with no children of her own yet, figured that she should be the one to go and get Pick and Cubbie in Ponca City. Cade didn't take much persuading. He was also saddened by the thought of those little boys being in that place. A few letters to Mrs. White and the arrangements were made for the transfer to take place on a sunny Saturday afternoon.

Pick and Cubbie had been apart for three months. They saw each other every now and then, running into each other's arms for quick hugs. The orphanage, quite overburdened with more children coming in every day or so, found it more orderly if all of the children were managed by age groups. Keeping family relationships up was not high up on the priority list. Too many children. Not enough time.

Pick learned quite early on to keep himself out of any controversy. He was a compliant and mannerly child. Cubbie, on the other hand, cried a lot. Of the two boys, Cubbie was the most sensitive in nature. He couldn't quite get the hang of things and found himself at the end of the paddle, ryzens or not, just about daily. So the day that Mrs. White came and got Pick from the dinner table, he was more curious than concerned, since he was pretty sure his "nose was clean." She took him to her office and told him to wait there for a moment and she would be back.

Cubbie, didn't trust that old woman for an instant. As soon as he saw her come his way, down went his head. Smack dab in the center of a pile of mashed potatoes.

"No! No!" he cried. "No spank me!" Mrs. White had as much disdain for Cubbie as he had for her.

She jerked him up, wiped the potatoes from his face, and blurted out, "Lionel, stop your crying! Come on now. Come with me!" Down the hall they went, Cubbie being dragged, kicking and screaming, all the way.

As Pick waited patiently in Mrs. White's office, it wasn't long before his ears perked up when he recognized the all too familiar wails coming from his little brother. He jumped up to grab a peek down the hall to see what was happening when out of the corner of his eye he saw a young man walk through the door of the office. He knew him! Was that... was that really his Uncle Cade? Pick couldn't contain himself for a second. He took off running toward his uncle. Uncle Cade laughed and patted Pick on the head.

"There you are, you little rascal! Where's your brother?"

"Waaaaaaaa! No! No pull arm!" All their heads turned to see that Pick's little brother, Cubbie, had been found. Cubbie, unaware of the audience, planted one swift kick to the shin of the exasperated Mrs. White.

"Ouch! You little, urchin!" Mrs. White, also unaware of the same audience, returned the favor with a quick swat to Cubbie's rear end. What a spectacle they were!

Chapter 15

Welcome to the 101 Ranch.
Lil' Pardners!

Aunt Nellie was Kip Watie's younger sister. She had recently married her sweetheart, Cade Overstreet, and as newlyweds, with the rotten state of the current economy, had both come to the realization that they barely had enough money for nothing more than a meager existence. The stock market had just taken a horrific crash, and people from all walks of life were feeling the pain of unemployment and despair. Cade, a house painter by trade, was discovering that it was hard to find anyone that had the extra income to hire someone to put a fresh coat of paint on their home or business, particularly when their cupboards were getting emptier by the day.

The misery index in the entire country was at an all time high, and to add insult to injury, a drought had settled into the state so severe that it wasn't long before the dry winds blew with great gusts from the west and the moisture robbing clouds of dust rolled in and enveloped the area with dark, black relentless waves of suffocating wind and dust. Crops were failing at a rapid pace, and the prospects of employment were grim.

Many of those that had earlier struck out westward and settled in Oklahoma could no longer stand the misery and were making the decision to pack up their belongings and head back east where they had relatives and the promise of work. Those with a bit of wanderlust still lurking in their dreams, continued onward toward California. The common reasoning was that at least both coasts had water, this place was nothing but a rimless bowl of dust!

Cade was finding a few odd jobs here and there, just enough to keep himself and his new bride from starvation. With each sunrise came the daily struggle just to survive.

Nonetheless, not a day went by that Nellie didn't crumble in a heap in her husband's arms as she bawled and bellowed over the fate of her brother Kip's children. Cade would listen and try to comfort her the best that he knew how. He was just a young man himself and was mired in the day-to-day worries of a husband trying to keep food on his own table. Cade had great sympathy for the Watie children, but as he held his wife in his arms, for the life of him, he couldn't come up with any solution to the dilemma. A few dollars change and some pocket lint were pretty close to about all he could count as his fortune.

He had to remind his wife daily that they would only be adding to the misery of the children. He assured her that where the children were being cared for, they most certainly had the promise of daily nourishment. Cade and Nellie both knew that they could barely feed themselves, let alone six hungry and growing children.

Cade went to the town square on a daily basis to mill around with other unemployed men to see if there was any word of gainful employment. Every so often, if a farmer had been fortunate enough to coax a crop from the parched earth, he would come to town to see if any able-bodied men were willing to spend the day at his farm working the fields. The pay was little, but little was better than nothing, and the men hoisted themselves up onto the wagons to head out for a day of work.

Cade Overstreet had come prepared for a day in the field as he was willing to do anything to keep a roof over their heads. The wagons were filling quickly and Cade had placed his hands on the sideboards to heave himself up and over when he glanced at a gentleman tacking up a poster on the side of the livery stable wall. Curiosity got the better of him as he stood back and watched the wagon pull away, headed toward the farm and work. For a split second, he felt as if he might have just jeopardized his chances of having enough money to pay their rent as the wagon disappeared around the bend. However, something in his gut told him that this just might be a worthwhile decision as he sauntered toward the billboard.

The numbers 101 were printed boldly in the corner of the poster. As he got closer, he could feel a rush of excitement as he continued to read the best news he had heard in weeks!! The 101 Ranch was hiring! Before he got halfway down the sign he saw "Skilled Painters Needed," and that was enough for him. He dashed to the livery stable and asked his friend, Nate Hadley, if he could borrow his rig for the afternoon so he could make a fast trip to Ponca City to check on a job. Without hesitation, Nate had Cade situated aboard the buckboard and on his way!

With the scarcity of employment, Cade knew that he better ske-daddle as fast as the horse could go to get a place in the employment line at the ranch. His father had taught him his painting skills, and Cade Overstreet was a master at his craft. No doubt he could do a very fine job, he just had to high tail it over there before the news of jobs would spread like wildfire, bringing hoards of unemployed from every nook and cran-ny in the region. In times like these, it was every man for himself.

Cade had the reins wrapped around a post and was bounding toward the growing line of men in a flash. He felt satisfied by the length of the line that he had made it before the onslaught that he knew was to come. Most of the men were lined up to apply for the carpenter positions.

Cade glanced around and his eye caught a sign that said, "Paint-ers Line Up Here."

Hot diggedy! He was first in line! The man at the table asked him the pertinent questions, and before he knew it, he was being told that he could start the next day and that there would be a house on the ranch for his family! The 101 Ranch! He would be living and working on the famous 101 Ranch!! He couldn't wait to get back to town to tell Nellie the good news! There was a bright and shining sun on the horizon!

In its prime, the 101 Ranch had comprised 110,000 acres. Col-onel George W. Miller, the founder of the ranch, had given rise to one of the most fascinating chapters of American history and added untold tales of wonder and excitement to the annals of the western frontier. Its Wild West and Great Far East shows were known around the world! When they weren't on the road performing for the great crowds and admiring fans around the globe, they would be headquartered at the Oklahoma ranch. Buffalo Bill Cody and Pawnee Bill Lillie would delight the crowds with their fast-paced and action packed performances. It was billed as "the most magnificent tented attraction ever put on wheels." Riding, roping, shooting, all at a thundering pace that kept the onlookers begging for more! The excitement was riveting! Indian war whoops would send chills and thrills down the spines of the audiences as "has been" Indian warriors, tamed only by broken treaties and the long end of a rifle held by the U.S. government, participated in reenactments and mock massacres. The only difference between what had been and what was portrayed was that the outcome was always the same—the white men would win and the Indians would surrender. Their falling pride was nevertheless overshadowed by the promise of payment at the end of each performance. Everybody needed to eat.

The glamour of the Wild West soon made famous stars from some of the local talent. Buoyed by their fame as wild and rowdy performers in the 101 Ranch productions, several actors were propelled to stardom—Tom Mix, Buck Jones, Hoot Gibson, and William Desmond Taylor all soon saw their name in marquee lights all around the world. The 101 Ranch had been a huge success. Colonel George Washington Miller had moved his family from Baxter Springs, Kansas to the sprawling acreage of the infamous 101 Ranch after several years of building his cattle empire in the southeastern parts of Kansas. By having a heart made of gold, he proved himself a worthy friend of the Ponca Indians by giving them food to eat when they needed it the most. When he needed a favor in return, all he had to do was ask and the Ponca tribe came to his aid without hesitation. They helped him as he moved his cattle operation to Oklahoma, and the 101 Ranch was born.

When the Colonel passed away his sons tried their best to keep the cattle ranch and the Wild West and Great Far East Shows operating in the black. Through adversities and tragedies that wasn't always the end result. Untimely deaths and economic struggles kept the show from ever again achieving the greatness it once knew. However, the few surviving members of the Miller family had decided in early 1929 to give it a go one more time. The show went back on the road.

Cade Overstreet couldn't have come to 101 Ranch at a more opportune time. There was a renewed excitement, and from years of neglect, there were houses, buildings, and barns all needing fresh coats of paint. Nellie was delighted with the news and it took her no time at all to gather their belongings, load them on the wagon, and prepare for the ride to Ponca City and the 101 Ranch.

Cade and Nellie settled into their house at the ranch that afternoon. It was one of several that housed the other hired hands, carpenters, electricians, and jacks-of-all-trades that were proud and excited to be a part of the renewal of the great old ranch. Nellie became fast friends with the wives of the other workers, and Cade went about the task of spreading his white paint on every structure he could find.

"Cade, can we at least go get the babies?"

Cade put down his fork and slowly wiped his mouth with his napkin. He had been expecting this conversation for several days. They had a furnished house, food in the cupboards, and a tidy sum of money in the bank. The orphanage where Pick and Cubbie were was eight miles from the ranch.

"Nellie, I have pondered this situation front, back, and sideways. I think we are both aware of the fact that the older children have settled in nicely at the boarding school. They are receiving an excellent education, and from my last conversation with Mr. Kagey, they seem happy. And I'm told they are thriving. The boys are involved in basketball and Iris and Alice have made a lot of friends and are doing well in school. I don't think it would be in their best interest to bring them from their stable environment to this small house out here on the prairie in Ponca City, as none of the other workers have children their ages. I feel that we should give up on the notion of uprooting the four of them after all that they have been through already. Mr. Kagey has assured me that they are fine. That leaves Pick and Cubbie. I have visited Mrs. White at the orphanage and informed her that we are prepared to come next weekend to bring the two boys to live here at the ranch with us."

Nellie Overstreet burst into tears of joy as she jumped from her seat at the table and threw her arms around her husband's neck.

"Thank you, Cade! I can't thank you enough." she sobbed.

She placed a kiss on his forehead and began to remove the dishes from the table to the sink. The sun was setting on the horizon as she stuck her hands into the hot, soapy water searching around for the next dirty dish. Around and around the plate went the dishrag she held loosely in her hands. She began to hear the squeak of the clean plate as she peered out the window into the distance.

"I can do this. I just know it."

Chapter 16

First Things First

Nellie Overstreet took one look at the two scrawny boys that peeked out from behind her husband Cade's pant legs. What a sight they were! Even at four years old, Nellie knew that Pick was going to grow up tall and lanky like his mother, Addie. Nellie's eyes landed on little Cubbie, and she swore she was looking right at her dead brother, Kip. Cubbie was the spitting image of Kip, and Pick was Addie made over.

"Come here and let me look at you two!" Aunt Nellie squealed as she headed toward the two youngsters. Even though she had out-stretched arms and a mile wide grin, Pick and Cubbie were not quite sure what to think. Instinctively they both grabbed at Uncle Cade's pant legs and held on for dear life!

"Now, don't you be afraid of me. You remember your Aunt Nellie, don't you?"

As a matter of fact Pick did remember his Aunt Nellie. He had vague memories of going to visit somewhere and Aunt Nellie would be there. As he loosened his grip on Cade's trousers, Pick realized that this place just had to be better than the orphanage. It just had to be.

When two-year-old Cubbie saw his brother Pick slowly walk

toward Aunt Nellie, he momentarily considered doing the same thing. However, he had no memory of Aunt Nellie or Uncle Cade, and after all he had been through at the orphanage, he didn't trust anyone. He decided to wait and see what was going to happen next. Aunt Nellie bent over and gave Pick a big hug. He hadn't had any affection in so long and her hug felt so nice. He blushed and felt warm inside. He felt loved for the first time since he went to the orphanage.

When Aunt Nellie went toward Cubbie, all of the horrible memories of Mrs. White and the orphanage came rushing back to the little boy, and he squared off in front of his Aunt Nellie and gave her a swift kick right in the shin!

Pick scolded his little brother. "Cubbie, don't kick Aunt Nellie! She's nice and she's going to take care of us!"

Cubbie began to cry. He was so confused. He had lost his parents, causing him to be ripped from the only home he had ever known and thrown into a dismal orphanage where all he could think of was cranky old Mrs. White, the smell of urine, babies crying all the time, and being bitten by a dog! It was going to take a whole lot more than outstretched arms to win over this little boy. His spirit was so crushed and aching. It was going to take a whole lot more.

Nellie was so taken aback. This was not how she pictured the way the welcoming party would go. Not in a million years did she expect Kip's baby to kick her smack dab in the shin.

Nellie Overstreet was in no way, shape or form prepared for what she had just signed up for. She was only nineteen years old, newly

132

married, and had no children of her own. Even though her father, Pickford, had died when she was very young, her mother Simmy had seen to it that her children had a stable and happy home. Nellie had never been subjected to suffering, rejection, or abuse. She had not a clue what the two little boys had been through.

In her simplistic and immature mind, she thought a few hugs, shelter, and home cooking would make everything perfect. Because of her naivety, Aunt Nellie expected an idyllic homecoming celebration. The two boys would run to her and scream with joy. She was their emancipator. They were free from bondage and could now live happily ever after on the 101 Ranch with their aunt and uncle.

Instead, she found herself cleaning up the messy pants of two-year-old Cubbie as he kicked and screamed and pulled away from her, making things a whole lot messier. Nellie remembered that he had been toilet trained before Kip and Addie passed away. Apparently life at the orphanage caused some set backs.

That was an understatement.

Chapter 17

Tony, the Soda Pop Drinking Bear

Aunt Nellie made sure that her two nephews had nice clothes, three square meals, and hot baths at the end of the day. Unfortunately, intermingled in the care taking of these little orphaned boys was a growing and seething resentment.

Aunt Nellie was not much more than a kid herself. At age nineteen, she had not reached the maturity she had needed to take on the task of raising someone else's children. Dead brother or no dead brother, Nellie resented cleaning Cubbie's soiled underwear. She tried time and time again to get him to tell her when he had the urge to go so she could walk him out to the outhouse behind their home.

Of course, through experiences at the orphanage, Cubbie sensed the resentment.

She was sort of patient at first, but the more soiled underwear she scrubbed, the less patient she became. Soon she found herself dragging Cubbie by the arm out the back door and slinging him toward the outhouse. She knew it was too late. He had already soiled his britches, but she was determined that Cubbie found himself near the outhouse by hook or by crook. She would show him the outhouse one way or the other.

The more she lost her patience with Cubbie the more the troubled little child rebelled. As far as he was concerned, his Aunt Nellie was no different than mean old Mrs. White. No affection offered and none returned.

Pick was beside himself. The fairy tale ending was turning into a nightmare.

Always the diplomat, Pick Watie found himself taking Cubbie away from Aunt Nellie and the house as much as he could. There was so much to explore at the 101 Ranch.

Even though the glory days of the iconic entertainment venue had waned, Pick and Cubbie never ran out of things to investigate. One of their favorite things to do was to go visit Tony, the soda pop drinking black bear that made his home just outside of the general store. Some days he would be in a cage. Other days found Tony lounging in his hole, which he had dug under the wooden porch in front of the store, secured only by a chain around his neck.

The contributing factor to whether Tony would be found in his cage or chained under the stoop was how much the cowboys drank the night before. If more than a few cowpokes got a snoot full and became rowdy, Tony's cage would be their home away from home for the evening.

Tony didn't seem to mind the slight inconvenience at all. His main focus was begging for a five cent bottle of soda pop from the stream of visitors that frequented the ranch. As the people approached the general store, Tony would come out of his hole and stand tall with both hands forward and belt out a screeching bear yodel. If he happened to be caged on any day, he would be reaching between the bars of his cage for a slurp of that sugary beverage. The visitors would go into the store, lay down their nickel and place the cold pop into Tony's waiting paws. Tony knew the drill. He would use both paws and hold the bottle to his mouth, slurping every last drop of the mouth watering liquid. As soon as the bottle was empty, Tony would sling it behind him and instantly begin to beg for more. He usually didn't have to wait long until another spectator offered forth a refreshing bottle of soda pop.

Aunt Nellie, relieved to have a break, gladly gave the two boys their daily nickels. She knew they would be heading to see the soda pop drinking bear, and she silently hoped they would take the long way around.

As they approached the fat, lazy, sugar satiated bear, Pick and Cubbie would begin to call his name. "Tony, Tony! We're here, boy!" It sure seemed to the little fellows that Tony recognized his two buddies and was very glad to see them. They were convinced that even if they didn't give him the soda pop he would still be their friend.

Coincidentally, Tony acted differently around the boys. Instead of standing tall and begging with his insistent yodel, Tony would sit down with his legs stretched wide apart and proceed to just stare at the half pint visitors. When they waved, he waved back. When they put their arms to their sides, so did Tony. Tony, the soda pop drinking bear, with the heavy chain around his neck, seemed to be telling the youngsters that he understood the weight that the two freckle faced little boys carried.

He had his problems around his neck, and so did they.

Chapter 18

God, Can You Hear This Prayer?

Pick Watie was born with a severe birth defect. His kidneys were deformed. They did not have the normal shape to them and looked like angry, knotted up fists.

Therefore kidney infections were an ever-present way of life for him. Ravaged with sharp, sheet-gripping, unrelenting pain, the young boy took to his bed with ridiculously high fevers at the most inconvenient times.

Inconvenient because it took him away from Cubbie. He was Cubbie's bodyguard and earthly savior. A five-year-old soldier, he never worried about himself. Lying in a pool of sweat, Pick would try to get up and get out of bed, knowing that at any given moment Cubbie would need him. Cubbie needed him a lot.

Especially on that day....

It started raining early that morning. Lightening bolts streaked across the sky sending loud pops and crackles up and down the pasture. Cubbie huddled in bed beside his older brother. Throughout the night, Pick had moaned and groaned, wracked with the pain that surged throughout his little body. The more he suffered, the closer Cubbie would snuggle in and hold his beloved brother tighter and tighter.

When tears of agony streaked down Pick's face, a matched set would find their way down the cheeks of his little brother. The only known remedy for the ailing boy was to flush the infection by drinking lots and lots of sulfur-laced water.

All throughout the night, Cubbie never failed to sense the correct time to coax his brother to drink up. A few times, Aunt Nellie would come into the bedroom to check on her nephew and give him a sip of water. That wasn't enough as far as Cubbie was concerned. He offered up the cup every hour on the hour, like clockwork.

At daybreak, Cubbie sat the water jug back down on the bedside table. In that instant, he was jarred all the way down to his toes by an electrifying zig zag bolt of lightening followed by a clap of thunder. Cubbie hated storms, and today he hated them more than ever. It had been a long night and he was exhausted.

The two-year-old boy was tired, afraid, and worried about his best friend in the whole wide world. Therefore, he was in no way prepared for that moment when the bedroom door came open, and he saw Aunt Nellie standing in the early morning shadow. His heart sank below the floor.

When the loud clap of thunder startled the little boy, Cubbie had dirtied his underwear.

Aunt Nellie had come into the bedroom to bring a fresh jug of sulfur water for Pick. As she neared the bedside table she knew instantly what she smelled. With a jerk, she grabbed Cubbie up by the arm and dragged him out of the bedroom. Nellie never said a word to the boy as she pulled him into the kitchen. His underwear was removed from his body and placed on a plate on the kitchen table.

"Eat it!"

His head was shoved toward the plate as he was forced to take a bite of his own feces.

"Stop! Stop, Aunt Nellie! Please don't do that to him!"

Pick stood in the doorway, his hollow eyes filled with terror and fury. He gripped the door-facing to hold up his weakened body. His labored voice was just above a whisper. With every ounce of strength he could muster, Pick headed toward Aunt Nellie.

Lost in her fury, Aunt Nellie hadn't even heard Pick's cry, nor had she seen him dragging himself toward the battle. The troubled young woman had finally reached her point of no return. Determined to finish this with the flair of a mad woman, Nellie Overstreet grabbed the little boy from the chair at the kitchen table and stood him upright and pushed him toward the basement stairway.

Her hand planted square in the middle of Cubbie's back and with a quick shove, the young child went tumbling down the stairs into the basement. She never blinked an eye. She couldn't have been more removed from the emotions of what she had just done. A little boy, a sack of potatoes, what's the difference?

The half-naked child made hardly a sound as his body bounced from step to step.

Cubbie wound up in a heap on the dark and damp basement floor. He began to whimper. Bright red blood oozed in striped formations down his legs. As he tumbled, they were scraped by haphazard splinters and nail heads. He had not broken any bones, and his head had landed in a pile of lime covered potatoes, saving his skull from any damage. Nellie remained motionless at the top of the stairs. The silence was broken by the sound of a kitchen chair hitting the floor.

Young Pick had made it as far as the table and had grabbed ahold of a chair to keep himself balanced. The chair and Pick hit the floor about the same time. Aunt Nellie turned around and saw that five-year-old Pick was out cold. His body was sprawled in the middle of the kitchen floor. The high fever and dehydration had sent him reeling until he passed out cold. He didn't make it in time to save his baby brother from the hands of his Aunt Nellie.

Almost in a hypnotic trance, Nellie walked over to the coat rack and proceeded to put on her raincoat and galoshes. She left the two children as they were and went directly to fetch her husband, Cade.

As was customary for Pick and Cubbie, they never failed to go to sleep without saying their prayers. Two nights before the incident, Pick had told God about the burden on his heart. He had prayed the best prayer that a five-year-old child could muster. His body was wracked with fever but nonetheless he reached out to the Lord and said all that he needed to say, "God, help me and my little brother."

Chapter 19

Short Miles but a Long Ride

There was not a single word spoken on that eight-mile trip as Uncle Cade commandeered the sedan along the streets of Ponca City, Oklahoma. Aunt Nellie did not accompany the children on this trip. She stayed at home, saying that she had to do the dishes.   It was kind of like soda pop bottles. When all the good stuff is gone and you don't have need for the empty bottle, you take it back to the store where you bought it.

Pick and Cubbie were being treated like soda pop bottles. They were being returned. Pick's emotions were all over the place. He watched Aunt Nellie place every piece of clothing they owned into two separate little bags. She wouldn't look at him. She busied around like she was the only person in the room. She had tried her best, she told herself. She just couldn't do it anymore. Maybe she was too young to have even tried to tackle something as demanding as trying to raise two little boys. She just couldn't do it anymore.

Did she have remorse for the abuse? Yes. She was swallowed up by it. Their Aunt Nellie was so ashamed for the horrible things she had done. That's why she couldn't look at them. She couldn't look at her two nephews and tell them how sorry she was that she lost her temper so many times. They were good boys. They were sweet boys.

She just didn't have patience to deal with the emotional baggage that came with those two freckled faces.

Uncle Cade had not known how bad it had gotten until that fateful rainy morning. He worked long hours at the 101 Ranch, and by the time he got home each night Aunt Nellie had already put the boys to bed. If they were in bed, she didn't have to deal with them.

Cade rushed back to the house after Nellie showed up at his workshop. She was crying uncontrollably. All she could say amidst her blubbering was, "I'm so so sorry. Cade, come home. I'm so so sorry." Cade wasted no time and scurried down the pathway to their house. Nellie was close behind, running with her head in her hands. In the mean time, Pick had come to and dragged himself down the stairs to retrieve his baby brother. When Uncle Cade burst through the door and headed down the basement stairs, he saw the two children huddled at the bottom sitting on a pile of lime-covered potatoes. Pick was pale and sweating profusely and Cubbie sat wide-eyed and motionless, covered in blood.

Nellie Overstreet told her husband everything. She placed her face in her hands and wept. She was so ashamed of what she had done to the two little, innocent children.

She explained to Cade that no matter how hard she tried, she couldn't control her temper. Uncle Cade couldn't believe what he was hearing. His heart sank when his wife told him the things she had done. He felt sick about what Pick and Cubbie had endured at the hands of their

144

Aunt Nellie.

He didn't know what to do. He knew that Nellie was done. She was telling him in no uncertain terms that she couldn't handle being their mother figure anymore. She was done. He agreed that they needed to be removed from her care, but where was he to take them?

They must take them back to the orphanage. It was mutually agreed. There was no other answer. No one wanted them before so they figured that no one would take them now.

Uncle Cade made the arrangements to return Pick and Cubbie to the orphanage the very next day. Unfortunately, though, Cade and Nellie Overstreet made a very selfish decision. They didn't want anyone to know that they had been such failures at child rearing, so they decided to not tell anyone that they were taking the boys back. As far as Angus Scott knew, Nellie and Cade had taken the boys in and all was well.

Trees and birds. Pick glanced out of the back seat window and saw trees and birds. He could barely think about what he was seeing. It had been so scary living with Aunt Nellie. He saw the good in her. He knew she meant well, but when she lost her temper it was "Katy, bar the door!"

He knew that his little brother couldn't handle any more of Aunt Nellie. The damage was deep and cut like a knife. He had protected his brother the best he could. He looked down at Cubbie. Little Cubbie sat next to his big brother and snuggled as tightly to him as he could as Uncle Cade's car pulled in to the driveway to The American Legion Children's Home in Ponca City, Oklahoma.

145

As the car came slowly to a stop, Pick looked out the car window. The precious little boy immediately recognized the orphanage. His insides began to crumble. Just like empty soda pop bottles, they were being returned.

Chapter 20

Poppa and Momma

A good night's sleep was hard to come by for Angus Scott. El-la's night tantrums were definitely a factor, but over the years, he had almost grown used to hearing her cry out those inaudible words. When she went to throwing her arms up in the air, yelling, "stop!" he knew he should just get up and go sleep on the old rollaway bed.

Many years ago he would try to console her. He tried every-thing he could think of like hugging her tight or gently nudging her until she would awaken. He was a patient man, but after so many hateful con-frontations in the middle of the night, he just decided to let sleeping dogs lie or something like that.

Angus hadn't recognized much about the woman that lay be-side him at night for many years. When he came home from the prison in New York, she was not the same woman he had married. He surmised that something horrific had happened to her, but try though he might, she was impenetrable. The truth was he had grown to love Jessie as if he were his own son. It was easy to do as Jessie had a heart of gold. From the beginning, the little boy had a humble spirit, almost as if he knew that he was an uninvited guest to the family. Set another plate and let him in.

Ella held the name of Jessie's father between two tight lips. She refused to go near the subject, and eventually, Angus grew weary of trying and just accepted the life that had been dealt his way.

He did love Ella. How could he not remember the good times? The times before there were demons rattling about in her brain. He had pity for Ella. He would never abandon her. He had pity and memories of their love from long ago.

How could Angus bring two little boys into this home? How could he? That's what had kept him tossing and turning since his son-in-law, Kip had died. Kip was a wonderful father. After Addie died, there was never a doubt that Kip would pick up the pieces and go on with their six children.

Angus had asked the Lord many times why He would take both of them and leave those children alone? After Kip came down with typhoid fever and it was evident that he was losing the battle, Angus heard one person after the other say that they had no room in their homes for Kip and Addie's six children. Times were hard, and there just wasn't anyone that felt like they could afford to add six more mouths to their tables. They weren't the only families in those parts that were suffering.

So many well-intentioned Christian churches had taken it upon themselves to establish boarding schools in North America. It was their understanding that in order for the indigenous people to be truly accepted into the Christian faith, they had to shed their heathen culture and become more like the White Man. They tried day schools, but their pupils were versed in the Christian way during the day at school, but as soon as the bell would ring, they would go back to their homes to speak their Native American tongues and dress in their Indian garb.

In the white, Christian minds, this hindered any progress toward their goals of acculturation of the Indian children to make sure they would go to heaven when they died.

"It is for their own good." That was the mantra. The Indians had to become more civilized in order to be Christian. Thus the boarding schools were opened, and Native American families were counseled, or forced, to give their children a chance for a better life by allowing them to come live at the boarding schools full time.

It was an expensive venture for the churches to open and run the boarding schools, and often, they turned to the government for assistance in order to keep the doors open. Eventually the schools became 100 percent government run facilities, and as the government began to take over the operations, the services slowly eroded. More often than not the Indian children were abused, raped, or used almost as indentured servants providing hard labor for the institutions. One school, however, was the exception. The Seneca Indian School in Wyandotte, Oklahoma was rated the number one Native American boarding school in the nation.

Thanks went solely to the two administrators, Joe Kagey and his wife Aline. They truly cared about the children. When the government only allotted twenty cents a day per student (that was to include food, boarding, education, shipping of the food and supplies, and medical expenses) Joe Kagey set forth his plan to make Seneca Indian School self-sufficient to a great extent. The soil in the northeast Oklahoma area was loamy and fertile, and it made perfect sense to Joe Kagey that they grow their own vegetables. To further that premise, he started an animal husbandry program thus not only providing farming and ranching skills to the students but adding meat and poultry to the school's larder. Besides their state regulated curriculum for education, the boys were taught auto mechanics and technical skills, and the girls were taught sewing, cooking and other homemaking skills.

Therefore when the Bureau of Indian Affairs opened up the school to all tribes, they also put a stipulation that admission be granted only to those students showing a need, especially orphans.

Agents of the Bureau of Indian Affairs were no strangers to the Native American communities around Dustin, Oklahoma. They had been going door to door for months canvasing the homes, looking for needy Indian children to place in the boarding schools. Typhoid fever had been running rampant in those parts leaving many one parent or no parent homes. The government agents did as they were mandated to do. Find the needy children and transport them to BIA run schools.

When Addie Watie died, it wasn't long before there was a knock on Kip's door. The BIA agent introduced himself and queried Kip as to his intentions for the care and education of his six children. Kip didn't hesitate to set the record straight for the government agent.

His sole purpose going forward in his life was to keep his children right by his side and see to it that they got the best care and education available.   The agent tipped his hat to Kip, thanked him for his time, and drove away. Little did Kip know that the government agent had already started a file on each of the Watie children, just in case.

Word got around fast that Kip Watie was infected with the "swamp fever" and was on his deathbed. Like a blaze, the word also got to the local BIA agent. He reached into his burgeoning satchel and pulled out the files for Iris, Augie, Alice, Joe, Pickford "Pick," and Lionel "Cubbie" Watie. He quickly noticed that the two youngest children, Pickford, age four, and Lionel, age two, were ineligible for the boarding school. He neatly replaced those two files and started to work on the information for the four older children.

To each folder he attached an application form. At the top of each form he drew a large star and wrote: Expedite admission to Seneca Indian School: Orphan. A large rubber band was placed around the four files, and the government agent placed a call to Mr. Joe Kagey at the Seneca Indian School in Wyandotte, Oklahoma.

"Mr. Kagey, this is Homer Bernson. How are you today?"

After the pleasantries, Mr. Bernson and Mr. Kagey discussed the upcoming arrival of the four Watie children, from Dustin, Oklahoma.

Was this government overreaching? Absolutely. Was there any question that Mr. Kagey would be welcoming Iris, Augie, Alice, and Joe Watie in a few days? No, there was no question as far as the government agent, Mr. Homer Bernson, was concerned. This was a pretty open and shut case for him. He was quite confident that after he gathered up the Watie children's files and drove over to the family home, where Kip Watie lay dying, he would procure the proper signature on the admission forms for Seneca Indian School and be arranging transportation by the day's end.

"Thank you for your cooperation, Mr. Scott. It is obvious by your signature on these forms that you love your grandchildren and recognize that it is in their best interest to be placed under the auspices of the Bureau of Indian Affairs. Furthermore, I can assure you that this monumental decision you have just made will secure a prosperous future for each one of these children. Yes, sir, they will certainly thrive at the Seneca Indian School." As Homer Bernson stood to leave, he shook Angus Scott's hand and took one last glance around the living room of Kip and Addie's home. If he had seen one he had seen them all. It was all in a day's work for Homer. He glanced at his pocket watch, realizing that he had plenty of time to call the school and put Mr. Kagey on notice that four more students were being added to the roster. As he made his way to the door, Mr. Bernson suddenly remembered something that he forgot to give to Angus Scott.

"Oh, Mr. Scott. Here is the contact information for the American Legion Children's Home over in Ponca City. They take in the younger ones. It's a shame that the two little ones can't accompany their brothers and sisters to Wyandotte, but I have heard good things about the care received by the orphaned youngsters at that home." He placed the sheet of paper on the table by the door, tipped his hat, and strode out the door, leaving Angus Scott standing motionless in the middle of the living room of his deceased daughter's home. His beloved son-in-law lay dying in the bedroom and Angus was coming to grips with the fact that he had just sealed the fate of his grandchildren.

All in a day's work for Homer Bernson.

Angus felt like the worst person on the face of the earth. The government agent put a wonderful spin on what he knew was the coerced removal of his grandchildren. The family and friends were immersed in their grief as they stood around the graveside of Kip Watie. No one seemed to notice the short, balding man off in the distance, standing by a tree in the Dustin, Oklahoma cemetery. Homer Bernson had a job to do and a schedule to keep. Jobs were hard to come by in those days, and Homer understood that if he didn't complete his orders, there were several men waiting to take his place. He was to pick up the Watie children immediately after the funeral, and he had every intention of being at their home in a timely manner.

There was a house full of visitors in the Watie home when Homer Bernson drove up the lane. They recognized his car immediately and knew exactly why he was there at Kip's home. This same scenario was happening all over the county. Families were being torn apart all over the area as Indian parents were dropping like flies with typhoid fever. Orphans were being made on a daily basis.

Friends and family members alike scattered like flies as Mr. Bernson walked toward the front door. It was evident that they loved Kip and his children, but they didn't want to be around for this at all. None of them were going to come forward to take the children into their homes, as they had their own problems.

Angus Scott was right among them on that. He told himself that his wife Ella was too mean to take in the six children. They would be miserable around her. She barely raised her own eight children, and he shuddered to think how awful she would be if he told her that Addie's six children were moving into their house. As Angus was trying to convince himself he shouldn't take the children, Mr. Bernson did a stand up job convincing him to let them go. So he let them go. He never slept another peaceful night after placing his signature on the paperwork to give up Kip and Addie's children.

Over the eighteen months since Kip's death, Angus had received notices from the Seneca Indian School informing him of the well-being of four of his grandchildren. He was convinced by the hand written letters from Joe Kagey that Iris, Augie, Alice, and Joe were thriving. On the flip side, it had been awhile since Kip's younger sister, Nellie, had written him with news about Pick and Cubbie.

He had been praying mighty hard for about two weeks, sensing the need for heavenly intervention of some sort. Ella Scott was going about her daily chores when she glanced over at the kitchen table and saw her husband, Angus, with his head bowed and his hands clasped in front of him. She had no clue whatever that her husband, Angus, was deep in prayer for Pick and Cubbie. Angus prayed before his meals and oddly enough he prayed afterwards too. Little did Ella know that the after meal prayers were Angus's plea that he would be able to digest Ella's horrible cooking and not keel over dead. Ella continued to sweep around him. The farm was never quiet. There were always chickens cackling, cows mooing or neighboring dogs barking in the distance. Today however, Angus's prayer was interrupted by the sound of a wagon pulling up in front of the house.

Ella scurried over to the window to take a peek, curious as to whom their noon day visitors were and was surprised to see her sons, Logan and Duff climbing down from the wagon being pulled by Old Tobe. It was hay-hauling season and Logan and Duff had been leaving before daybreak and not returning until past dark. Something must have been wrong for them to show up at noon.

Logan Scott was the first one to step into the house. He made sure he did double duty scraping mud from his boots on the edge of the step. He had no desire to give his mother any reason to go off on him in a tirade. Yes, he knew quite well how many times a day she swept the floors. Following close behind was the older of the two brothers, Duff. He had been out in the front yard using his straw hat to beat any remaining bits of hay off his britches. Poppa had said a hurried, "Amen" and rose from the table to meet his two sons in the living room.

"Everything all right, boys? Nobody hurt?"

Duff looked square at his father and without taking a breath began to spill the news.

"No, Poppa. We just heard something that we figured we needed to come tell you as quick as we could. We was in Gray's to buy some twine and ran into Mr. Parks. It seems he just got back from Ponca City visiting his sister. While he was there he ran into Cade Overstreet at the hardware store in town."

"Is this news about the younguns, Duff? Are they all right?" Poppa sat down in his rocker and leaned forward, bracing himself for what he supposed would be an onslaught of something he didn't want to hear.

As for Ella, none of this conversation had sparked her interest, and she had a cow to milk. So without as much as an "hello" she tootled her way out the back door. Logan couldn't wait any longer and picked up the story right where his brother Duff left off.

"Poppa, Nellie and Cade took our sister Addie's babies back to that goll durned orphanage! Been there nigh on three months now and never told nobody. We ain't at all happy about it, and we knew this would send you reelin' too."

Angus Scott's face reflected his true Scottish roots. The more he thought about what he had just been told, the redder his face got. It seems that Mr. Parks was able to ascertain from Cade that he and Nellie had run out of patience with the two children and had taken Pick and Cubbie back to the orphanage three months prior and didn't tell anyone until now. It made Angus sick to his stomach to think about it. He knew he had to go get them.

There was not a doubt in his mind that he had to go get those two little boys. They were Addie's babies. Addie's babies needed him, and he did the only thing he could think of to do at that very moment. He prayed.

"God, please help me through this"

Three days later, Angus Scott slung his old straw hat upon the top of his head and hefted himself up over the side of the buckboard. Ole Tobe, his faithful, long eared mule, was ready to go at the first flip of the reins.

The sun was hot that morning as it bore down on the back of his neck. He knew he was burning daylight as Ponca City was quite a haul from Dustin and he had already gotten such a late start. Ella was having a really bad morning. She refused to cook him any breakfast and was busy pacing back and forth on the front porch. She was fit to be tied. He had told her last night that he was going to the orphanage to pick up Addie's babies. He was going to bring Pick and Cubbie to live with them.

"I don't want no more children to raise in this house! There won't be no food left for us. Them two fellers will eat it all!" Ella's parting words were echoing in Angus's head.

He could still see her standing on the porch stoop hollering and stomping her feet as he drove away. A deep sadness engulfed him. That wasn't his Ella standing there shaking her fist and spewing all kinds of hurtful things. Ella would certainly have held loving arms open for Pick and Cubbie if she were still in her right mind. Ella was gone, and a mean old witch had taken up roost in his wife's head. She was like a bubbling teapot. If the fire was down, she would just simmer, but mercy sakes, if the flame took a notion to rise, Ella would spew and spout and rattle!

Nevertheless, he still loved that old woman. He loved who she had been, and if he could, he would chase away those demons that had moved into her mind. Before he left he made it a point to stop her long enough to encircle her in his arms for a hug. He gently kissed the top of her head.

"Now, Ella, I will be back tomorrow evening. You get the house ready for the boys."

Ella ran her fingers through the hair on the top of her head and placed her chin in her hand. "I just don't know if we will have enough food around here to feed two more people. Those two boys will probably eat us out of house and home!"

After phone calls to Joe Kagey at the Seneca Indian School, Angus was convinced that Iris, Augie, Alice, and Joe had adjusted well at the boarding school. Bringing them to Dustin now would certainly disrupt their lives. They were receiving a top-notch education, and being fed hearty meals on a regular basis. The country was in the throes of the Great Depression, and Angus knew that taking on the two smallest grandchildren would be a hard endeavor on the meager pay of a share-cropper. The four older children were thriving and he knew he had to focus on Pick and Cubbie for now.

He had made up his mind that those boys needed to be with family. He reasoned that Ella on her bad days had to be better than the orphanage on a good day. They would just have to learn to live with this, just like he had.

Since Ella was on strike from kitchen duties that morning, Angus made himself a lunch to eat along the way. Esther Holmes had brought by some fresh picked apples earlier in the week, and two nice and juicy ones found their way into Angus's knapsack, along with a handful of fresh raw peanuts and a couple of day old biscuits. Esther was an old friend and neighbor of the Scott's. She and her family had come to Oklahoma from Arkansas around the same time as Angus and Ella.

Esther had a soft spot in her heart for the Scott children. Maybe it was a woman's intuition, as she could tell that Ella hadn't always been the cold-hearted person that was the mother of those precious and well-mannered children.

Ella held a deep, dark secret. Esther was convinced that somewhere in Ella Scott's cold, hardened heart, there had once lived an entirely different spirit. Over the years, Esther would see little glimpses of her. Little short spurts of gentleness. Even playfulness. Often Esther would feel sorry for the family for having to endure Ella's sorry excuse for cooking and bring them baskets of home baked goodies.

Over the years of showing up on Ella's stoop bearing gifts, Esther had witnessed several fleeting appearances of what must have been the old Ella. The one that Angus Scott fell head over heels in love with many years ago. On some days, Ella would almost crack a smile when Esther would reminisce about the Holmes and Scott children playing together, but more often than not, Ella would scowl at Esther and tell her that she didn't remember any such thing and that Esther just needed to go on home before she took after her with her broom. Esther felt sorry for Angus and the kids, and she even felt sorry for Ella. Demons had a hay day in that woman's head, and Esther never knew when the storm would surface.

Esther had promised Angus that she would keep an eye on Ella while he was gone. Good friends are like gold. With several stops to water Old Tobe and give him a handful of oats, the trip to the orphanage seemed to go on without end. The sun was setting, and Angus knew that he had about 12 miles to go to reach Ponca City. He was tired and sore and decided to pull off the road and sleep for the night in the bed of the wagon. He had sent word to the orphanage that he would be coming to get his grandsons the following morning. He knew he better get some rest for the long trip home with the boys tomorrow and fell fast asleep as soon as his head hit the sack of feed that he had chosen for a pillow.

Angus Scott had not remembered having a dream in a long time, but that particular night, he had the most vivid vision! As he slept, he found himself sitting in a rocking chair on the front stoop of his house. He was rocking back and forth to the rhythm of the summertime bullfrogs croaking their love songs to some lucky bullfrog girls. "Ree row, ree row." Low and melodious the bullfrogs crooned. As he sat and rocked, Angus felt a sense of peace and happiness wash over his body. He hadn't felt so comforted in many years. "Ree row, ree row." He was so relaxed he almost felt like he was floating. From the distance, he heard the laughter of children. As he turned his head to see where the sounds were coming from, he found himself standing on the porch stoop looking toward the old gate that led down to the stream. He saw the blurry figure of someone coming through the garden gate. He took his handkerchief from the pocket of his overalls and began to wipe his eyes.

"Must be something in my eyes."

As he lowered the handkerchief to put it back in his pocket, he saw her. It was Addie! His beautiful daughter, Addie! She was smiling and laughing and, with her, holding each one of her hands, were her two babies, Pick and Cubbie!

160

"Hello, Poppa!" She shouted with glee as she ran toward him.

The boys were ecstatic! They couldn't take their eyes off their mother. The three of them together, what a glorious sight. Angus was overcome with a sense of pure, sweet love!

"Here you go, Poppa! I know you will love them and take good care of my little boys! I love you!" The dream began to fade, and Angus awoke with a start. He was lying in the back of the cold hard wagon. His arms were outstretched as if they were waiting for someone to get a big hug. Cold sweat ran down his temple. Was that real? Did he really just see his precious daughter?

"She brought them to me," he said in a whisper.

Chapter 21

Home at Last

A little child's heart can be broken and shattered into innumerable pieces. However, the mending is miraculous, and forgiving is non-negotiable. Young Pick Watie was told by one of the orphanage workers to put all of his belongings in the tow sack. He wasn't told why. As far as that goes, as long as he had lived at the orphanage, he was never told the "why" of anything. Just do it, and don't ask questions.

For some unknown reason, the little five-year-old boy stopped what he was doing and looked around the room. It was cold in the boys' dormitory. Always cold. A shiver ran down his spine and Pick wasted no time as he stuffed what few belongings he had into the makeshift luggage (the tow sack was an emptied flour sack). He was too young to read the words "Washburn Crosby's Gold Medal Flour" displayed across the top of the flour sack, but his memory was certainly fresh enough to recognize that the same pattern embellishing the cotton cloth in the flour sack had also been used to make dresses for his sisters, Iris and Alice and... Momma!

Pick fell to his knees and buried his little face into the fabric of the flour sack. It felt soft against his skin. He could just imagine himself running up to Momma, as he had so many times before, gathering her dress into his hands, and burying his face into the folds of cloth. He would giggle, and she would scoop him up into her arms and smother his rosy cheeks with kisses! The indescribable sensation he felt when he touched the fabric of the flour sack to his skin held him spellbound. The heartbroken five-year-old child was suddenly immersed in feelings that he had held deep in his heart for so many long and painful months.

He had a flashback of happier times. He saw himself laughing with his brothers and sisters in the cozy little house that he once knew as home. He could almost feel himself wrapped up in the warmth of the embraces coming from his Momma and Poppa. It was such a safe place to be— wrapped in their loving arms! He began to cry. Breathless sobs. Long and hollow.

He longed for his parents and his brothers and sisters. The joy that he had felt a few minutes before had melted away as his longing turned into an overwhelming sense of loss. A lone tear streaked down his freckled cheek. He had held in the pain for so long. He was much too young to comprehend everything that the world had thrown at him at this point in his life, but Pick Watie was beginning to discover something about himself. A trait was surfacing in this child that would carry him throughout the rest of his life. He was developing wisdom.

He was already an observant child. He knew that obedience was quite often followed by good things. Next he stood up, wiped his tears away with the sleeve of his shirt, did one last big stuffing motion to his clothing in the sack and gave a twirl to the top. He slung the sack upon his right shoulder and headed out the door. He lowered his chin to his chest and closed his eyes and heaved a big, heavy sigh. He didn't know who would be waiting at the end of that long hallway or where they would take him, but one thing he prayed for more than anything else: "Lord, please let someone love us."

He knew him.

Pick knew that it was his grandpa, Angus Scott, standing in the doorway of the dormitory. Angus held his old straw hat in one hand and little Cubbie's hand in the other.

"Son, you ready to go home with me?"

Chapter 22

Preparing Them for Ella

The trip back to Dustin, Oklahoma was long, hot, and bumpy. Angus Scott was not a talker, and the two little boys were so unsure of things that they just sat quietly next to their grandfather, little feet dangling and little hands gripping the seat.

"Hep, Tobe! Hep! C'mon, Tobe!" Angus would call out to the mule as he flicked the reins.

The old wagon rocked back and forth and rolled up and down for miles. It had been an unusually wet summer. The dirt roads were so washed away in spots that it took every bit of might that Old Tobe could muster to pull the wagon down, up, and out of the holes. Time and again, the old mule would strain against the harness as he pulled the buckboard forward. It was as if Old Tobe knew his responsibility. The old man and the two little boys were headed home. Hours went by, and Angus knew his young passengers were hungry. In anticipation of the journey back home, he had only taken a few bites of his lunch the day before and when he saw a good place to stop, he pulled the reins to the right and told Tobe to whoa with all intentions to share the remainder of yesterday's lunch with his grandsons. Old Tobe obliged the command to pull over without hesitation, as he was ready for a drink and a nice handful of oats.

"You fellers hungry?" Angus asked as he hopped from the wagon and began to secure the reins.

"Yes, sir," Pick spoke just above a whisper.

Angus had marveled at how much Pick looked like Addie. Cubbie was the spittin' image of Kip, but Pick looked like Addie. Old Angus's heart ached for these two little boys. Kip and Addie had left behind six precious children, and Angus's heart hurt a considerable amount for these two babies.

"Well, jump down and help me feed and water Old Tobe, and I'll git you a bite to eat."

Their faces broke into wide grins, and the two Watie boys ran to the back of the wagon to get the food and water for the mule. Angus proceeded to throw back the oilcloth that covered the feed sack when he noticed a small, bundled parcel in the corner of the wagon. He knew he hadn't put it there.

As he peeled back the paper, he knew exactly what it was. Ella had sent lunch. Three biscuits. Three apples. Lunch for three.

Angus shook his head, took his handkerchief from his pocket and wiped his brow, "Here you go, boys. Here is lunch."

Old Tobe drank the remainder of the water in the bucket and munched contentedly on the oats offered eagerly from the little cupped palms of the two youngsters. Pick and Cubbie had already made fast friends of the mule as each one took turns scratching his ears.

They were about two hours away from Dustin when Angus started to speak.

"I need to tell you boys about your grandmother. She has had a nervous breakdown, and her mind ain't all there. I can tell you that for sure. She can sometimes be meaner than an old snake, but she loves you nonetheless. You will treat her with respect, as she really don't mean no harm. She's just a troubled soul."

The two little fellows listened as their grandpa spoke.

Even in their youth, somehow they knew trouble was brewing.

Chapter 23

Gettin' a Belly Full

By the time Angus pulled up to the house, the two boys were fast asleep. They had nodded off about ten miles down the road. When their heads had started to bob, Angus had pulled the wagon over and gently lifted the weary children and placed them in the floorboard of the front of the wagon by his feet.

"Pick, Cubbie. Wake up. We're home."

Old Tobe had come to a complete stop and was waiting patiently to be led to the barn when Pick and Cubbie raised their heads. They were somewhat disoriented and began to rub their sleepy eyes. Where were they? It was dark, and all they could hear was the distant hoot from an owl. The screen door slammed with a vengeance behind Ella as she trotted down the steps of the porch.

"I hope no one is hungry because I don't know if we have very much food in the house!" Angus jumped down from the wagon and without looking her way, spoke to his wife.

"Now, Ella, you know full well that all three of us are mighty hungry, and I am thinkin' that you could muster us up a meal."

Ella perched her hands on her hips as she took a look at her two little grandsons. She seemed to show about as much compassion for the two orphans as she would have shown for a tick on the back of the dog. Ella huffed. "Well, Esther brought by some stew. I don't know fer sure how much is in the pot, but I was hopin' it would last us a while. I'm not so sure now that there are more mouths to feed."

With that announcement she whirled around and went back into the house. Pick reached over and grabbed Cubbie's hand as they both stood staring at their grandpa. Angus didn't miss a beat.

"Boys, help me put the mule up for the night, and we'll go eat some stew." The three weary travelers shuffled toward the barn. Angus led the mule inside and pushed Old Tobe's ears forward as he removed the harness. It was obvious that the old mule was right where he wanted to be for the remainder of the night. He didn't budge. Angus reached down and tousled his grandsons' hair and headed toward the house, two little boys in tow. The lantern flickered as the children entered the home of Angus and Ella Scott.

Pick had memories of being in this home, but Cubbie was too young and had no recollections at all. Ella had placed four bowls heaping full of stew on the table and the aroma reminded them all how hungry they were. Pick and Cubbie lingered by the front door as Ella and Angus took their places at the table.

"C'mon, fellers. Come sit down and eat." There were no long rows of tables filled with hungry children, and this was not the orphanage. Both boys were suddenly overcome by their emotions, and they both began to cry. They were so hungry and so tired, but all they could do was stand there and bawl. Their grandfather stood up and lumbered over to the boys. With one fluid motion, he picked them both up, one in each of his arms and carried them over to the table.

"Don't you smell this stew? Our neighbor, Esther Holmes is a real good cook, and she made this special for us. Come on let's git your bellies full."

He settled them both at a place at the table. They knew when he lowered his head that he was going to pray over the meal. Pick remembered that his Momma and Poppa had always prayed over their meals, and it was also a ritual at the orphanage. The one consistent thing in their young lives had always been prayer. They had been taught that no matter what a person thought their troubles might be, there was always someone that had it a whole lot worse. Always thank the good Lord for everything, even if it is just being able to take a breath of air.

"Lord, bless this food, and let it nourish our bodies. Amen."

Pick and Cubbie reached for their spoons and began to slurp up their food. Angus handed them each a biscuit that had been slathered with butter as they plowed into the hearty bowl of stew. Spoonful after spoonful was lifted to their mouths. They were in their own little worlds as they filled their stomachs with the delicious soup.

At the other end of the table, she sat. Ella hadn't taken a bite. All she could do was stare at the two children sitting at her table eating her food. Two additional mouths to feed. Where is the food going to come from? Both boys looked up at the same time. They looked toward their grandmother as her lip turned up and her dark eyes peered toward them both. She spoke just above a whisper.

"Stuff guts."

Chapter 24

Settling in with Family

Time passed, and the two boys settled into life with their grandparents in Dustin, Oklahoma. They got used to seeing the steady flow of aunts and uncles in and out of their home.

Uncle Jessie had garnered a job in Tulsa and married a proper lady named Cora Mae. Uncle Jessie and Aunt Cora Mae loved coming from Tulsa to check on their little nephews. Jessie's job paid quite well, and more often than not they would bring gifts for the boys. There would be little wooden guns or toy soldiers. Aunt Cora Mae was concerned about Pick and Cubbie's hygiene, so she always tucked a couple of toothbrushes and a sturdy tube of toothpaste in the gift bag. Little did she know that as soon as their sedan was a mere trail of dust scooting its way back to Tulsa, Pick and Cubbie would be using the toothbrushes to dig trenches for their toy soldiers, and that fat tube of toothpaste was like a gooey stream of candy. They had that tube sucked dry in no time.

Aunt Cora Mae would have been proud that at least for a few hours their breath was nice and minty. Uncle Adair had moved to Texas to start his career and family. Aunt Maisie and Uncle Jubal found themselves ranching and farming cotton in Ruidosa, New Mexico. Uncle

Douglas moved to Eufaula, and Aunt Esme married Uncle Carter and stayed around Dustin. Uncle Logan was the city marshal in Dustin and was married to a flighty lady named Ruby Dee, and Uncle Duff lived close by with his wife Deloris. There were so many people coming and going, and they all called Angus and Ella "momma and poppa," so it didn't take Pick and Cubbie long to do the same. It felt good to have a momma and a poppa. Aunt Esme and Uncle Carter were the most frequent visitors, and Pick and Cubbie became very close with their three boys, Jack, Harlan, and Otis. When the Caudell family showed up, the five boys headed for the woods and were not seen again until dark.

It didn't take any time at all for Pick and Cubbie to hammer out parts for their cousins in their finely scripted antics in the forest. Their never-ending imaginations had them being World War I soldiers, Persian pirates, and cowboys and Indians.

When they tired of the play acting, cousin Jack, with his familiar stutter, would find a stump and declare that right there in the woods they were going to have church! Six-year-old Jack Caudell could bring on the hellfire and brimstone with the best of the traveling preachers he had seen in the brush arbor services. He quoted whatever scripture he could remember. His most profound sermon was surely the time he took a long sideways glance at his captive audience and banged his fist upon the wooden makeshift pulpit and declared, "This w-w-w-world is made out of a w-w-w-woman's side!"

All four of the freckled face boys in Jack's congregation nodded their head with certainty. Yes sir, Jack must be r-r-r-right!

176

Chapter 25

Julia Rose

Being a sharecropper in the sand hills of Oklahoma in the 1930s was a living testimonial to unending labor, little pay, and hard times. The dust storms were relentless and eroded the fields that had once boasted rich and bountiful topsoil. Many a sunny day would turn black as night as the torrent of dust, scooped up by the dry, hot wind, would cut a swath of darkness across the plains of Oklahoma. Day after day the wind would come with a fury, making a barren wasteland out of the rented property that Angus, Ella, and the boys called home. Bound by a pact that a sharecropper held with the landowner, rent was to be paid by the first crops and the family got what was left.

Pick and Cubbie had settled into life with the Scotts, and Pick was enrolled in the Dustin, Oklahoma, elementary school. There was more money in the Dustin schools, and therefore, each class had their own room and their own teacher.

Pick was taken to school the first day by Uncle Duff. Momma Ella had packed Pick a disgusting lunch of cold, hard biscuits and gooey, tasteless gravy, and had placed it in a piece of cotton fabric tied in a bundle. Duff had business in Dustin that day so he volunteered to come by and take Pick to school. When he left the Scott's house with the youngster in tow, he glanced down at Pick and saw that his faced was covered in dirt from the morning chores. His overalls were a filthy mess. Duff Scott figured he could try to wipe the dirt from Pick's face with his handkerchief, but there was no hope for the overalls. They would just have to do. He dipped the corner of the cloth in the rain barrel and gave Pick's face a once over. Calling it good, he loaded his nephew onto the wagon and headed toward town.

Even though Pick had been accustomed to groups of children from his time at the orphanage, there was something different about walking into the classroom of Dustin's school. All eyes looked his way. All Pick could see was a sea of combed hair and shining, smiling faces. Pick was instantly self-conscious. It was a feeling he had never experienced before. He had never been around children that looked like this. They looked clean. He looked down at his clothes and saw that he was a filthy mess. His hands were dirty, His clothes were dirty. He was dirty. He hated how he was feeling. He wanted to run and hide.

Until he saw Julia Rose Devon.

She lit up the classroom like a marquee. Auburn hair with a big pink bow sitting sideways on the top of her head. Rosy cheeks. Dressed to a "t." Pick had never set his eyes on anyone so beautiful in his life. He blushed like an overripe tomato. Julia Rose was in the front row right beside the teacher's desk. She was smart and pretty. Pick felt puppy love like no other puppy had ever experienced.

Sitting directly across from Julia Rose was Lon Holcomb. Studious and a Mr. Smarty Pants. Julia Rose was smitten with Lon. Pick wasn't sure if it was fate or folly but Mrs. Bellmon pointed to the desk directly behind Julia Rose and instructed Pick to sit down. He was so nervous he could feel his body shake like he was stricken with the heebie jeebies. As soon as he found his place at his desk, Pick Watie put his dirty hands between his legs and hung his head, afraid to look up. He just knew if Julia Rose turned around he would surely melt like a candle right where he sat. Mrs. Bellmon rose from her desk and went to the chalkboard. The rest of the day was a blur to Pick. All he could remember was staring at the back of Julia Rose Devon's flowing and perfectly combed hair.

When Mrs. Bellmon took the big bell from her desk and raised and lowered it to make it ding and dong to signal the end of the school day, Pick stood up from his desk to leave. Julia Rose turned at the same time, and the two of them were face to face.

"Hi, my name is Julia Rose Devon. You can call me Julia, like everyone else if you want."

Pick Watie was struck dumb as a post. His voice was nowhere to be found. He did muster a shy smile, and as he was struggling to say hello, Julia Rose said, "see you tomorrow, Pick Watie." She was gone in a flash. Running toward Lon breathlessly shouting, "Wait, Lon! Wait for me! You can walk me home, if your mother doesn't mind!"

She was gone. Just like that. Poof.

Little did Pick know that when Julia Rose caught up with Lon, Lon had asked her what she was saying to that dirty new boy.

"I said hello, Lon. I know he is dirty, isn't he? Bless his heart. He is a Watie. Momma told me that he lost his momma and daddy and had to go to an orphanage. He lives up on the mountain with his grandpa and grandma. I hear that his grandma is ill. He probably doesn't have anyone to help clean him up."

Lon stuck his nose higher in the air. He had no time for such useless small talk. Pick continued to be smitten with Julia Rose. He was a good student and fast learner, but it was extremely hard to concentrate when such a beautiful creature sat squarely in front of him every single day.

Julia Rose was a popular student, and it was no surprise to Pick when she was voted to be a May Day Princess at the Maypole Dance. Pick grabbed his brother Cubbie by the hand and headed back to town the following Saturday to take part in all of the May Day festivities. They ate all the pie they could stand and played games with all of the other children in the town. The highlight of the day, however, was to be the Maypole Dance.

Pick and Cubbie Watie climbed in the big tree closest to the field where the poles had been placed into the ground. They wanted to get a bird's eye view and didn't want to miss a single thing.
Long strands of colored fabric cut into strips had been secured to the tops of each of the six poles that had been securely tapped into the ground. Each pole stood about 15 feet tall.

A hush came over the crowd as the Maypole princesses began to walk toward the poles. There were ten princesses per grade, six poles total. Sixty lovely young girls dressed in flowing chiffon dresses took their places and bent over in unison to pick up their strand of brightly colored ribbon. Each girl wore a floral headband of freshly picked spring flowers, in preparation to herald in the beginning of spring. A formidable group of town fiddlers, joined by Earl Jenkins, with his bagpipe and local Irishman, Wesley O'Malley, and his concertina, all stood ready.

At the signal, they began to play their best rendition of "Magpie Lane." The children wove in and out and plaited the ribbon to the pole. The crowd was delighted by the precision of their steps. As was the tradition, as soon as the ribbon was snug against the pole, the princesses did a reversal and unwound the ribbon, much to the admiration of the spectators. Pick and Cubbie were awestruck. Perched upon a sturdy branch, their jaws dropped in amazement. They had never witnessed anything like the Maypole dance. Pick had never witnessed anything so pretty as Julia Rose Devon as she flowed in and out among the ribbons. When it came time for the announcement of the Maypole Queen and the Maypole King, it didn't surprise Pick one bit as Julia Rose Devon and Lon Holcomb were chosen to represent the festivities as their royalty.

As much as a schoolboy crush could spring forth a desire, Pick knew that he would never forget Julia Rose Devon as long as he lived.

Chapter 26

Fannie and Porter Devon

The Devon boys lost their mother when they were just young children. Joseph Thomas Devon, Sr. buried his wife and decided to give his nine boys a change of scenery and moved them all lock, stock, and barrel to southeastern Oklahoma from Tennessee. J.T., as he was called, had spent several summers in Oklahoma trying his hand at farming peanuts. Each summer, he took the older of his nine boys, and they made their way out of the mountains and headed to the rolling hills of Oklahoma. J.T. had befriended an Oklahoma soldier when they were marching together on the Western Front during World War I. The two men bonded immediately when they found that their southern accents twisted the pronunciation of Alsace-Lorraine in quite a similar fashion.

Several battles and joint life saving measures later, the war ended and the two men gave each other bear hugs and promised to be friends for life. They stuck to their promise and John Henry Calhoun and J.T. Devon stayed in contact after their service ended at the conclusion of the war. After many invitations for J.T. to come spend a summer in Oklahoma on John Henry's peanut farm, the wanderlust grabbed hold of J.T. and he took John Henry up on the invite.

J.T. Devon never fit in to the mold of the rest of his family. The Tennessee Devon clan had migrated from England in 1838 and had established a good living for themselves in Tennessee as bankers, hoteliers, and shopkeepers. J.T. didn't like to dress up and he felt mostly at home when he could be out in the sunshine planting a seed of something or other into the Tennessee soil. He was the black sheep of the family, and he didn't mind that moniker one iota. Cotton farming was depleting the once fertile soil at the foothills of the great Smokey Mountains, and it didn't take too many letters from John Henry to convince J.T. Devon to come take a peek at Oklahoma.

J.T. became so fond of Oklahoma, it was like pulling hen's teeth to get him to return each fall to Tennessee. His boys loved it too. They had made friends with the locals, and each trip made them miss their eastern home less.

Olivia Devon had her foot solid on the Tennessee ground. She would never leave her beloved state of Tennessee to go live with the "heatherns" in Indian Territory all the way out west in the wasteland that had to be waiting in Oklahoma. No matter what picture her husband and sons tried to paint for her of the beauty and culture waiting on the other side of the Mississippi, she refused as politely and defiantly as her southern temper allowed.

J.T. and the boys yearned for the feel of the earth in their hands and the promise of hearty crops around the bend. To them, Tennessee was a strangler, robbing them of their chance to breathe clean air and feel the sun beat down on their backs. Oklahoma called to them from the prairie. Their hearts had no strings attaching them to Tennessee.

Joseph Thomas Devon did not nag or wheedle his wife with his desires to move his family westward. It was the measles that sealed the fate for Olivia Devon. She passed from her beloved earthly home in Tennessee to her heavenly home in glory at the young age of thirty-seven. She left behind her husband, J.T. and their nine boys. Soon after the last shovel of dirt was placed upon Olivia's remains, her husband and the nine boys left Tennessee and headed for Oklahoma, the "Land of the Red Man." They never looked back. John Henry Calhoun was happy to sell a few acres of his land to his good friend J.T. Devon when he arrived by covered wagon with his nine strapping boys in tow. The Devon boys were pleased as punch to call Oklahoma their new home. The peanut farming was a fairly profitable venture for J.T. and his boys.

They grew to be strong, handsome and hard working young men, and it wasn't long before they all found wives and started having children of their own. Porter Edward Devon, J.T.'s youngest son, had gone back to Tennessee to fetch his long time love, Fannie Beth Bingley, married her in a beautiful ceremony and proceeded to load her and her trousseau into the same covered wagon that brought his father, himself, and his brothers to Oklahoma. Fannie loved Porter with all of her heart, and if Oklahoma was where Porter was going to be, she would be there with him as long as they both shall live.

Porter and Fannie Devon purchased a few acres to raise peanut crops in Dustin, Oklahoma soon after he got a job as a night watchman with the St. Louis and San Francisco Railroad (The Frisco). He also supplemented their income by setting up a little shop out back in the shed to cobble shoes for the people of Dustin. With his own hands, he built them a modest home on the edge of their property to house their growing family.

Their firstborn child was a girl they named, Pearl. Next up was their only boy, Rory, named after Fannie's father. Rory was followed by his sister, Hilda Ruth. Love abounded in that home, and soon afterward, Fannie gave birth to a tiny girl they named Ellen Elizabeth. Little Ellen's birth coincided with an horrific outbreak of the whooping cough, and six weeks later, the baby lost her hard fought battle and was buried in the Dustin cemetery. Three more daughters followed as Julia Rose, Carlene, and Jennie Lou rounded out Porter and Fannie's family, and life in Oklahoma went forward for the two lovers from Tennessee.

Chapter 27

A Peek at Easy Street

Porter was a good provider for his brood, but the depression and the lasting effects of the horrific winds that made a dust bowl out of the Oklahoma territory took their toll. Times were just flat out hard. It was hard to keep mouths fed and backs clothed, but no one worked harder at it than Porter Devon. He was a proud man, proud of his beautiful wife and their children who were the lights of his life. They were poor, but so was just about every other family in the town. Poor but happy.

Then came the phone call. Julia Rose Devon was eight years old when she overheard her mother, Fannie, talking to Uncle Gibby on the telephone. Uncle Gibby was Fannie's only brother. When the Devon clan decided to move to Oklahoma and Fannie went with Porter, she was the only one of the Bingley children to ever leave Tennessee. Uncle Gibby and the other sisters Beatrix, Bronwyn, and Clementine all lived near each other in the Nashville area.

"Hello, is that you, brother Gibby? My oh my it sure is good to hear your voice! How is Hermione? Good, good... Yes, it sure is... My, my that's good news.... What? Say that again, brother. I'm just not sure if I heard you correctly. Yes.... Yes.... Oh, praise God, Gibby! That is the best news I've ever heard! Yes, I will watch for it… Sign it and return it to you. Glory Be! Oh, and I love you too, sweet brother of mine! Give my best to the family! Goodbye."

Fannie Devon hung up the phone and stood with her mouth gaping open and both of her hands placed directly upon her heart. It was as if she didn't hold her heart in, it would pop right out of her chest!

"Porter! Porter!" Fannie went running right out the back door with six children right behind her. Fannie found Porter out in his cobbler shop working on a pair of boots for one of the Mason boys.

"Porter, you will just not believe the phone call I just received from my brother Gibby! My heavens, Porter, we're going to be rich!"

Porter was not one to get too overly excited about a whole lot, but it did perk up his ears when he heard his wife enunciate the word "rich."

Porter rose from his bench, wiped the oil off his hands with an old rag and stood up to face Fannie.

"What in tarnation are you talking about? Slow down; take a breath; and let me hear it."

The words came tumbling out of Fannie's mouth like an overflowing bucket. It seems that Fannie's brother, Gibby Bingley, had gotten a letter from the English government. The letter informed Gibby that after several years of searching and verification, they had deemed that he and his sisters were the sole surviving heirs to the fortune of their late cousin who had perished upon a ship that sank. The Titanic.

Fannie told Porter that she vaguely remembered her distant

cousin. Apparently he had made his fortune in real estate. It seemed that he owned several parcels of land in the United States and several in Great Britain at his untimely passing, and now Gibby, Beatrix, Bronwyn, Clementine, and Fannie had been given title to all of their cousin's holdings!

Money straight from heaven, that's what Fannie deemed their good fortune. She didn't hesitate to lament the passing of her cousin but gave the glory to God that if anyone was going to receive the windfall, she felt blessed to know that it was them!

Porter Devon looked away from his wife, sat back down on his cobbler's bench, and said, "I will believe it when I see it, honey. I don't mean to bust your bubble, but you need to stop and think a minute. Your brother Gibby is about as shifty as they come. You know I'm not one to talk ill of anyone, especially kinfolk, so I will just say again. I will believe it when I see it."

Fannie knew that her husband spoke the truth about her brother Gibby. Nevertheless, she hoped, that once, just once, one of Gibby's schemes had some meat behind it. Ten days later, a brown envelope showed up in the Devon's mailbox addressed to Mrs. Fannie Beth Devon. The return address was to a pompous and multiple surnamed law firm in Nashville, Tennessee.

Fannie's hands trembled as she tore open the top of the parcel. Inside the envelope were two sheets of paper. The top one was a hand scribbled note signed with affection from her brother Gibby. At his direction, Fannie was to go to the second page and place her signature and

189

the current day's date on the aforementioned dotted line.

"... and darling sister, Fannie, as you will notice, I have not had our attorney include the bothersome legal documents. I know you place your trust in me that all is in order, and I can assure you that it is. I have had similar packets mailed to Beatrix, Bronwyn, and Clementine. Please sign your name on the dotted line, and mail this back to Mr. Willingham in the enclosed, self-addressed envelope. As you can see, Bart Willingham has attached more than adequate postage for the return. Give my best to Porter and the children. Loving you, Gibby."

Fannie did not see any reason to hesitate to sign the document, place it in the enclosed return envelope and hand it to the postmaster for immediate handling. Upon placing the life changing document into the dutiful hands of Dustin's postmaster, Fannie, with the small crease of a smile upon her face, walked toward the door and placed her hand upon the doorknob.

"I can buy some nice fabric for dresses for the girls and myself. Porter and Rory can finally get some new dungarees and a nice coat of paint on the porch would sure spruce things up around the house! And Christmas! Christmas will be such a fine celebration! Toys and dolls and a fine fat hen with all of the trimmings! We can invite the whole family." Fannie's mind was spinning with excitement as she grabbed little Jennie Lou's hand and headed back home. Porter had already left for his shift as the railroad night watchman, so Fannie would explain what had transpired when her husband returned home the next morning. A twinge of sadness crept into her glee. She knew how Porter felt about her brother.

More times than not Porter had rolled his eyes at the mention of the latest brainstorm from the Tennessee Breeze, as Porter Devon nicknamed her brother Gibby Bingley. Fannie knew that up until now, none of Gibby's grand schemes had brought forth anything more than the lost time it took to listen to them. Time, as far as Porter was concerned, that he would never get back.

Fannie had to admit to herself, even though this one sounded like the real deal, she had her doubts about the outcome of the signing of that document.

"He didn't send the documents that go with the signed form, Fannie? Really? Holy smokes, Fannie! Trust or no trust, he should have had the decency to let you read for yourself what you are attesting, in order to sign your name to a legal document! " Porter Devon rarely showed his temper in front of his family, but this particular occasion was a display fit for a Fourth of July celebration.

Fannie had waited to approach Porter about the letter from Gibby and the attorney. She had not slept a wink all night due to the uneasiness she felt creeping up on her. It took a bit of courage to follow him out to the barnyard where he was feeding the chickens their morning corn, but she put on her best smile and let the information come forth. After hearing his wife tell the happenings of the day before, Porter Devon picked up the feed bucket that he had placed on the ground and threw it as hard as he could against the fence. It hit with a clang and just by happenstance the handle hooked on a piece of barbed wire. The bucket kept swinging and clanging repeatedly against the post. It was a good thing that there was the sounds of the clanging bucket because Fannie did not have adequate time to place her hands on the ears of her daughter, Carlene, when Porter let loose with a few choice words. In essence, the air turned a shade of blue, and Fannie Beth Devon stood with her jaw wide open as her young daughter Carlene repeated every single word that spewed from Porter Devon's mouth.

It was a sight.

Chapter 28

Don't Speak Ill of Kinfolk

Pages on the calendar flew by one at a time, and there was no word from Gibby announcing the amount of the check that would be headed their way after the sale of their deceased cousin's real estate holdings. The sound of crickets came over the mountains and through the woods from Tennessee to Oklahoma. Porter Devon refused to talk to his wife about Gibby and the dead cousin's money. Porter knew all too well what had happened. The signed sheet of paper that Fannie Devon sent back to the lawyer in Tennessee gave her permission for Gibby Bingley to be the sole heir to the windfall from their long lost cousin.

Brother Gibby and his attorney were the only ones who shared in the profit from the sale of the property. The other sisters, Beatrix, Bronwyn, and Clementine had all been as trusting and had not hesitated to sign the sheet provided by "their" attorney. So that was that. Any hopes of receiving money from Gibby or the attorney went down, just like the Titanic.

Fannie forgave her brother in her heart. She couldn't have gone the rest of her life with hatred toward the only brother she had, and she knew full well that he would have to be accountable for his own actions someday.

As for Gibby, he never brought up the cousin, the money, or the Titanic again. Fannie never mentioned it to her sisters either. She decided that God would provide for her and her family with abundance. She was convinced that there was a reason God had for her not touching any of her cousin's money. She was a woman of great faith and decided to let God alone be the one to judge others.

Chapter 29

Greener Pastures

The current landowner came to Angus Scott with the news that he had sold his land and was moving to California. Angus and the family would have to move due to the fact that the new owners were bringing a large family that would be farming the land. By word of mouth, Angus heard of a small parcel of land in nearby Ryal that was available for sharecropping. So a month later Angus, Ella, Pick, and Cubbie said goodbye to Dustin and found themselves living a few miles away in Ryal.

Ryal, Oklahoma was nestled in the sandy hills on the outskirts of Henryetta, Oklahoma. Sharecroppers and railroad workers provided the majority of the livelihood for the tiny community where the main street boasted a post office and a general store. The schoolhouse could be seen in the distance if one stood on the stoop of the post office and looked due north.

The school housed all 12 grades in one small room. There was an unreliable pot bellied stove that the schoolteacher, Miss Penelope Washington, often coaxed to warm the chilly air by striking it directly on the flue with the butt end of an ax. Chunks of creosote could be heard rattling down the stovepipe, clearing the way for the ventilation to feed the flames and turn the chilly room into a warm and toasty haven for learning.

Each morning, all 14 students would stand erect, with their right hands cupped upon their hearts to recite the Pledge of Allegiance to the United States of America. Fourteen hands. Some were chapped and dirty, weathered by the daily chores completed in the wee hours of the morning. There were cows to be milked, scoops of scratch to be scattered to the chickens, and water to be gathered by the buckets full and hauled up to the houses from the Canadian River. Age made no difference in the work done by these hands. The little ones had their responsibilities right along side of their older brothers and sisters.

Work. The majority of the children were very well acquainted with work. Before school and after school, they would work. They knew no other life but work and work some more. There were, however, a few hands of the privileged. Soft hands and scrubbed nails. These hands belonged to the children of the few affluent citizens of Ryal. There was no drudgery of morning chores for them. They would lie nestled in their featherbeds until their mothers came quietly into their bedrooms to gently wake them up for another day of school. A warm and heaping plate of breakfast awaited them. As they were seated at the table, their mothers would tuck a cloth ever so carefully under their chins. The birds would tweet a cheerful melody outside the sunny window.

"Did you fill yourself up, my precious? Would you like another

196

piece of bread and butter to tide you over until lunchtime?" Their mothers would smile and brush the backside of their hand on their children's cheeks as a loving gesture before the youngsters headed back into their rooms to dress themselves in the warm clothing and sturdy leather shoes that their mothers had set out for them. It was another pleasant day. They had not a care in the world as they scurried off to school.

Pick and Cubbie Watie, however, lived in the other world. Their morning started as they heard the cast iron door slam on Momma's cook stove. They knew Poppa had gathered a bundle of wood and placed it in the bottom of the stove for Momma. They also knew she was fixing the biscuits. (At least she called them biscuits. Pick and Cubbie called them "rocks.") It was time for them to get out of bed and fetch a pail of water for Momma. Even though their shirts and overalls were thin and worn, they slipped them on without a moment's hesitation and headed right out the door. They had no shoes. Last year's shoes had worn out a couple of months before, and Mr. Box, the traveling shoe salesman, had not made his rounds to these parts and wasn't expected for another two weeks. If they hurried, they would make it down to the creek and back up in time to warm their feet by the stove before their toes began to go numb.

They had a well-worn path down to the icy water. Due mainly to the proverbial, yet unspoken, pecking order, Pick would lead the way, and Cubbie would follow as fast as his short legs could carry him and the empty bucket down the trail.

After they let it sit sideways in the water until it was full, Pick would grab the other side of the handle, and the two of them would hoist it up out of the creek. They tried not to slosh the water out of the cold metal pail as they turned to go back up the hill looking like bookends. It was more often than not a smooth operation, but every so often, they would lose their balance and tumble face first into the frosty creek. That was the last thing they wanted to do on an icy morning. With only one set of clothing to their names, they knew that Momma would hang the wet clothes by the stove, but time, not being on their side, would not allow their shirts and pants to be more than soggy when they had to put them back on to head out to feed the mule. Luckily, the water gathering today had been successful, and this was turning out to be a good morning for the boys. They very carefully weaved along the pathway, heading back up to the house with the water for Momma.

The reeds from the cattails loomed high over their heads. With the sun peeking out over the trees, Pick turned to his little brother and shouted, "Um! Me Tarzan! You, Cheetah!" and right on cue, Cubbie would immediately reply in his best Cheetah screech, "EE, EE, OO, OO, EE, EE!"

They laughed and laughed, and the water sloshed around but did not spill. This was a good morning!

As they came out of the woods with their bucket of water, they saw Momma standing in the doorway. "Hurry up! Get that water in here, and quit yer lolly gaggin'!"

Tarzan and Cheetah emerged from the jungle and found themselves standing at the bottom of the steps to the porch. Back into reality, Pick and Cubbie deposited the bucket by the front door and headed over to the barn. Old Tobe, the mule, was braying his disgust that his breakfast had not been delivered to his feedbag a lot sooner and didn't mind a bit who heard his complaints. Pick poured the feed as Cubbie held the bag, filling it to the brim. Next the boys hurriedly hung the feedbag on a nail in Old Tobe's stall. With a few scratches on his ears, the cranky mule soon forgot his misery and buried his nose right down in the grain as content as he could ever be. The colorful rooster crowed and strutted as Pick and Cubbie ran back into the house. Poppa had already headed out to the fields to plow, and the boys were excited to be finished with their chores so they could head into town for school.

They both loved spending the day at school. The screen door slammed with a bang behind them as they settled at the table for breakfast. Momma had calmed down some and proceeded to slide a plate in front of each boy's face. Breakfast was a biscuit with Momma's gravy in the middle. If the biscuits were rocks, her gravy was the mortar. The food hung like boulders in their throats. Washing their breakfast down with milk was not the relief they hankered for as Momma often lost track of the expiration period on the freshness of the milk.

Most of the mornings, Pick and Cubbie were greeted with sour and curdled milk. They each grabbed up their glasses and chugged down the thick liquid as fast as they could. There was only one thing worse than eating mortared rocks and drinking sour milk. If they went to school without breakfast, their stomachs would growl. They did not appreciate the looks and giggles they would get from the other school children if their bellies began to rumble and beg for more food!

199

With the last gulp barely down their throats, both boys scooted backward in their chairs, jumped up, and grabbed their lunch bags from Momma and hurried out the door. They were footloose and fancy free as they skipped merrily down the pathway, leaving their bellyaching grandma behind them as they scurried off down the road to the Ryal schoolhouse.

"All right, class, I would like you all to turn to page four of your primers and we will continue our discussion on the founding of our country." No one ran a tighter ship than Miss Penelope Washington.

Chapter 30

Easin' Around Ella

Pick and Cubbie loved to make their grandfather Angus laugh. He would sit in his rocker on the front porch and watch their antics as they scrambled up the old tree in the front yard. They were so animated! Angus wasn't much of a talker but he loved to laugh at Pick and Cubbie. When something struck him funny, he would squint his eyes. His face would begin to turn red, and his abundant belly would start to jiggle up and down. Not a sound would come out of his mouth but he would look like he was about to explode! The funnier they would be, the redder his face would get!

They even learned to live with Ella. Without a doubt, children are the most forgiving of God's creatures. Ella could be mean, that's for sure, but every so often, the grandmother from the past would come to the surface. She would just peek out and show a bit of kindness. The boys soon learned that her bark was meaner than her bite and that a "hit or miss" stitch on a patch on their overalls was better than no patch at all.

They appreciated the fact that she never failed to hand them their lunch every morning before school. She would thrust it into their little hands and give them one last scowl before she whirled around to run out the back door to shoo off the old black crow that was perched atop her freshly washed clothes. She was determined not to be outsmarted by some old bird that thought he could just sit anywhere he wanted and do his business anywhere he chose!

"Shoo! Shoo! Git off my clothes, you dirty ole bird!"

Yes, Pick and Cubbie accepted Ella Scott as she was, most days.

The economy continued to be in the gutter, and times were hard. But the people around those parts of the country had figured out that the recipe to a good life was often the ingredients offered up in the most simple forms of pleasure.

With that in mind, without a doubt, one of the best things that ever happened to the two orphaned brothers was the day that their grandpa brought home Bulger. Angus had been gone for about an hour when Pick and Cubbie saw the wagon coming down the road. The boys had been told to stay home and help their grandmother weed the vegetable garden.

Pick looked up first. The sun shone bright that morning and he had to shield his eyes with his hand to see his grandfather coming down the lane in the distance. Old Tobe was trotting with an anticipation that a bag of feed must surely be waiting for him in his stall in the barn. Cubbie stood beside Pick as they both squinted their eyes to see that Angus was not alone on the buckboard. There beside Angus was a dog. Not just any dog, mind you, but a muscular dog with his chest so prominently on display! He was half bulldog and half German shepherd. Bugler was headed their way, and he looked like a Roman soldier in a chariot!!

Without speaking a word, both boys dropped their hoes right where they stood and began to run toward the wagon. Could it be? Could it be that their grandpa had made a secret trip somewhere and procured this magnificent animal for them?

They had never had a dog of their own. They often played with their Creek Indian friends down the road and those boys had several dogs that were their constant companions. Pick and Cubbie often marveled at the loyalty of their friends' dogs. Oh how they wanted a dog to call their own!

They ran so fast they were totally out of breath by the time they reached the wagon.

"Is he ours? Can we keep him? Please! Please! Let him be ours!"

Angus's round belly began to jiggle, and his face turned redder than ever. He looked down at his two grandsons and with a twinkle in his eyes said "Well, I ain't quite sure yet, boys. I guess if you promise to rub my feet tonight I could be persuaded to let him stay."

Pick and Cubbie clamored up the side of the wagon in a flash! They threw their arms around the dog, and crescent shaped grins covered their faces from ear to ear as Bulger returned their welcome with slurps from his wet and sloppy tongue.

The whoops of laughter and Bulger's approving barks announced the group's arrival as the wagon pulled up in front of the house. Angus, Pick, Cubbie, and Bulger were all caught up in the moment of happiness until they saw the likes of Ella Scott, hoe raised high over her head, come swirling like a dust storm around to the front of the house! She was fit to be tied!

"Just git yourselves right back out to the garden and get back to weedin'! I don't have any recollection at all of tellin' you two hooligans that you could jest up and go runnin' off! I've never seen the likes! And, Angus Scott, what in the all mighty have you drug home? We don't have enough food to feed all of these mouths and now you come with a worthless dog that's gonna do nothin' but hang out on my doorstep, beggin' around for some food that we ain't got! You better be thinkin' about the next trip you'll be makin' and that one is gettin' that mutt outta here!"

Yessiree, Ella Scott, was hopping mad, and it was obvious to the gaping mouths of her audience that it might take just a tad longer for her to warm up to Bulger. Ella threw her hoe down and stomped up the back steps and headed straight into the house. She was still mumbling something about not having enough food when the door slammed behind her, drowning out any last syllables that might still be hanging in the air.

The enraptured audience, Angus, Pick, Cubbie, and Bulger, although meaning not one ounce of disrespect, lowered their heads but peeked up enough at each other to see that grins were being worn by all.

As for Bulger, it was obvious he had found a home. He trotted himself right up the porch steps and sat down in front of the screen door. He smelled something, and the boys hadn't had time to warn him about the lack of quality service that he might receive from Ella's kitchen. All he knew was he was hungry and whining had often helped him out in the past, so whining it was going to be. So there he sat, whining away, when—KERWHAP! Poor Bulger didn't know what to think as Ella took her best shot and threw one of her shoes straight from the kitchen toward the front door screen. Direct hit!

Bulger high tailed it toward Angus and the boys coming to an abrupt halt right behind Angus Scott's left leg. Poor Bulger's chest was no longer in the warrior pose as he shrank behind Angus, wide-eyed and trembling.

Angus Scott took his straw hat off with one hand and scratched at his chin with the other, and in a matter of fact sort of way said, "Well, boys, I guess we'll have to give Bulger a nice bone to satisfy his hunger for awhile. Looks like the friendship between your grandmother and this dog might have to be gradual in its course."

Days turned into weeks, and Bulger had totally captured Pick and Cubbie's hearts. An incredible bond was instantly formed between those two little boys and their dog. There were no Cowboys and Indians adventure in the woods, no late evening watermelon heist, no "sans clothing" swim that didn't include Bulger. Heck, Bulger even got to join Tarzan and Cheetah and play the part of Boy. He made a great Boy. Pick and Cubbie tweaked the Boy parts to fit Bulger just fine, and Bulger never left their sides. He was like a member of the family. He eventually got to sleep in the house as even Bulger learned how to ease around Ella.

It was soon obvious that Bulger had immense intelligence, even if he was a dog. The first sign of it came when he, like a knight in shining armor, came to rescue the damsel in distress! One cloudy day Ella was out back scrubbing clothes on the washboard when Bulger came charging toward her. Right between her two long legs he went! Before a split second could actually be split, Bulger had seen the copperhead snake making its way toward Ella's ankle and with one fell swoop sank his strong teeth deep into the sides of the looming enemy!

He shook and shook the venomous snake until he was assured that it had met its fate. The hero of the day turned with an air of confidence and released the defeated foe from his jaws and placed it directly at the feet of his newly indebted servant, Ella Scott.

Now, truth be known, Ella didn't scoop her savior up into her loving arms and run directly into the house and fetch a feast good enough for a king, but in her own way, she let Bulger know that she would be forever grateful if he did hang around her a bit more. She even located an old piece of burlap and placed it in the corner by the boys' bed in case Bulger might find his way into the house at night. Scraps of leftover food soon found their way into an old bowl that Ella just so happened to place in a spot on the back porch conveniently by the other old bowl that was filled with fresh water. In a similar fashion, as the others that lived in the house with Ella, Bulger discovered that even though he had never been accustomed to the likes of Ella's cooking, as intolerable and hard to swallow as it was, it did keep his belly full.

Chapter 31

"My Mother the Queen of My Heart"

"The Miracle Rider" starring Tom Mix was playing at the Morgan Theater over in Henryetta. Pick and Cubbie stood staring up at the movie poster tacked up on the wall of Gray's Mercantile in Dustin, Oklahoma. Pick Watie was introduced to Tom Mix at the 101 Ranch when they lived there with Aunt Nellie and Uncle Cade. Cubbie Watie was too young at the time to remember being around Tom Mix, but Pick had told him enough that he felt like he knew him too.

Tom Mix was their hero. Unfortunately neither of the two boys had a plugged nickel to their names and the price for admission to see Tom Mix was five cents a piece. They needed to figure out a way to earn some money and fast!

Pick was a natural on the guitar. Since he was a little boy, he would sit and watch Uncle Duff strum his guitar and sing. Uncle Logan would accompany Duff with his fiddle as the two young men entertained for hours from the front porch of Poppa Scott's home. When Duff placed his guitar in young Pick's hands, it didn't take the boy long to learn the chords and the melodies. Pick had found his true passion when he held the guitar.

Cubbie loved to sing. Long after their uncles, Duff and Logan, went to their own homes, Pick and Cubbie would continue to sit on the porch and play the guitar and sing. They were a dynamic duo.

Eureka! Pick spotted it first.

"Look, Cub! It's a talent contest!"

There next to the movie poster was another notice. There was to be a talent contest in Henryetta that coming Friday night!

"We can do this! We'll enter this contest!"

The prize? A month of movie passes for two at the Morgan Theatre!

Uncle Logan came up with the hook. When the two youngsters came running up to the house, a breathless Pick stopped right in front of his uncle and said, "Uncle Logan, Cubbie and me are gonna enter a talent contest! The prize is a month of movie tickets at the Morgan! Will you help us?"

A barn door sized grin covered Uncle Logan's face from ear to ear as he stood to greet his nephews. He looked down at the two freckled faces, scratched his chin, and said, "Well, I don't see why not! I tell you what; I've got just the song you fellers need to do. Git up here on the porch and we'll do it. And if I can give you any advice, you gotta make the ladies cry."

After a morning of jugglers, yodelers, barbershop quartets, and poetic recitations, Pick and Cubbie Watie were set to perform next. The sign-in sheet listed them as The Two Orphans. Uncle Logan had picked the duo's name and the perfect song for his nephews. He just knew handkerchieves were going to be sopping wet with tears. They were the only child act entered in the contest, and as they made their way to the center of the stage, looking like two soulful ragamuffins, a hush came over the crowd. Pick and Cubbie took off their hats and held them to their hearts.

In a soft voice Pick said, "We would like to dedicate this song to our dear mother in heaven."

The hats went back upon their heads and as Pick strummed the opening chords, his little brother began to sing a song by Jimmie Rodgers, "Mother The Queen of My Heart."

There wasn't a dry eye in the house. The Two Orphans won first prize hands down and hitched a ride the following morning with Uncle Logan and found themselves seated in the front row wide-eyed and totally immersed in the tale of the Texas Ranger, Tom Morgan, played by Tom Mix. When they got home they reenacted the whole movie. Pick, being the big brother, got to be Tom Morgan. Cubbie was Zaroff and of course Bulger was Chief Black Wing. They stopped the takeover of the Indian lands until it was time to feed Old Tobe.

Over the next several months, the Two Orphans swept every talent show in the county. As fast as Hollywood could churn out the next B western, "Mother The Queen of My Heart," kept them sufficiently supplied with front row seats. It was the summer they would never forget.

Chapter 32

The Fateful Tale of Jimmy D.

Growing up running through the woods, climbing fences, shinnying up trees for hours on end helped to make Pick Watie a stellar athlete. Tall and lanky with natural speed, he could run rings around anyone in every race. If there was a foot race to be held, first place always went to Pick. No one challenged him, and because of his kind and fun loving nature, he was a welcomed addition to any team.

At the opposite end of the spectrum, if there ever was a sullen class bully in Ryal, Oklahoma, it was Jimmy Dyson, Jimmy D. for short. Jimmy D. had a sorry attitude, and the primary targets for his aggression were the younger boys at school. He never had to worry about going hungry. That was for sure. When he finished the lunch that his mother had packed that morning, he would saunter over to the bench where the younger boys were eating, and if someone's lunch looked good to him, he would reach over their shoulder and grab what he wanted. It wouldn't do a bit of good whatsoever to complain. Jimmy D. never hesitated to grab one of them by the arm, look in their face and threaten them under his breath.

"Don't you even think about tellin'. I'll get you good and I mean it." Another hungry boy denied his own lunch by the likes of Jimmy Dyson. It was a daily ritual.

One of Jimmy D.'s favorite targets was a scrawny, freckled face kid Cubbie Watie. Jimmy Dyson only had to take one taste of Cubbie's lunch to realize that his dog ate better food than Cubbie. It might have been the equivalent to hog slop to Jimmy Dyson, but the lunch of hard biscuits and cold lumpy gravy, prepared with disdain by Ella Scott, was all that Cubbie had to eat. It was eat or go hungry.

Jimmy D. took great pleasure in grabbing Cubbie's lunch and throwing it on the ground. Fire lit up his eyes as he took his oversized shoes and stomped on Cubbie's meager lunchtime fare until it was a gooey, muddy pulp of dirt, biscuits and lumpy gravy.

Cubbie put his face down on his arm and sobbed. He arrived at school hungry and now he would go home hungry too. Jimmy D. laughed his haughty laugh, put his hands on his hips, and turned around to face Cubbie at the lunch table. It was a beautiful spring day in Ryal. The birds were singing and children were playing out on the playground. The old wooden picnic table was nestled under a big oak tree at the edge of the schoolyard, and sitting on the benches were four frightened boys. Smiley Chasteen, Orvie Winters, Bobby Dolan, and Cubbie Watie. They sat motionless, staring at the monster that taunted them day in and day out. Jimmy D. was relentless in his never-ending quest to think of a new way to torment them and they knew it.

"If I find out that any single one of you tells anyone about anything I have ever done to you, I will hang you by your ankles right here in this tree! And don't you forget it!"

All four boys gulped in unison. They had no intentions of telling a soul. They could each feel an imaginary rope tightening around their ankles. They were scared for sure, but they would continue to keep mum.

Cubbie knew that if his brother Pick got wind of what Jimmy D. was doing, there would be hell to pay. Jimmy D. was a big boy, but there was no doubt in Cubbie's mind that Pick Watie could hold his own with the lumbering bully. In fact, he came close to telling him that Sunday, but the cat got his tongue and the feeling of rope on his ankles overcame his good sense to just let his brother help him one more time. His stomach growled so loud it sounded like a pile of potatoes rolling out of the back end of metal washtub. He was mortified each time the sound of his stomach roared and the giggling classmates commenced. He still decided to stay mum for now.

Chapter 33

Hell to Pay Sometimes
Involves a Dentist

Jimmy D. got more and more brazen each time he confronted the four boys. He gave up just tormenting them at lunchtime and carried it over to before and after school antics. He was relentless. He had gotten his bluff over on them and was quite confident that this was all being kept "between friends."

That summer, Ryal, Oklahoma added a gymnasium to their school, and Pick decided he was going to try out for the basketball team. He and his friends had been practicing with a make shift goal consisting of a bottomless fruit basket that they had nailed to a tree in his buddy, Jenkins Macfarlane's, back yard. They had found an old deflated basketball in the trash. It had not one bounce left to it, but after they plugged the hole and wound paper tape around it many times they at least had a ball that they could aim and shoot toward the fruit basket.

They had never played organized basketball, but that didn't put a damper on their confidence. The way they figured it, no one else had ever played basketball either, so it was a level playing field. The day of tryouts came, and all of the boys that were interested in finding a spot on the team gathered at the south end of the basketball court. They were to be coached by their math teacher, Mr. Campbell.

Mr. Campbell had served in the military and had played basketball on an Army league. He was eager to get the team organized, and what better way to start than to send everyone out on the court to dribble and shoot. Pick knew practically all of the boys that were on the court. There were a few that he couldn't remember the names of, but he had seen them around the school. One particular boy that he saw out of the corner of his eye caught his attention.

It was Jimmy Dyson.

Pick Watie had never been the judgmental type. He believed everyone deserved at least a fighting chance in this world, and Jimmy Dyson was no exception. Pick knew that Jimmy D. was different than the rest of the boys that went to Ryal school. He couldn't quite put his finger on it though. Jimmy was a quiet loner most of the time. There were a few boys that he hung around with sometimes. Pick was pretty sure they were from Jimmy D.'s church. Other than that Jimmy D. stood out in the crowd as a solitary, somber, and sullen kid. Pick had heard some schoolyard chatter about Jimmy D. bullying some of the younger boys, but Pick had never witnessed it. So he decided to let things be for now and enjoy the afternoon of basketball tryouts.

Coach Campbell paired the boys off and coincidentally, Pick found himself paired with none other than Jimmy D. They were to do "one on one" exercises, taking turns on offense and defense.

Pick was on a roll. He found the sweet spot, and the ball sailed right through each time he launched the ball toward the basket. Defensively his long arms seemed to block every single shot that Jimmy D. fired.

A mile wide grin stretched across his face. Organized basketball was really fun, and Pick was having a great time. In his mirth, however, he failed to see the powder keg that was his practice partner. Jimmy D. was steamed, fired up, and hotter than a match head. Jimmy did not like to lose, even if it was just practice.

Pick was in the alleyway heading toward a straight shot into the basket. As he took one last step before he raised his hands to shoot, Jimmy D. slid his size 13 right into the pathway and the next thing Pick knew he was sprawled out on the gym floor looking straight up into the rafters.

Accidents happen, and in sports there are plenty of opportunities to get into the way of an errant foot. Pick gathered himself up onto his elbows fully expecting Jimmy D. to be standing in front of him to offer him a hand up.

Not so much.

Jimmy Dyson had calmly walked over to the side of the gym and was wiping his face with a towel. He never looked Pick's way, and it was obvious that an apology was not in the cards. Pick Watie got clotheslined, side armed, and elbowed by Jimmy D. the rest of the practice. There was no exchange of conversation from either party. The dance on the gym floor proceeded until the coach blew his whistle, signifying the end to practice.

Several of Pick's friends came up to him after practice and asked him in no uncertain terms if he was aware of the fact that Jimmy Dyson had his number. Being Cherokee Indian, Pick Watie could often be a kid of few words. Speak only when spoken to, and if you can't say nothin' nice don't say nothin' at all. Words to live by as far as he was concerned. He assured his friends that what they witnessed was just a rowdy practice, and boys would be boys. Pick told them he would see them at the gym the next day and headed home to do his chores. As he walked down the road toward his house, he looked ahead and recognized his brother Cubbie and a couple of Cubbie's friends.

"Wait up, Cubbie!" Pick started to sprint toward the boys as they turned around to wait for him to catch up. "Hey, Orvie! How's it going, Smiley!"

Pick placed his hands on the two boys' shoulders. Then he turned toward his brother, Cubbie, and tousled his hair.

"Hi, Pick. How was practice? You make the team?" Pick noticed all three boys talking, but none of them looked his way. There was a mixture of feet shuffling and turning their heads around as if someone said something behind them. It didn't take two seconds for Pick to spot it.

"Cubbie Watie, where did you get that shiner? Smiley why is your shirt torn? You three been fightin'? Come on now, give. Tell me what happened."

Mum was still the first word in their dictionary and Smiley and Orvie found themselves making all kinds of excuses that they just heard their mothers calling them, and they ran off. Cubbie was left there with his brother. His head was down and tears were beginning to make a little stream down his dirty face.

"You gonna tell me, Cubbie?"

"I cayn't, Pick! There ain't no way I can tell ya. It would be really bad for me and my friends. Let's just go home and feed Old Tobe and then go swimmin' with Bulger."

Cubbie turned to start to head toward the house when Pick gently put his hand on his younger brother's shoulder.

"Let's talk after swimmin', Cubbie. Maybe we can figger this thing out. Don't worry about it. Let's just go on home."

After the silent walk home, chores done, Momma Ella's attempt at supper choked down their throats, Pick and Cubbie headed toward the creek. Bulger must have sensed that something was different about this trip. Instead of charging ahead of the two as if he was a scout for a wagon train, he lingered back close to the boys. Bulger had a good intuition for trouble.

Pick and Cubbie Watie could each skip a rock to almost an eight jumper. Zoom went the slick rocks one after the other. When the pile of flat stones depleted, Cubbie sat down on the side of a big tree that had fallen down in the last wind storm.

With a gulp and all the courage he could muster, Cubbie began, "Pick, do you know Jimmy Dyson?"

Cubbie no more had the "n" sounded out before he looked over at his brother and saw Pick's head jerk in his direction.

"What about him, Cub? What do you know about Jimmy D.?" Pick's forehead was furrowed deeper than a row dug fresh for planting. He spilled it. Cubbie was like a volcano in the midst of the first wave of eruption. He oozed out every detail of torment that had been dished his way at the hand of Jimmy Dyson, the grand finale being the reason for the black eye, torn shirt. and dirty faces. Jimmy D. had not taken it well ,being outplayed on the basketball court by Pick Watie, and decided to take his aggression out on the kid brother and his friends. While Pick and the rest of the team were changing clothes after practice, Jimmy D. was confronting Cubbie, Orvie, and Smiley by the back door of the gym.

Fury shone in Pick's eyes as Cubbie relayed the details. He had been mulling over the episode on the basketball court and was trying to think of a diplomatic way to handle practice the next day, but after listening to Cubbie, all bets were off.

It would be difficult to run out of nice things to say about Pick Watie. Even if the word bucket was turned upside down and shook really hard, there would always be one more thing brought to mind to describe the sweet kid. Many children that had been through what he had endured from such a young age would turn out bitter, angry and confused.

Confused was the one thing that Pick Watie was not.

Lying in the dark in a hell hole of an orphanage, listening to his little brother cry and beg for him to come get him, the pages of his life to come had been written across the four-year-old Pick's heart.
Do good. Be kind.

That he had done very well. He was a good person and was kind to everyone. As the years progressed, Pick had made his mark. Any time a group of boys got together for a game or adventure and needed a team captain, they didn't look farther than Pick.

He always liked to give others a second chance. Redemption was there for the asking.

He had even planned on trying to reason with Jimmy D. The trouble that he had caused Pick in practice that day surely had a story behind it. Maybe something terrible was eating at Jimmy and a good talk would iron things out.

That was before his kid brother spilled the beans. And they were a rotten mess of beans at that. Nobody messed with his little brother and got away with it. The gloves were off, and they revealed a pair of pretty angry knuckles.

"He said he'd tie all of us up by our ankles if we told anyone, Pick. I'm skeered!"

Pick Watie bent down and scooped up a limb that had fallen from a tree and held it in his hands for just a moment before he tossed it into the water. By the time it had sank to the bottom, he had decided how he was going to take care of Jimmy D.

"Let's go home, Cubbie. Don't worry. I'm gonna take care of Jimmy D. None of y'all need to worry an ounce."

That was good enough for Cubbie. He trusted his older brother beyond measure. It was as much as done and put away as far as he was concerned. Pick would handle Jimmy D.   It got handled and put to bed. That's for sure.

The next afternoon, Pick and his classmates gathered at the gym to continue their quest for a coveted spot on the newly forming basketball team. Sure as rain in the springtime, the coach pointed to Jimmy Dyson and Pick Watie to be partners. Jimmy looked at Pick and with his lip turned up, tossed the basketball he had in his hands toward Pick and said, "I'll be defense."

Pick began to bounce the ball and look for an avenue around Jimmy that would lead him to the basket. As he took his first step, Jimmy D. stuck his foot out and Pick's body went flying across the gym floor. Jimmy laughed under his breath as he watched Pick pull himself up off the floor. Pick's jaw was squared, and his hands formed two solid fists as he walked slowly toward Jimmy D.

Jimmy Dyson never knew what hit him. Pick continued toward Jimmy with unspoken determination, reared back his fist, and planted it right into Jimmy D.'s mouth. Jimmy looked at Pick with horror! Blood gushed from his lips as he began to spit. Jimmy Dyson spit out his top four teeth. Right there on the gym floor was Jimmy's smile, swimming in a pool of blood.

The coach told Jimmy D. to get a towel and wipe up the mess and go on home. Practice resumed when the coach blew the whistle. He never mentioned the incident to Pick, and it was pretty much a given when the boys picked Pick Watie as their team captain.

Jimmy Dyson soon thereafter moved with his family a few miles away to Henryetta and Cubbie and his friends never missed a bite of lunch again.

Chapter 34

Life Ain't Fair

Addie Watie's older children were good about writing letters to Poppa on a regular basis. Mostly in a joint effort written by Iris and signed by the other three, Augie, Alice, and Joe.

Seneca Indian School had provided the four children with a good education and allowed them to be close to each other. Pick and Cubbie would sit at Poppa's feet and hang on every word that he read from their brothers and sisters. This particular letter was tinged with sadness as Iris related to Poppa and the boys that she, Augie, Alice, and Joe were in for some big changes in their lives. It was almost graduation time for the four of them, and they would be leaving Wyandotte, Oklahoma. The boys would be going to high school at Chilocco Indian Agricultural School, outside of Ponca City, Oklahoma where they had chosen to be enrolled into the auto mechanics, training program. The girls would be transferring to Haskell Indian Nations University, in Lawrence, Kansas. They would be continuing their education in more of a college setting.

Iris asked for prayers from her family for a smooth transition for them all. She lamented that she didn't quite know how they were going to handle being separated, but it was obvious, from their past experiences, that for all they knew they didn't have any choice or say in the matter. However, she promised to write as soon as she and Alice arrived at their school.

Therefore, after several weeks, Poppa received a letter from Iris and Alice. They had settled in nicely in Lawrence, Kansas. Both were very beautiful Cherokee young women and relayed to Poppa and their brothers that they had been chosen to be cheerleaders for the school and that Iris had been crowned as the homecoming queen for Haskell's football team. Iris asked Poppa if he had heard from the boys over at the Chilocco school, knowing full well that letters would be few and far between without Iris sitting there writing them for them.

Poppa responded to Iris and Alice that he had gotten a short note from Augie that they were both on the basketball team and that they had to study a lot and there wasn't much time for writing letters.

Angus Scott was relieved to know that Addie's older children were safe and happy in their respective schools. It gave him a great peace of mind. Fall turned into winter and on that December day, Angus Scott received a telephone call from the Dean of Students at Chilocco Indian School. The dean informed Angus that he needed to come to Ponca City immediately, as his grandson, Joe, was near death.

At age 16, Joe had been a star basketball player for the Chilocco team. Three weeks prior to the telephone call, Joe had rubbed a blister on his heel during basketball practice. The pair of socks he was wearing had a hole in the left heel, and the exposed part of his heel met the friction from his shoes and caused a blister. The dormitory mother had been coating the blister on Joe's heel with a concoction of salve and ointment, but it festered and got a horrible infection. Joe Watie was now in a coma with lockjaw, and the doctors didn't give him but a few hours to live. Poppa hung up the phone and sank to his knees. He prayed long and hard for his grandson, Joe.

Next he called his sons, Addie's brothers, Duff and Logan and told them to come over and make arrangements for Pick and Cubbie to stay with one of them since he didn't want to leave them alone with Ella. Angus grabbed a bag and threw in a few articles of clothing for himself, placed his old straw hat on his head and hurried out the door. There was no time to waste.

It seemed like it took forever to get to Ponca City as Angus pushed the accelerator to the floorboard of his old Ford truck. He barely had it in park as his feet hit the pavement of the hospital parking lot. Angus Scott's heart raced as he ran as fast as his arthritic body could carry him. He glanced up and saw a red and white sign signifying the entrance to the hospital. Talking to God and to his deceased daughter Addie as he climbed the steps. "Oh, Addie, I'm almost here. I will do everything I can...."

"I'm Joe Watie's grandfather. Can you tell me where I can find my grandson?"

The lady at the desk stood and walked Angus down the hallway to a room. The door was shut. She knocked gently, stuck her head in the room, and announced that the patient's grandfather had arrived.

A nurse in a starched white uniform approached the doorway and motioned Angus to come into the room. The grey haired grandfather took his hat off of his head and placed it with both hands upon his chest. He walked slowly toward the bed where he could see his grandson lying silently in a sea of white sheets and blankets. Joe was barely breathing. The nurse pointed toward a chair that was pulled up beside the bed and offered it to Angus. It was then that Angus heard someone crying softly behind him. He turned and saw his grandson, Augie, sitting by himself on the floor in the corner of the room, with his arms wrapped around his knees and his head in his hands. Angus's heart sank to his feet at the sight of his grandson crying in the corner.

"Why, Lord, why?" sobbed Augie.

"Mr. Scott, the doctor just left." The nurse's voice rose above his grief. "Joe's internal organs have shut down, and by the doctor's assessment, your grandson's time of passing is very near. I will leave you and Augie here to be with him. Please do not hesitate to call me if you need anything. I am right outside the door."

Angus walked over to Augie and placed his hand on his grandson's head. "Son, do you want to stand here by Joe's bed with me so we can say goodbye to him together?"

"Yes, Poppa, I do." Augie took hold of the hand that his grandfather was offering and stood up. They both walked slowly over to the bed.

Angus looked toward the window and asked his grandson Augie to open it up a bit to let some air into the room. There wasn't a lick of a breeze, and the room was so stuffy, Angus hoped that even a little air was better than nothing.

Augie stood by his younger brother's bed and placed his hand on Joe's pale one. Joe began breathing in a shallow and methodical pattern. His eyes were closed. Augie wondered if Joe could hear them. He wondered if Joe knew that his brother was there with him. He wondered if he was in the present, unable to respond, or was he in the past reliving his childhood with pleasant memories whirling by like a picture show. He also wondered if there was such a thing as the soul leaving the body ahead of time, while the physical body stayed behind and slowly ended.

Was Joe in pain?

Just the thought of his younger brother suffering was more than Augie could bear. "Poppa, this just ain't fair. How can my brother be dyin'?"

The tears were an endless stream down Augie's face. At eighteen years old, Augie had grown to be a strong and handsome young man. This ordeal, losing his brother, took him back to so many years ago when he said goodbye to his mother and his father.

At this moment in time, Augie was eighteen going on seven. Raw pain and heartbreak swarmed around him as he cradled his brother's hand in his own. Was that a breeze? Poppa Angus and Augie both turned their heads at the same moment. The curtains that covered the hospital room window billowed with a sudden puff of wind. Joe's hand went limp, and with slight release of his last breath, he was gone.

It went unspoken, but Augie and Angus were convinced that angels scooped up their loved one and carried him away. Joe was such a

227

good kid. He deserved the angelic escort to the Pearly Gates. As he stood in the cold and unwelcoming hospital room, looking down at the peaceful face of his kid brother, Augie Watie knew he never wanted to let go of the lifeless hand that he grasped. As if by the grace of God, he suddenly had a vivid image of his brother running toward their momma's waiting arms.

In a moment of unbridled grief, Augie turned to the window and screamed his brother's name. There was a glimmer of hope that maybe, just maybe, Joe could hear him one last time. He wanted Joe to know that he never wanted him to doubt for one second that he loved him with all of his heart.

"Please let my brother Joe hear the echo of his name and know that it came from me," Augie muttered under his breathe.

Even though Joe's soul had left his body and what was left was the earthly shell of a young man too young, Augie Watie begged to stay with his brother for just a while longer. The nurse obliged and told him she would be back to get him in 15 minutes. Poppa followed the nurse out the door, giving Augie a few moments alone with his precious, younger brother's dead body.

Augie wanted to stay with Joe until the warmth of life left his body. He wanted to talk to him, like brothers talk, for one last time. He wanted to assure Joe that he would miss him and that he would think of him every day for the rest of his life.

Augie stroked Joe's cheek, and if he could, he would grab him up and take his brother away, somewhere. They would leave this cruel world behind and go on one last squirrel hunt together. They would eat watermelon and tell jokes and toss a basketball back and forth to each other. Most of all they would put their arms around each other and hug a tight hug. A strong, loving hug and never let go. Never let go.

"Augie, it's time to go, son."

They didn't know how they were going to break the news to Iris and Alice.

Angus and Augie had left the hospital after making arrangements to have Joe's body transported back to Dustin where he would be buried beside his parents, Kip and Addie, back by the fence and the rambling roses in the Dustin cemetery.

Angus knew he needed to call the girls and tell them that he had purchased train tickets for them, and they were to board the train from Lawrence, Kansas to Dustin, Oklahoma at eight o'clock in the morning. He had talked to the school and had asked that Iris and Alice be brought to the office so that they wouldn't be alone when he called to tell them the sorrowful news about their brother.

The allotted amount of time had passed, and Angus knew his granddaughters would be in the office, wondering why their grandfather was calling. He took a deep breath and spoke to the operator,

"Miss, please connect me with Haskell Indian School in Lawrence, Kansas. Yes, ma'am, I will hold on."

He could hear Iris's voice on the other end of the telephone. "Hello, Poppa. Is that you? Is everything okay, Poppa? Are Pick and Cubbie okay? Poppa? Poppa?"

"Iris, Iris, yes this is Poppa. Iris, I need to ask you to grab hold of your sister's hand while I talk to you, do you hear me?"

"Yes, Poppa" Iris's voice was just barely above a whisper.

"I've got her right now, we are here, Poppa."

Nothing could have prepared them. Their brother Joe was gone and they were devastated.

They never looked out the window of the train on the long ride to Dustin. The flat lands of Kansas passed by and turned into the rolling hills of Oklahoma, and they never saw a blade of wheat or a limb of a tree. Their friends had helped them pack their bags, and they didn't even remember who drove them to the train station. All the girls could do was cry and think about the pain in their hearts over the loss of their sweet brother.

Family, commotion, friends and food. It was all a blur. Nothing could have prepared them for this at all. The day of Joe's funeral was one of the snowiest in the history of Dustin. The turnout was low, as it was three days before Christmas and many of the old timers couldn't gather the strength to face the north wind and mounting snowdrifts. It was a short, but certainly meaningful service. The threat of frostbite loomed as the temperature dipped below zero. The Watie children had been here before. The cemetery in Dustin had an eery hold on them all. Their parents were here in this place. They realized that Kip and Addie's souls were in heaven, but nonetheless, there were two headstones with their parents' names engraved across them, which was the earthly address for their remains. Years had passed but the pain was still as hard to bear as the day they last stood in this corner of this place.

A familiar pile of dirt was heaved up beside their mother's grave. Young Joe would be lowered into that hole. All too familiar. They would soon be leaving this place again, and the realization that their brother would now have an address for his earthly remains here in the Dustin cemetery was hard to comprehend. Momma, Poppa, and now Joe.

They lined up to touch Joe's coffin one last time. Iris, Augie, and Alice, Pick and Cubbie. One by one they filed by to say one last farewell to their sweet brother. Their tears no more left the corners of their eyes when they froze half way down their faces.

Cold, numb, and heartbroken.

Chapter 35

The Blind Bootlegger

Losing their brother Joe was a terrible tragedy, but it did allow the older children the extra time to spend at home during the holidays. The girls and Augie were able to make up for a lot of lost time with Pick and Cubbie before heading back to their prospective schools to start the new semester. It was wonderful to be together again. They had a nice Christmas dinner at Uncle Carter and Aunt Esme's. Guitars and fiddles heralded in the holiday as the cousins Harlan, Otis and Jack Caudell sang while Uncle Logan and Uncle Duff strummed and fiddled hymns and merry Christmas tunes. Pick and Cubbie even performed a duet for the family.

It was very festive. Uncle Logan and Uncle Duff made it even more festive for themselves with the addition of hootch. Aunt Esme would have chased her brothers off with a broom if she had any idea that when they stepped outside to smoke on the back porch, Uncle

Logan and Uncle Duff pulled the bottles of libation from their pants pockets and took a couple of good long swigs. Uncle Carter was a Godly man, but knew his brothers-in-law were good men and didn't think it would do any harm if they enjoyed themselves a bit. He was aware of the bottles in their pockets but chose to look the other way. Where did those bottles come from?

The day after Joe's funeral, Uncle Logan sidled over to Pick with a big grin and asked him if he wanted to go on an adventure. He told Pick that it was about time that he started learning about the world, and heck, it might even help some hair start to grow on his scrawny chest.

Cubbie was told to stay home and take care of Bulger and Tobe. Duff and Logan told Cubbie that Pick was older than him and that sometimes, older brothers got some extra privileges.

Pick Watie felt himself grow about an inch right there on the spot. This was the first indication that he was reaching the turning point in his life from boy to man. It felt good, kind of scary, but good.

Pick always looked up to his two uncles. They were solid men, a lot on the ornery side but solid. No doubt in his mind that wherever it was they were going, he figured it would be just as Logan described it—an adventure.

Logan pulled the choke on his old car and started it up as Pick and Duff climbed in for the ride. It wasn't long before they were tooling down the road, heading north toward Dustin.

The sun had set and the dark of the evening was pulling the shades down on the horizon. Logan stuck his arm out the window to motion a fruit truck to go around him. When the view was clear, he turned and started down a dirt road that ran parallel to the river. Just north of the Dustin cemetery. There was an old house about 500 yards ahead.

Pick was surprised that he never knew this house was down

this road. In fact, he was amazed that he had never even noticed the road. Logan idled the car about 100 yards from the house. With his left hand he reached down and turned off and on the car lights. Three times. They waited, and in a few seconds, they could tell that someone was on the front porch of the old house swinging a lantern back and forth. That was the all clear signal. Uncle Logan parked the car under the old blackjack tree. Pick knew at that instant that this visit was one of many that his uncles had made down this road. He sensed familiarity.

Logan turned around and looked at Pick sitting wide-eyed in the back seat. "Pick, don't even think of opening your mouth. Keep it shut and don't you be looking around at anything. Walk behind me. If I run, you better skeedaddle."

A chill ran straight down every disc of Pick's spine. A little fear wasn't about to stop him though. He didn't want to miss whatever this was, no way. The two men and their youthful sidekick slowly approached the front porch of Lena Wainwright's shack. Her son, John Wainwright, stood in the dusk holding a flickering lantern.

"John." Duff and Logan spoke with a nod.

"Boys." John returned the half nod as he grabbed for the old wooden spool that now served as a doorknob and pulled the screen door open. Logan, Duff, and Pick followed closely behind John. Pick came in last and held the door until it closed silently. His knees were knocking like a woodpecker beating his beak on an old tree.

The house was filled with a smell that Pick couldn't quite put his finger on, Liniment? Horse salve? Medicine? Naw, it wasn't medicine they were here for.

"Who we got here, John?" The raspy voice came from a corner of the living room.

"Scotts." John was a man of very few words.

Lena Wainwright was blind as a bat. She had lost her sight as a young girl. When she was seven years old, she had finished her chores and decided to take a nap in her parents' barn. She had inadvertently left her coal oil lantern burning down in the stall. The old milk cow decided to scratch her belly with her hind leg. One kick was all it took, and the lantern tipped over. And while Lena was sleeping, the barn went up in flames. During her escape, young Lena lost her footing. A flaming beam struck her face, marring her pretty features and turning her world into darkness for the rest of her life.

Darkness inside and out.

Lena Wainwright had endured unmerciful teasing and taunting. She had no eyesight and never saw her scars, but by the cruel names she had been called, it wasn't hard for her to feel some sort of relief that she couldn't see her image in a mirror. Bitter. She had turned into a bitter and hateful old woman. When she was in her early thirties, a drifter was seen hanging around her place for awhile, and by the time he had moved on down the road, Lena had given birth to her son John. If Lena had sight, she would have known that her son John was the spitting image of the drifter. Good thing she couldn't see, she might have had resentment toward her son. That drifter had done his fair share of knocking Lena around. His fair share and maybe enough for someone else too. So when the day came that Lena was pretty convinced that the scent of that man was a thing of the past, she breathed a sigh of relief to know that he was long gone. It was a hard life for her and her son.

The local charities and townspeople did what they could to help Lena provide for herself and little John. It wasn't much but it was the best they could do. Several years after John was born, Lena gave birth to a daughter. She named her Sarah. The wagging tongues of the community whispered that Sarah was the daughter of a local politician. He had been spotted sneaking around Lena's shanty at all times of the day and night. However, there were conflicting rumors to that assessment. It seems that there was somewhat of a constant stream of men trying very hard to be discreet and inconspicuous as they pulled out of that dirt road onto the highway.

Dark rumors swirled around the mysteries lurking down that old dirt road. Too much activity to just be happenstance. Some kind of business was being transacted at the home of Lena Wainwright. The "spit and whittle club" holding pow wows in front of Gray's General Store had come to the general conclusion that it was pretty much a given that Lena Wainwright was up to no good. When John got big enough to tote a shotgun, the charity packages were not so politely declined by the squarely pointed barrel of a rifle. It seemed that Lena had somehow become self-sufficient.

Lena Wainwright was the local bootlegger. The blind bootlegger. She was a mathematical whiz and imparted her skills upon her son John when he was just a young boy. They were a team.

Lena was sitting behind a makeshift desk. Two old barrels with a wide plank of used lumber laid across them, an old three legged stool and Lena Wainwright was set up for business in her stark and unfurnished living area. The only thing happening in that room was business. Strictly business.

John and his shotgun stood guard over his mother and her pile of cash. No small talk allowed. Lena ran a tight ship and didn't want any feds snooping around her place. The "mystery man" that had fathered her daughter, Sarah, had helped set up her business.

Prohibition had come and gone in the country, but in this southeastern part of Oklahoma, one couldn't get any drier than Hughes County.

Many a parched whistle around those parts had been wetted by Lena Wainwright. You name your poison. Corn likker, moonshine, rye whiskey, bourbon, or any rot gut concoction that could be bottled and corked. Lena Wainwright was happy to oblige.

Her sources were silent and her shipments were secretive. Delivered in the middle of the night. To top that off, there was probably never a more tight-lipped group of men than those walking across the threshold to enter Lena Wainwright's house. It was Dustin, Oklahoma's answer to the Secret Society.

No occupation or religious conviction could keep the never-ending stream of customers from turning down that hidden pathway alongside the lazy river. When a person had a hankering for the taste of the Irish Handcuffs, blind faith in the saving grace of teaching a Sunday

School class over at the First Baptist Church of Dustin the following Sunday washed over them. Repentance would come with the morning light. But tonight we drink.

Preachers, farmers, politicians, teachers, and lawmen. They all knew Lena, and Lena had profited nicely when they forked over their dough for a bottle of hootch. One dollar bills. Nothing larger.

The drill was to walk into the room, stand in front of Lena, look at Lena, and state how many bottles they wanted to purchase. It didn't matter a lick that Lena couldn't see anything out of those dark and empty eyes. She demanded that her customers show her enough respect to face the proprietor of this establishment. Besides that, it helped to hear them when they faced her.

Judge Hiram Bilby had just garnered himself a nice bottle of the snake water and was starting to walk past Duff, Logan, and Pick when he turned around and tipped his hat toward the kitchen, "Good evening, Miss Sarah."

Fire lit in the eyes of John Wainwright. "Judge, you ain't nothin' to me. Don't you ever speak to my sister again."

Judge Hiram Bilby looked at John Wainwright and laughed. Haughty and supercilious. The Judge owned this county, and he knew it. John Wainwright would be on his knees one day and be facing the balding and big-bellied Dishonorable Judge Bilby.

"John Wainwright, you can only imagine the things I would like to do to that pretty sister of yours. You can only imagine..."

The Judge nodded his head at John and with a mile wide grin

walked directly past the fiery eyed young man brandishing the sawed off shotgun.

John Wainwright knew that Judge Hiram Bilby not only owned Hughes County, he had also staked his claim on every square inch of the comings and goings of Lena Wainwright and her family. They were indentured servants to that old man, and he would never let them forget it.

If there was one thing John knew for sure, he would go down in a blaze of glory if that old geezer laid one fat finger on his sister. Many had tried.

Sarah was a beautiful, young girl. Pick knew her from his school. He had never gotten to know her more than just a nod or smile. She kept to herself most of the time with her face stuck in a book. Pick had overheard the conversation between John and the judge. Sarah. Sarah Wainwright? Would that be the Sarah that was in his class? He

peeked around his uncle Duff's shoulder and sure enough there she was standing in the kitchen in Lena Wainwright's home.

Her eyes met Pick's, and he knew immediately that she was mortified. Her cheeks rushed cherry red all the way down to her neck. Sarah had never seen one of her classmates in her mother's home. Her secret was out, and she felt so ashamed.

Sarah hated her home life. She did not hate her mother though. She knew what her mother had endured throughout most of her life. Sarah pitied her mother to a certain degree, but she drew the line at her mother's chosen profession. It was wrong, and Sarah knew full well that her mother and her brother could be sent to prison for many years for bootlegging.

The illegal aspect of the goings on in her home were not what had Sarah Wainwright in distress. It was the clientele. John Wainwright was an attentive soldier in his quest to protect his mother's pile of cash and to keep his mother's customers away from his sister. He stayed as close as he could to both of the women, but there was more than one occasion when John would have to make a restocking run to the barn for more bottles of product and a local patron with a snootful would shuffle over to Sarah, get her cornered and try to get a squeeze or pinch her posterior. Most of the tomfoolery was accomplished when the customers came in twos. One would try to cop a feel and the other would distract Lena.

Pick Watie felt so sorry for Sarah. He had seen her sitting by herself under a tree at school with her nose planted in the classics. She had no friends, and now he knew why she kept to herself. What a life she must have to endure. He felt a tinge of rage when old Judge Bilby paraded past him. Poor Sarah!

"Two moons, one rye whiskey." Duff placed his order as he walked toward Lena.

"Three dollars."

Uncle Duff laid down the three one-dollar bills and took the bottles of liquor from John Wainwright's hands. Lena picked up the money and ran her fingers up and down each dollar bill. When she was satisfied that the correct amount had been garnered to purchase her wares, Lena nodded toward her son John.

"You can go on now, boys. Pleasure doin' business with you again." John pointed toward the door with his sawed off shotgun and the three customers scurried out of the Wainwrights' house. Pick, Duff, and Logan piled into the automobile and headed back toward Dustin. Pick couldn't help but be sad for Sarah Wainwright. He knew he was going to have a nice Christmas holiday with his family but he couldn't get his mind off Sarah. Sarah's home life just had to be dismal.

Chapter 36

Saving Sarah

January brought the next semester at Dustin High School, and Pick was on a mission. He was going to talk to Sarah Wainwright. Pick Watie had a heart for people and had always been a champion for the underdogs.

Not only could his younger brother, Cubbie, attest to that fact, one of Pick's most ardent fans was Hobey Hawkins. Hobey was cross-eyed and tongue-tied. He was bullied mercilessly, unless Pick was around. Pick stood up for Hobey when no one else gave a rip about the pitiful kid.

The school-yard bullies moved away from Hobey if they saw Pick coming toward the swings on the playground.

"Me can swing too, can't me, Pick?" Pick's heart melted as the tow headed youngster looked up at his knight in shining armor.

"You betcha, Hobey. Hold on,and I'll send you to the moon!"

Hobey squealed with delight as Pick gave him a big push. Sarah Wainwright was like Hobey Hawkins. She needed a hero, and Pick Watie was determined to let her know that she could count on him.

"Hi, Sarah."

Sarah Wainwright jerked her head up at the sound of his voice. Her faced turned red as she fumbled for the book that had fallen into her lap.

"Please leave me alone. Please. I don't want any trouble. Just leave me alone."

"Sarah, I just came over here to see if you wanted to go to the picture show this afternoon with my brother and me. I promised Cubbie I would take him to see Pinocchio. It's supposed to be pretty good.

Wanna go with us?"

Her jaw dropped.

"Sarah, let's don't talk about the rest of anything right now.

Do you want to go have some fun?"

She sat there on the grass. It was a typical Oklahoma winter day, typical because the weather in Oklahoma was never typical. The sun was bright and shiny, and Sarah couldn't resist bundling up and enjoying the warmth against her skin. She sat on the grass, staring up at the lanky kid that had just said a very nice thing to her. Sarah had no idea how to respond to kindness. She and her family were shunned and mocked. Kindness was foreign.

It was as if a pitchfork was poked in her back. This is your chance for something normal in your life, girl. Speak up! A rush of emotions pulsed from her head all the way down to her toes. Her lips parted and the words came out. She was surprised to hear her voice. It sounded normal.

"Okay, Pick. I'll ask my mother if I can go. I will meet you

244

there, but don't wait too long outside if I'm not there."

The blush on her cheeks remained long after the tall, good-looking teenager walked away. She had never been to the picture show in her life. Sarah knew that Pick Watie was a nice kid. Everyone knew Pick, and she had no doubt that his intentions were gallant. She just didn't know why he would be asking her. Sarah took a deep breath, felt the sunshine on her face, and escaped back into chapter three of Jane Eyre.

"What will mother say?"

Pick and Cubbie approached the theatre just as John Wainwright drove up with his younger sister, Sarah, in the passenger seat. Pick overheard her brother tell her that he would be waiting outside the theatre as soon as the movie was over.

John Wainwright looked toward the two Watie boys. Pick's eyes met John's, and it was a telling moment. John's eyes said it all, "This is my kid sister and you better take good care of her or you will definitely live to regret it."

Chapter 37

All the Girls Like Him

For the first time in her life, Sarah Wainwright was someone besides the daughter of a blind bootlegger. She was a normal teenager hanging out with her friends. The more time Sarah was able to spend away from her home, the less time she had to worry about gropers and pinchers. She could walk down the steps of the old shack by the river and head into Dustin and be free. Free to be just a regular girl.

John Wainwright was somewhat relieved that his sister Sarah had found friends. It was one less thing that he needed to worry about. He knew she was safe hanging around the likes of Pick Watie, his brother Cubbie, and their cousins Jack, Otis, and Harlan. They were all church going kids with good reputations around town. He didn't worry much until the last few times he dropped Sarah off in front of Gray's.

He had to admit, he had some reservations about the new kid that started showing up in the group. Something about that smiling bastard worried John Wainwright. The kid with the possum grin. He couldn't quite put his finger on it. Just an uneasiness. He was going to have to ask some of his mother's customers what they knew about that kid. Johnny Prescott was his name. Johnny Prescott and that dang grin.

Johnny Prescott was Pick's new best friend. Friends were easy to come by for Pick. He was such a likable kid. Everyone wanted to be his friend, and Johnny Prescott was no exception. The Prescott family had just moved to Dustin, and it wasn't long before Johnny was enrolled in school and found himself sitting right next to Jenkins Macfarlane. Jenkins was Pick's long-time, boyhood friend. Johnny was soon invited to hang out with Pick, Jenkins, and the rest of the boys.

The one thing that stood out about Johnny Prescott was all the girls liked him. He had a swoop of blonde hair that hung, just right, down on his forehead. Just above his eyes. Oh and his eyes. They were the clearest blue eyes one ever did see. Seemed to the giggling teenaged girls in Dustin that they could just get lost in those crystal blue eyes, like an ocean on a clear day.

If a pretty girl walked by Johnny Prescott, he would turn his head and let out a whistle. A wolf whistle was what they called it. One might think that the girls would be offended at the kid with the infectious grin whistling and ogling at them in such a crude way, but the instant they turned around and saw the blonde hair and blue eyes of Johnny Prescott, they would just melt. Right then and there. On the spot.

He knew it too. Took him awhile to figure it out. He was a boy, mind you. Everyone knows it takes young boys a bit of pondering and wondering to figure things like that out. Johnny figured it out. It was a calculation of sorts. Yoyos, tops, and girls. If you held them just right, you could set them spinning. It just took practice.

Yes, all the girls liked Johnny Prescott. He sure did like them back, but there was one girl in particular that he spotted at the First Baptist Church social that made him do a double take.

"Pick, you and Jenkins go on over to the sack race. I'm feeling thirsty and I'm going over there to get me a drink of punch." Johnny winked at Pick and pointed to the old apple tree where the drink table was set up. There were two young ladies dipping out ladles of punch for the thirsty crowd. It was the two Julias, as they were called by those that knew them. They were inseparable friends. Julia Lorene Mason and Julia Rose Devon.

"There's someone over there that I've been wanting to meet." Johnny Prescott smiled and started his stroll toward the table.

Pick's head did a double take. There she was, his dream girl, Julia Rose Devon. He had just moved back to Dustin after Christmas and hadn't had a chance to talk to all of his former classmates. He still had a thing for Julia. The years had not swayed his affections for an instant. He fell in love with her the first time his eyes took in every ounce of her beauty. As far as he knew, she was still pledged to Lon Holcomb. Just that name churned his stomach something fierce. He couldn't stand that phony.

A sudden spike of jealousy struck Pick's gut. Was Johnny Prescott going to smooze Julia Devon or Julia Mason? It sure better be Julia Mason. Pick knew he didn't have a chance with Julia Rose Devon with that stinking Lon Holcomb in the picture, but he would be danged if he was going to let Johnny Prescott flirt with the girl of his dreams and get away with it!

"Uh, hey, I'm thirsty too! Wait up and I'll go with you." Pick caught up with Johnny, and the two young men wandered over to the table to talk to the Two Julias. Flashy Johnny Prescott went immediately toward Julia Rose Devon. Pick's Julia Rose. Pick almost tipped over the table trying his best to squeeze in front of his friend to ward off any eye contact between the grinning Johnny Prescott and the unsuspecting Julia Rose.

"Why, hello, Pick Watie. I haven't seen you in years. My how you have shot up! You are a lot taller than you were in second grade!" Pick's heart melted in a puddle.

He could almost feel it leaving his body and oozing down to the ground as he realized that Julia Rose Devon knew who he was.

"Hi, Julia! I'm glad you remembered me. My family just recently moved back from Ryal to Dustin, and if I can say anything about you, its that you have gotten even prettier than you were in second grade." Pick's face was lit up like a Christmas tree.

"Oh, now you're making me blush! Julia, do you think we can serve up a couple of cups of punch for these thirsty boys?"

The next move was as smooth as a baby's bottom. Johnny Prescott scooted Pick to the side and picked up a punch cup,

"Hello there, my name is Johnny Prescott. I'm new to Dustin and from what my friend Pick says, you have been lighting up this town with your beauty for a long time. I'll hold my cup if you want to ladle some of that punch into it. Now did I hear correctly? The name connect-

250

ed to such a beautiful flower as you is Julia Rose? My, my, my." Johnny brought the brimming cup of punch up to his lips with one hand and with the other he ran his fingers through the swoop of blonde hair falling down his forehead. "Yes, miss, my, my, my...."

Julia Rose Devon seemed to have instantly been transported to another planet in a far off galaxy. And for that matter, when Pick looked over at Julia Lorene Mason, she too was standing there with a googley-eyed look. Staring off into those blue eyes of Johnny Prescott!

"Hello, I'm back with more jars of punch, girls!" Pick Watie knew that this was the first and last time he would ever be glad to see the likes of Lon Holcomb. Lon hoisted two large canning jars filled with lemonade punch up onto the table. The two Julias were brought back to reality by the thud.

More people began to show up to be served and the hustle and bustle of activity shuffled the focus from visiting with the two teenaged boys to dipping the ladles into the beverage.

As Pick and Johnny began to walk away, Julia Rose stuck her head up above the crowd and shouted, "It was good to see you again, Pick Watie! And nice meeting your friend Johnny!"

Pick glanced back over his shoulder just in time to see Julia Rose beaming a huge smile at her boyfriend, Lon. The pain that scene caused him was bothersome. Why did he get a knot in his stomach over her? He could never have that girl. Never in a million years. The knot was like an ache. Like something that had a string tied to it that when the

251

ache happened the string would pull on his heart or his brain or something. He wasn't quite sure about all the emotions going on inside of him. They were new, and he didn't have a clue how to sort them out.

What he did know at the moment was he found it hard to stay aggravated at his friend Johnny for slobbering all over the two Julias when right up ahead of him, he was all sidled up to Nelva Sue Jones. Johnny Prescott was a rounder. That was for sure.

Chapter 38

Aunt Esme and
the Sunday Afternoon

Aunt Esme Caudell, Jack, Otis, and Harlan's mother, and the Watie boys' departed mother's sister, was one of Pick and Cubbie's favorite people in the world. Not only did they love hanging out with their cousins, their dear Uncle Carter, and eating Aunt Esme's wonderful cooking, they also felt a kinship to her that they were certain was like a beam of light that connected them to their mother. They barely remembered their sweet mother, but certain mannerisms of Aunt Esme always brought a flood of memories and good feelings to the two boys.

They could see their mother's face in Aunt Esme's.

As Pick and Cubbie Watie became young men, it became more and more important to Aunt Esme to try and steer them away from trouble. She had raised her three boys to be good Christian men, and that influence did not fall on deaf ears with her nephews. Esme knew that her deceased sister, Addie, would be so proud of her two boys and she certainly wanted to keep it that way.

Pick could sense that something was whirling and brewing inside Aunt Esme that late summer afternoon. Church had been a blessing to them all, and Aunt Esme and Uncle Carter didn't hesitate to invite Pick and Cubbie to their home for dinner. She had cooked a freshly plucked hen and had just finished pinching off the last of the strip dumplings, letting them slide into the boiling pot of broth. A touch of fresh cream and a half scoop of butter and they would be ready to eat in about twenty minutes.

Aunt Esme grabbed up her apron and used it to open the oven door. She was cooking a pan of corn bread and reached in and touched the top with her fingers to check it for doneness. Twenty minutes would be perfect for the cornbread too. Dinner was almost ready.

Pick was sitting in his favorite Sunday afternoon spot. In the corner of Aunt Esme's kitchen was an old milk stool. Aunt Esme had sewn a nice cushion out of left over fabric from one of her dresses many years ago. It was all worn out now, but Pick asked Aunt Esme not to change it. He had been occupying this corner in his aunt's kitchen for so many years, he didn't want to change a thing. He loved listening to Aunt Esme tell the stories of when she and his mother Addie were little girls. He could hear those same stories over and over, and each time it seemed like the first time. Change wasn't always good as far as Pick was concerned. It was as if that old tattered cushion had listened to those stories along with him and he just couldn't bear the thought of throwing it away.

Cubbie and the three Caudell boys would customarily go hang out in the barn until Aunt Esme called them for dinner, but Pick preferred to sit on the old stool and visit with his beloved Aunt Esme, smell the wonderful aroma coming from her stove and hanging on every detail of all of her old stories.

Today was different.

Pick had pulled off his boots and plopped down on the old stool. He wiggled his toes as if to tell them to breathe and be happy for a while. Aunt Esme busied around in her kitchen. Pick tried to get her going on a story or bring up something interesting that he heard in the sermon, but she wasn't taking the bait. Pick Watie knew that sign well. She was mulling over some kind of trouble, and that trouble was making her brow get all furrowed.

"How are your grades, Pick?"

"Oh, they're real good, Aunt Esme. We're learning about the history of World War I, and I'm really enjoying it!"

"That's nice, son. What about your friends, Pick? I've been hearing some talk, and I want to hear about it from you and not from some wagging tongue down at the butcher shop. I've talked to Jack, Otis, and Harlan, and they told me their side of it, but I want to hear from you. Tell me about Sarah Wainwright. I hear she has been running in your same crowd. Explain to me how that came about. Did my brothers take you to that house by the river? Your Uncle Carter thinks I am not aware of their shenanigans, but I know full well what my brothers Logan and Duff do with their free time. When is the last time you saw them at church?"

Pick looked at his Aunt Esme and shrugged his shoulders.

"You're right. I don't remember either." Aunt Esme answered

her own question with truth. "Pick, those two men, my beloved brothers and your uncles that love you dearly, don't always do exactly what they are supposed to do, but the Lord knows they are good men. Good hearts, the both of them. I won't for one second stand here and say that I agree with their drinking. I know they do it. They are grown and can make their own decisions, but if I find out that they took you to that Godforsaken house of Lena Wainwright's, I will tan their hides! Tell me, Pick. Is that how you came to being friends with Sarah Wainwright?"

An out. Inside and outside of his body there was an inaudible sigh of relief. His dear Aunt Esme had tossed him that last question and left him an out.

"Aunt Esme, Sarah Wainwright became my friend because I felt sorry for her. You know how in the Bible it says do unto the least of my brethren, and I shall do the same thing to you? From the first time I ever heard that, I knew that I couldn't treat people bad, Aunt Esme. We are all God's creatures. Poor Sarah, she had no friends. She's not like her ma, Aunt Esme. She is really nice and sweet, and did you know that no one in this town had ever invited her to church? No one, Aunt Esme. Not one single Christian walking around Dustin ever took the time to invite that girl to church."

"Well, my word, son. I am proud of you!" Aunt Esme walked toward her nephew and wrapped him in her strong arms and gave him a huge hug. "I'm glad to think that you are witnessing to the lost and taking a notion to be kind to someone with as sad of a home life as Sarah Wainwright. Proud as I can be. Now, will you go ring the dinner bell and

256

call the boys and your Uncle Carter in so we can eat this bountiful meal that the good Lord has provided for us?"

Pick, feeling so relieved that he did not have to rat out his uncles regarding that Christmas time "adventure" did not hesitate for an instant before he sprang to his feet and headed out to the front porch to ring the bell. It was true that he had been witnessing to Sarah Wainwright. Pick had a strong belief that he needed to tell someone that had never owned a Bible about Jesus. It was true that he approached Sarah to be his friend because he felt sorry for her. All of that was true, and he could bow his head during Uncle Carter's prayer at the dinner table and not feel like he had mislead his Aunt Esme in any way, shape, or form. He was also glad that she didn't push for an answer to her question about going to Lena Wainwright's house with Uncle Logan and Uncle Duff. Nope, he did not lie and he was relieved that he didn't have to throw his uncles under the bus. "Can I please have another scoop of dumplings, Aunt Esme? These are delicious!"

Chapter 39

Hearts Are Made to be Broken

It was evident to everyone around them, but Pick was oblivious. Sarah Wainwright had fallen in love with the tall good-looking young man and he didn't have a clue.   They were constantly together. Always in a group setting, with Jenkins Marfarlane, the Caudell cousins, Johnny Prescott, and the twin sisters Nelva Sue and Naomi Jones. Pick was a gentleman toward Sarah, Nelva, and Naomi. He was sweet, kind, caring and a lot of fun. He was the clown of the group. He could make funny faces that would send them all into fits of laughter and tell the silliest (and cleanest) jokes of the day.

One of the funniest things he did was mock Johnny Prescott. Johnny laughed as hard, if not harder than anyone else when Pick tipped his hat forward on his head and pretended to make a move on a girl. Pick was famous for his props, so the girl in his skit might very well be the nearest mop, broom or shotgun.

Pick Watie had the persona of Johnny Prescott down pat. He had the moves and the lines, and his friend Johnny ate it up. He considered it a form of flattery, if not downright jealousy, to be portrayed as a ladies' man always on the prowl for a new love interest. Besides that it was good for laughs and he loved Pick like a brother. It was just good clean fun.

Pick always was the last one to leave. He never failed to wait with the three girls until their rides showed up and they were safely on their way home. This night was no exception as Pick and Sarah stood at the street corner and waved as Naomi and Nelva's father drove them home. It was a bit chilly, but Sarah refused Pick's offer of his jacket.

"No thanks, I like it on the cool side, and John will be here in no time anyway."

Sarah laughed as she turned around and saw Pick hanging upside down in the tree that shaded the corner. He had climbed that tree so fast she didn't even know he had left her side.

She had fallen hard for this goofy guy, but something about the way he acted told Sarah that she was no more to him than a very dear friend. Just like a sister.

"Do you have a girlfriend, Pick?"

"Yes, I do, Sarah. Her name is Lulabelle." Pick was matter of fact with his answer as he jumped down from the tree and began to dust off his britches. Sarah burst out laughing. Lulabelle was an old stray dog that liked to follow Pick and Cubbie around town.

"Lulabelle! Now you two make a very handsome couple!" Sarah joked. "Honestly, I seem to think that you have some kind of secret girlfriend, Pick. Do you? Do you have a secret girlfriend?"

Even in the dark, Sarah could tell that Pick was blushing a crimson red all the way from his cheeks down his neck.

"Aww, Sarah, let's don't talk about that kind of stuff. I don't have any secret girlfriend. Now that I've let the cat out of the bag about me and Lulabelle, it ain't a secret no more. Isn't that John coming down that way?"

That was all she needed to know. Pick Watie had a crush on someone. It broke her heart to realize that he didn't like her the way she liked him right now. However for the time being, she knew she was real and in his life and available to be his girlfriend. She didn't know who this secret crush was but Sarah had determination and wasn't going to give up quite so easily. She was going to hang on tight.

Chapter 40

His Daughter's Heart

Porter Devon was pretty much surrounded by a sea of Devon women. His only son, Rory, had joined the Army the morning after President Roosevelt shocked the nation with the somber announcement that the Japs had just bombed Pearl Harbor. He was transported out shortly after standing in the high school gym in nothing but his undershorts with all of the other patriots. Feet were observed for nice arches—flat feet were not allowed in the United States Army.

Porter Devon's son passed his physical with flying colors, and he and his nice high arches were bussed in short order to Fort Sill within the week, leaving Porter with a house full of women. His two oldest daughters, Pearl and Hilda Ruth, had recently gotten married, and their husbands were on the same bus as their brother-in-law Rory Devon, ready and willing to right the wrong brought upon their country. Pearl and Hilda Ruth were settled in their little homes in Dustin, within walking distance to their parents' home.

Fannie Devon and her daughters Pearl, Hilda Ruth, Julia Rose, Carlene, and Jennie Lou made quite a gaggle. Added to the mix was Julia Rose's one-year-old daughter, Violet. Julia Rose had gone and married

Lon Holcomb. Julia's father, Porter, never whittled so many whistles in his life as when the whole Julia Rose and Lon saga was in full swing. Lon was a momma's boy. For the life of him, Porter could not see what Julia Rose saw in that Lon Holcomb.

She had been swept off her feet by Lon by the time they were in the second grade. Lon was always squeaky clean and never failed to be at the top of his class in scholastics. Julia Rose swooned at the thought of Lon. Porter's idea of a suitable mate for his daughters certainly wasn't in a package like Lon. Porter's daughter, Julia Rose, always came in second to Mother Holcomb, and that alone burned Porter to the core. All of Porter Devon's daughters were his heart, and his hands were tied when it came to Lon and Julia Rose. Porter's wife, Fannie, chided her husband if he attempted to thwart the romance between Julia Rose and Lon. Porter had Lon pegged a mile away, and he saw nothing but heartache ahead for his daughter if she went through with the marriage to the likes of Lon Holcomb.

When Lon would show up at the Devon house to court Julia, Porter barely gave that rascal the time of day.

"Good evening, Mr. Devon. Is Julia Rose home? I know I am late, but my mother had a pressing matter that needed my assistance, and I guess time just slipped away. I know I should have called..."

Lon's neck craned to peek inside the screen door to see if Julia Rose was nearby. He hoped he could just avoid her father altogether, but it never failed that Porter Devon was on the front porch every time he came calling. Just like a gatekeeper.

Porter barely looked up from his whittling. Lon was oblivious to the fact that as he babbled on and on about his mother, Porter Devon rolled his eyes and poked his pocketknife farther down into the wood. Julia Rose appeared at the front door as Lon placed his hand on the door handle.

"Lon, there you are! I thought you said you would be here by seven. We've missed the start time for the picture show." Julia couldn't hide her disappointment from her suitor. She knew that Lon's mother was quite demanding, and it sure was taking its toll on their relationship.

"My exquisite, Julia Rose, have I told you that you are the most beautiful woman in the world?"

Porter Devon was within earshot of the flattery that bubbled out of Lon Holcomb's mouth.

"Shyster..." Porter muttered as Julia rushed into Lon's arms. "I hate it when you don't call. It worries me, Lon." Julia's lower lip protruded in a pout.

The two lovebirds walked down the lane from the Devon home, headed to town to try and catch the remainder of a movie. Julia Rose was begging to see "Best Foot Forward" with Lucille Ball and Gloria De-Haven, but Lon usually got his choice and they would more than likely spend the evening watching, "Adventures of the Flying Cadets" starring Johnny Downs.

Porter Devon was nearing the end of his patience with the way Lon Holcomb treated his daughter. It seemed to Porter that the more Lon catered to his mother and left Julia Rose hanging, the more his daughter,

Julia, flung herself at Lon.

Porter's nickname for Lon was Poindexter.

"Fannie, what is it going to take for our Julia Rose to see that Poindexter doesn't take her feelings into consideration for a minute? I've just about had it with that pointy headed devil!"

"Porter, honey, you know you can't meddle. She's going to do what her heart wants to do and there's not a thing that you or I can do about it. I see it too, and I've tried to talk to her, but she is madly in love with Lon and headstrong to boot!"

It was useless and Porter knew it. She was going to marry this Poindexter. He also knew that it would just be a matter of time before she would need a soft place to fall.   Like clockwork, the movie never happened that night. Lon's mother's "pressing needs" pressed on and on and on.

When Lon walked Julia Rose to the door, he planted a soft kiss on her lips. Before he could whisper goodnight they heard stifled giggling inside the house. Carlene and Jennie Lou were hiding behind a chair and couldn't contain themselves as they peeked out the window at their sister and her boyfriend cuddled together by the screen door. Julia Rose turned to Lon and smiled and waved goodbye as her evening with her suitor came to an end.

"I'm going to get me two little sisters!" She laughed as she came to their hiding place.

"We saw him kiss you, Julia Rose!" Julia blushed as she sat down beside the two girls.

"How was the movie? Did you get to see Lucille Ball?" They were anxious to hear every single detail that Julia Rose would share of her evening out with her guy.

No, there was no movie. She explained to her sisters that on the way to the theater Lon felt the pressing need to stop and look in on his mother. While they were there, Mrs. Holcomb decided that she needed some coal oil added to some lanterns and a sudden headache prompted Lon to make an ice bag for his dear mother to place upon her forehead. Julia was so proud of her dear Lon. He was such a devoted son and had such a tender and loving heart. It was okay, she told her sisters, that they missed the movie. She just knew that they could catch another one soon.

The saga wound around and around and before long Julia Rose Devon became the wife of Lon Holcomb. The blushing bride just knew that her place in Lon's heart was elevated higher as she looked down at the ring upon her finger.

Her father, Porter, brooded. Julia Rose deserved far better than someone like Lon Holcomb. Lon's mother insisted that the bride and groom move in with her. She had plenty of extra room, and it would be good for the young couple to not have to worry about having enough money for rent. They could live with her for free.

And live with his mother they did. Yes, they did.

Violet Rose Holcomb was born on April 25, 1945, to Lon and Julia Rose Holcomb.

Porter Devon knew exactly what Julia had hoped for with the birth of this baby. He saw Julia Rose practically stand on her head for

267

the last year to get attention from her husband. With every passing day, it seemed that his daughter, Julia, fell farther and farther back into the shadows of Lon's devotion to his mother.

She thought he would be thrilled to find out that he was going to be a father. Well, at least she thought it would be something to take his attention away from whatever whim Mother Holcomb had concocted to keep him busy with her.

Unfortunately, the new baby and his wife were just passing fancies to Lon Holcomb. He and his mother had decided that he should join the Army, and two weeks after Violet Rose was born, Lon Holcomb left for basic training in Fort Sill, Oklahoma.

As he prepared to board the train, he gave a cursory hug to Julia Rose, kissed the forehead of his baby, Violet, then turned to say goodbye to his mother, and there before God and everyone, lost total control of his emotions. He wept like an infant as he held his mother's face in his hands. Porter Devon witnessed the whole scene. He was just coming on duty as the night watchman for the train, when he stepped out onto the platform and saw Julia Rose's disappointment as her husband, Poindexter, babbled on to his mother about how he was going to miss her so. Porter was seething.

Chapter 41

Julia Rose Finds Her Spine

Julia Rose and her baby daughter found themselves spending more and more time at her parents' house. With Lon across the ocean and the United States fully engulfed in war, his mother couldn't contain her disdain for her son's wife and barely noticed her first grandchild, Violet Rose. Her whole life was centered around her son, and judging by the flow of mail, Lon Holcomb most assuredly spent more time writing his mother than marching with his platoon.

It was almost nauseating, and Julia Rose had just about had her fill. She had sent plenty of informative and cheerful letters to her husband and kept him updated on all of the cute things that their little Violet would say and do. At first he attempted to send a few quickly scribbled notes her way, but eventually he resorted to scrawling a line or two at the end of the letters to his mother, "Mother, please tell Julia Rose hello for me, and kiss my precious daughter, Violet."

How could she have been so blind? Why didn't she listen to her mother and father? She knew that they tried ever so delicately to talk to her about what they saw in Lon Holcomb. He was a momma's boy. She knew it now and felt so stupid and so trapped.

Lon was due home on leave in a few days, and Julia Rose was attempting to insert excitement into her emotions. Honestly, she had quit missing Lon when the first letter from bootcamp arrived. Was the letter addressed to her? No. The first letter that Lon Holcomb sent after he left Dustin was to his mother.

Julia felt duped.

Lon had been granted leave, and on his arrival date, Julia Rose decided to dress in her prettiest seersucker dress, the one with the red roses embroidered on the lapel. She did her best to emulate the latest hairdo worn by Betty Grable, spit curls up on the side with the back rolled under. Two squirts of rose water on her neck and a dab of bright red lipstick.

She deemed herself ready to check the pulse of her husband as he departed from the train.

"I don't know why I'm doing this," she muttered to herself.

As for sweet little Violet, she couldn't have been dressed cuter if she was the Gerber Baby! Julia Rose went all out getting her baby ready to go to the train station. Ruffles and bows from her head to her toes!

Mother Holcomb, pulled a handkerchief from her purse and dabbed a couple of tears from her eyes.

"I am trying to keep from crying, Julia. I am so excited to see my boy it has just about brought me to tears. I've checked the schedule twice. It looks like the train should be here any minute now."

And arrive it did. The whistle blew to announce its arrival as the train slowed and the steam spewed. Excited families stood on the platform of the depot waiting anxiously to welcome their soldiers, sailors, and marines home to Oklahoma. American flags and handkerchiefs fluttered in the air.

Julia Rose found herself filled with strange emotions. She really wanted to have a good marriage. She had married Lon with all of the right intentions. Had she been madly in love with him or had she been in love with being in love?

"Mother!" Lon raced to embrace his mother and smothered her cheeks with kisses.

"Oh, son, you are a sight to behold! Let me look at you" she held him back at an arm's length as tears of joy streamed down her face.

He beamed at his mother and laughed out loud as he took her handkerchief from her hand and began to wipe her tears away for her.

"And there are my girls!" Lon turned to look at Julia and Violet. "Pretty as pictures and all dressed up to see their man!"

He reached for Violet and raised her in the air and bounced her up and down a few times as she giggled and cooed. After settling Violet in the crook of one arm he reached with the other to give a sideways hug to Julia Rose. She could have easily been a neighbor or a sister. There was not an ounce of passion in the token embrace that she received from him standing there on the train depot platform. It had been a year, and she got a sideways hug. "Welcome home, Lon."

That evening as they sat around Mother Holcomb's table, feeling stuffed after a hearty meal of roast chicken and all the fixings, Lon turned to Julia Rose and began, "Julia, dear, Mother and I have been discussing our future and we both have agreed that the boarding house has just about run its course here in town. Mother is tired of the day-to-day grind and would like to sell out and move to the farm in Hanna. Of course, you, Violet, and I will be moving with her. When the war is over and I come back home, home will be the farm in Hanna! Doesn't that sound wonderful?"

Julia Rose Holcomb could have been knocked over with a feather. She had visited the old farm on many occasions where Granny and Grandpap Holcomb lived before they passed away. It was a dump. There was nothing there but a rundown old house covered in deteriorating shingles and a couple of ramshackle outbuildings.

Lon never let on that if he noticed that Julia was sitting there with a furrowed brow, speechless and terrified.

"We're going out there tomorrow, and I will show you our new home! Mother already has a buyer for the boarding house, so we plan to be moved before I have to report back to duty."

That night, Julia Rose got ready for bed. Before she went upstairs to their room she looked into the kitchen and saw Lon and his mother totally wrapped up in a long-winded conversation. It was obvious Lon was more interested in every minute detail of his mother's comings and goings for the last 12 months than he was in spending time with his wife. That was quite all right with her. There it was. She said it. She knew as she climbed the stairs to her bedroom that she had no feelings for the man that she married. He had no longings for her either, and that was fine with her.

Tomorrow would be hard.

Chapter 42

You Want Me to Live Where?

When Julia Rose woke up the next morning, she looked and saw that Lon's side of the bed had never been slept in at all. He and Mother Holcomb had spent the whole night talking.

She dressed herself and Violet and went down the stairs for breakfast.

"There are my sleepy heads!" Lon was just too giddy for words.

After a breakfast of coffee and toast, Julia climbed into the backseat of the car with Violet, while Lon and his mother occupied the front seat, as usual. It took them about 30 minutes to navigate the muddy dirt roads to the farm in Hanna.

Much to Julia Rose's chagrin, nothing had changed. If anything, it had gotten more run down than before. Lon ran to his mother's side of the car and helped her out, and off they went almost at a gallup toward the house.

Julia Rose was left to get herself and her baby out of the backseat. She was a lot like her daddy, Porter. She began to slowly seethe. By the time she caught up with her husband and his mother, she could tell by their actions that they had already laid out some of their plans. They were standing out in the barnyard in front of what looked like an old coop.

"Julia dear, here is where we are going to live." Lon had his arm extended as if he were expecting a king to walk out the door of the coop.

"We might be you, Lon, but we is not this baby and me. I will not put my daughter in this coop." Her spine had finally grown. She even felt herself standing taller than ever before and it felt fabulous!

"Oh, yes, you will. Mother and I have discussed this and we agree that we can make a home here." Lon and his mother were double-teaming Julia Rose but she wasn't budging.

"Never."

"You don't have a choice, Julia."

"Oh, but I do, Lon. I do have a choice."

"What is your other choice?"

"Divorce. I want a divorce from you and your mother."

There was not a lick of a breeze that day as Lon Holcomb, with his mother by his side, stood toe to toe with his wife. It was over.

Lon drove her back to the boarding house where she gathered her and Violet's belongings and waited on the porch for her daddy, Porter. She never shed a tear. All she felt was the weight of the world being lifted off her shoulders.

Porter Devon had waited patiently for this day. It didn't come a day too soon for him.

"Tootle loo, Poindexter."

Chapter 43

Johnny Prescott Makes His Move

About the time it took the ink to dry on Julia Rose's divorce from Lon Holcomb, Johnny Prescott decided to throw his hat into the ring as her next suitor. Johnny had learned at a very early age that there were two kinds of women. The first kind of woman was the one that could be enticed into his embrace with a wink and a promise. The promise simply being that she would be the center of his attention until the next one came along. He had enjoyed the company of many women that fit that description. Brief encounters. Satisfying, romantic, brief encounters.

The second kind of woman was the one that he wanted to have on his arm in public. The fresh faced beauty that his mother would proudly drop her name in the neighborhood quilting bee. A good, Christian woman. Johnny Prescott knew that Julia Rose Devon Holcomb fit that description to a tee. There were no behind the hand gossips proclaiming that Julia Rose was now a divorcee. Her reputation stood steadfast. The good folks of Dustin stood with Julia in the split with Lon. His reputation spoke volumes. They cheered Julia Rose on, and eyes lit up when she entered a room with her beautiful blonde haired baby in her arms. Julia was definitely one that any momma would want on her son's arm.

The savvy Johnny Prescott knew that in order to score the nice girlfriend, he would need to be discreet with the not so nice ones. Only his closest friends knew that Johnny Prescott led two lives, and Pick Watie was one of the ones that had witnessed both of them, first hand.

Pick had accompanied his friend Johnny on treks to Okemah, Oklahoma. Okemah was just far enough away that Johnny could be the smooth operator and make his moves without damaging his reputation back home. Pick would observe his friend with amazement. He had no desire to be like Johnny Prescott. If it weren't for the way his friend Johnny could be a cut up and make Pick laugh, he probably would have been just as happy staying back home in Dustin. Pick was discovering his manhood and independence but had no desire to be a rounder like Johnny Prescott. More often than not, he would sit in the corner of the cafe watching his friend sweet talk the waitress, and his mind would wonder again.

The wheels in his mind would travel to that place. He had seen her walking down the sidewalk not two days ago. She had the hand of her little daughter, and the two of them were strolling at a leisurely pace stopping long enough to gaze into the windows of the shops on that side of the street. Her hair was perfectly combed with smart spit curls sweeping the sides up like a movie star. She was dressed in a pretty cotton skirt with a white blouse tucked into her slim waistline.

Pick memorized every detail as he followed her at a prudent distance. His heart was fluttering, and his legs were wobbly at the sight of that beautiful woman. He wanted her so badly but knew that the chances of her giving him the time of day was slim to none. She was a Devon, and he was a Watie. Both good families, but he was convinced that she deserved better than him. He had nothing to offer her but himself. In his way of thinking, she was a princess, and he was a pauper.

Nothing made him feel as good as thinking about her. He had always loved her. It had been from a distance, but he knew he loved her. Julia Rose was his dream girl.

"Watie! Quit your daydreaming, son!" Johnny Prescott was ready to head back home.

Apparently this was one of the few nights that he wouldn't disappear for a bit, leaving Pick to talk to the late night patrons at the all night diner until he came back, lipstick on his face and collar.

"That broad scratched me good, Pick." Johnny said with a laugh as he wiped the bits of blood from the lines crossing his cheeks. "I guess I wasn't her type."

Johnny Prescott was careful to protect his choir boy image. He never missed a church service, and if there was an old lady that needed an arm to hold on to as she feebly crossed the street, he raced to crook his elbow. Charm was his middle name, and he could blow smoke with the best of them.

The next morning started out as normal as they come for Pick. He had a part-time job at the garage on the far north end of Main Street and was headed to town for parts. The spring wind was blowing his hair as he drove his boss's car with all of the windows down. He felt carefree and happy. Jimmy Wakeley's "The Covered Wagon Rolled Right Along" was his favorite song at the time, and he sang it to the top of his lungs.

Suddenly, from the corner of his eyes, he saw a sight that nearly caused the car to skid as he slammed on the brakes. If a breaking heart could make a sound, the crash inside Pick's body could drown out a train wreck. Nevertheless, the two of them never noticed the commotion as Pick Watie brought the old car to a halt about 50 yards from the corner. Johnny Prescott and Julia Rose were standing in front of Gray's Mercantile, wrapped up in conversation. Wrapped up like two cuddling lovebirds. Julia and Johnny. Pick was almost nauseous. His head was pounding, and his heart was crumbling. Not Johnny Prescott. Oh, how he wanted to jump out of the car and run up to Julia Rose and warn her about the fox in the henhouse that was Johnny Prescott. How could he though? Julia barely knew him. They nodded and spoke briefly if they ever crossed paths on the sidewalk or church. She was always kind to him. She had no idea that he was madly in love with her.

He sat in the driver's seat watching them as he realized that it was not his place to interfere in another person's life. She was a grown woman and could make her own choices. Who was he to think that she would even listen to him for one second? He couldn't betray his friend and stand there and blather Johnny's hidden secrets right there on Main Street. It just wasn't his place.

She was already enamored with the smooth talking, blonde-haired salesman, and Pick knew it. Johnny Prescott could talk the coat off of the back of an Eskimo in the frozen tundra. It just wasn't his place.

Chapter 44

What Are Friends for Anyway?

President Roosevelt couldn't have made his point any clearer to the citizens of the nation. The Japanese had bombed Pearl Harbor, and every furious, patriotic, and able-bodied American man that wanted revenge found themselves standing in line to join the fight for the honor of the fallen sailors in Hawaii.

Pick Watie and Johnny Prescott of Dustin, Oklahoma were no exception. The two friends couldn't wait to join and fight for their country. And join up they did. They stood together as they filled out the necessary paperwork to be a part of Roosevelt's team. They chose to be sailors in the United States Navy. They were told their departing date and the time to arrive at the designated location to report for duty as recruits for the United States Navy from the great state of Oklahoma.

The following Tuesday, along with a gymnasium filled with fellow patriots, they raised their hands and took the oath. "I, Pickford Watie (and, recited in unison, with all the other Oklahomans standing there on that day) do solemnly swear that I will support and defend the Constitution of the United States against all enemies, foreign and domestic; that I will bear true faith and allegiance to the same; and that I will obey the orders of the President of the United States and the orders of the officers appointed over me, according to regulations and the Uniform Code of Military Justice. So help me God."

As a sense of pride washed over them all, a veteran chief petty officer immediately ordered them to remove their shoes and roll up their pant legs. He began shoving mops and buckets filled with soapy water their way.

"Swab this deck!"

The gym floor was instantly filled with barefoot recruits, pushing sopping mops back and forth in front of them. They had just been told in an obvious way that they were now the property of the United States Navy.

After the gym floor glistened, they were all handed their order sheets. Written at the top of the sheet, Pick saw that San Diego, California would be his location for basic training. Johnny Prescott's sheet said the same thing. Pick had never been out of the state of Oklahoma, and now, he was going to be headed for the west coast aboard a Greyhound bus. When the call to arms was sounded by President Franklin Delano Roosevelt, many industries in the United States found themselves scrambling to replace workers that left to fight in the war.

Greyhound bus line was no exception. They lost 40 percent of their male workforce when the first round of "Defend Your Country" posters were tacked up around the bus yards. Greyhound soon found themselves scrambling to hire female drivers to fulfill their government contracts to transport soldiers, sailors, and marines to the east and west coast.

Pick Watie and his friends knew exactly what they needed to do as soon as they saw the poster on the post office wall that said, "Sub Spotted—Let 'Em Have It!" Lend a Hand. Enlist In Your Navy Today. And they did.

The cold north wind was whipping around the end of the bus as Pick, Johnny, and the other recruits from southeastern Oklahoma boarded. They all did an instant double take when they saw a woman sitting in the driver's seat of their bus. A woman bus driver? It was unfathomable to think that all of these men were to be transported across the continent with a female behind the wheel. They knew they didn't have a say in the matter, but it was unsettling to say the least. A woman bus driver?

Heads were shaking in unison as they found their places aboard the vehicle. What was this world coming to? Route 66 helped to facilitate the greatest mobilization for the war effort of patriotic Americans. Prior to the start of World War II, a young Army captain, Dwight D. Eisenhower, saw first hand, as he and his command were bogged down in muddy roads near Fort Riley, Kansas, that if the country ever needed to be ready to assemble for a major world war, they better have good roads. Millions of dollars were allocated to the modernization and stabilization of Route 66 from the central United States westward.

Furthermore, the government didn't hesitate to concentrate on building most of the military training bases on the west coast due to the moderate temperature and mild seasons. Therefore many Midwestern naval recruits found themselves bound for San Diego, California along the corridor cut by Route 66.

Most of the travelers slept the entire trip, but not Pick. He was fascinated with the scenery as the bus rolled from state to state. He had no idea as he headed westward, from the tree speckled rolling hills of Dustin, that he would soon have to crane his neck as he looked out the window to see the tops of the craggy plateaus jutting with magnificence toward the clouds. Sunlight brought the desert around Albuquerque, New Mexico. Pick couldn't take his eyes off the huge cacti lining the highway like soldiers.

"These soldiers are all surrendering." he chuckled to himself.

As they crossed the California border, the bus driver pulled the vehicle to the side of the road and turned off the engine. Ensign Jerry Willoughby, the accompanying officer, stood up, turned around, and began to make his way toward the back of the bus, pulling down black-out curtains on each window as he went.

"Don't even think about touching these windows or you will find yourself walking home. Desert or no desert." They rode the remainder of the trip in darkness.

When they arrived at the San Diego Naval Base, the majority of the men from Oklahoma had no idea that a vast ocean lined by sandy beaches and swaying palm trees was just beyond the horizon. All that would be visible were concrete walls and barracks. Welcome to the Navy, boys!

The ensign arose and pushed the handle to open the door to the bus. He faced the passengers. Wild eyes and dropped jaws ensued as they heard a loud voice just outside the door of the bus. It instantly reminded Pick of the time Uncle Logan and Uncle Duff found a raccoon inside the chicken house. The air turned blue as the anonymous voice told each and every one of them to begin to depart the bus not later but now. Obscenities that Pick had never heard before filled the air. They were frozen to their seats, afraid to move. Unfortunately for one wise acre, he learned a lesson the hard way.

"I don't have to put up with..."

A bulldog that had morphed into a human being jumped into the bus and grabbed the joker by the shirt and dragged him immediately off the bus. He was slammed to the pavement and with one foot on his back, the officer shouted again, "You girls have to the count of one to start shimmying your asses off that bus."

The bus couldn't have emptied faster if it was engulfed in flames. They were standing and facing the entryway into the San Diego Naval Base, ready to report for duty. They were in awe as their eyes landed on the large sign at the top of the gateway.

"Welcome Aboard. Your are now men of the United States navy. The tradition of service demands your utmost effort. Give it cheerfully and willingly."

Boot camp was a breeze for Pick Watie. Lean and strong, the hardworking, young man could scale any wall, master any obstacle course, and run faster than a jackrabbit. He accepted every command with a true sense of duty.

The recruits were each issued a non-working rifle to march

with, and it was their responsibility to hold on to it throughout their time in boot camp. Pick was thrilled to carry his rifle, working or not. Handling a firearm since he was a young boy was a way of life for Pick and the men from the woods in Oklahoma. If they couldn't shoot their swiftly moving targets, they didn't eat. Simple as that. Eventually, they were each given their own working rifles. The recruits were then taught to thoroughly clean and disassemble them at a breakneck speed. Word of the loss of life from across the big pond poured in daily. Pick Watie and his fellow seamen knew that they were about to embark on a mission to protect the honor of their country, and the even more glaring and unspoken truth was that they each knew not every one of them would live to tell about it.

There was an eerie awareness of the fragile times in which they were living. Pride, honor, commitment. You bet. The possibility that they may die fighting? Eerie awareness.

Upon arrival at the base in San Diego, they were immediately issued their clothing. It all reeked of mothballs, and after wearing the items for awhile, it took some time for the sailors to regain their sense of taste. Everything tasted like mothballs for the first few days. Stencil pens were used to mark their names on all of their clothing and their ditty bags. Inspections were not pretty, and they soon learned the tremendous value in recognizing the definition of the word "spotless."

Settling in to barrack life was a matter of learning to get along with others to the highest degree. Pick a bunk. No the other one because that guy sitting on the lower one is a heck of a lot bigger than you. Thank you very much.

Chow lines. Some complained but not Pick. In comparison to Momma Ella's cooking, the food that was heaped onto the metal plate in front of him was akin to something that might be rated with five stars in a Parisian restaurant or even better.

The daily life of a Navy recruit consisted of rigorous training. Drill, drill, drill. Inspections. Drill some more. Hand scrubbed laundry. Spit shining of their newly issued shoes. Tug o' war, ropes courses, guard duty, weapons and ordinance training, career selection, classifications and general testing. The daily grind behind the walls in the sunny city of San Diego, California, was rigorous and given to exacting standards of discipline and self-restraint. The biggest complaint coming from the majority of the sailors was when they would pull mess duty. Just to think about the endless pile of potatoes that needed to be peeled on a daily basis was enough to make a lot of the guys want to scale the walls and run back home. There was one sailor in particular that actually looked forward to mess duty. Pick Watie counted the days until mess duty. He just loved it.

Guard duty was so monotonous, and it bored him to tears.

Mess duty, however, was never boring, especially after he met his new friend, Earl Millette. The self-proclaimed "coonass" from Nawlins, Loozyanna. Pick had never even heard of Nawlins. He had heard of Loozyanna in his geography class in Dustin, but it took him awhile, after talking to Earl, to figure out that his teacher had totally mispronounced that state's name. All the time he thought it was Looeezee-anna.

Earl and Pick hit it off instantly. They spent hours swapping stories about trapping possum, shooting rabbits and squirrels, and comparing notes on the best techniques for crawdad huntin' in Oklahoma and mudbug catchin' in Nawlins. They laughed until they were silly about all of the ribbing they got from fellow recruits for their similar southern twangs.

"Pick, I'm a'gonna brang this here plate over to the captain."

"Earl, my bidey is achin' from all the drills. You reckon we'll ever stop bein' so dang sore?"

On many occasions, the pile of potatoes dwindled down at a steady pace as Pick and Earl explained to their fellow peeler, Duke from Boston, exactly what it was that they just said.

In the best Bostonian retort he could muster, Duke asserted, "You two boys talk so slow I could run all the way around da block at Toidy Toid and Toid Street before you even finished the woid hello."

Hometown friends are great, but Pick felt the distance growing between Johnny Prescott and himself. Johnny longed to be a man of the world. Pick just longed for home.

Johnny was spending more and more time with the partying sailors and often came back to the base well hung over from the effects of their bar hopping and girl chasing. Pick and Earl often chose to remain on base rather than chance a barroom brawl. Furthermore, neither man had the desire to mingle with the women that hung out in the bars waiting for a tryst with a sailor. More often than not, if Earl and Pick did venture off the base, it would be strictly for sightseeing. The San

Diego Zoo in Balboa Park was by far their favorite hangout. They would make each other howl with laughter when they tried to see who could do the best imitation of the monkeys and gorillas. Good clean fun. Earl was in love with his high school sweetheart, and had no desire to look at another woman.

Delores DeWitt was waiting back in Nawlins for him when he completed his tour of duty. Earl loved his dark eyed Delores with a passion. He would fill many mess duty hours filling Pick in on all of the Cajun delights that his Delores could cook in her Loozyanna kitchen. Red beans and rice, jambalaya, shrimp creole. Earl would have Pick's mouth watering just talking about her cooking. Delores could kill and clean a squirrel and have it in a pot and on the table ready to dab the juice with a piece of hard crust French bread in no time at all. Mudbugs too. Earl demonstrated the age old method of using a thumb to pop the head off the crawdad, suck the juice and bite off the tender morsel of meat, all with one hand.

Pick became fast friends with Earl. They had so much in common. Hunting, fishing, family that they loved and missed, and women back home. Earl's was real though. Pick knew his was just a notion in his mind. He would give his right eye to think that Julia Rose would be the one to greet him upon his return to Oklahoma. That particular vision was always the last thought before he would doze off to sleep each night. Upon waking up, however, he knew it was not in his cards.

Chapter 45

Anchors Aweigh!

The weeks in basic training in San Diego seemed to fly. In their off-duty hours, the new recruits found themselves hanging by the radio more and more. The news from the African and European battlefronts was coming in at an alarming pace. The war was raging and was proving to be vicious and deadly. With each and every newscast, the hairs on the back of the sailors' necks stood straight out. They were riled, and they were ready to go into the battle with full force.

Pick, Earl, and Johnny Prescott would be shipping out the next day and heading for the continent of Africa. Pick and Earl would find themselves in the most vulnerable positions on the entire ship. Their jobs would be gunner's mates. They would be on the deck of the battleship prepared at a moment's notice to man the ammunition. Raw and ready, they stood tall in their respective saddles. Late night conversations were filled with fist pumping, boasts, and build-ups. They would do their best to stand up against any wayward submarine or battleship. Uncle Sam had called them, and they were there to answer!

During the first few weeks of the voyage, it was not uncommon to see rows of seasick sailors hanging over the edge of the ship as the remainder of their last meal was heaved and hurled into the foamy sea.

Pick, Earl, and Johnny were no exceptions. Green. Pick told Earl that if his face got any greener, he would have to get a spear and gig him for supper. Earl jokingly shot back at Pick, "Pickford, at least I make it to da side to lose mine. You betta watch it. Dey might think you been sneakin' a few nips. You are a' weavin back and forth like one of dose buoys out dat away!"

Most of the days passed without any more than monotonous and sometimes hazardous ship duties. Earl and Pick spent most of their waking hours on the deck of the battleship tending to their specific orders. The bright sun glistened across the breakers like jewels in a pirate's booty. Through experimentation, Earl and Pick discovered that if they rubbed their shirtless bodies and faces with the linseed oil that was used on the ship, they ended up with nice golden tans. Two young and carefree men serving their country aboard a battleship, bronze, and ready for battle.

It was not a drill.

The air raid collision siren was sounding. The ship was in full-blown action to prepare for an attack. An enemy submarine had been sighted and was heading toward their ship. "All hands on deck! All hands on deck!"

Pick and Earl manned their stations. They were each assigned to their own weapon. Their duties were to help keep it loaded and in working order. Ready to fire and defeat the enemy that was swiftly approaching. This time there was success! The oncoming submarine was rendered useless, and those aboard perished. Sweat ran down their brows. That was a very close call.

They awaited the all-clear signal to sound, but it was not going to happen soon. Again the siren wailed. To the starboard, or "senior," side of the vessel they could see a kamikaze pilot heading his airplane toward the ship that was sailing beside theirs. Dive bomb. Direct hit! Massive damage. Man the guns again. Where did that guy come from? Sitting ducks they were, but nothing was going to keep the gunner's mates from revving up the fight! All of the days and endless hours of drills had paid off, whereby the entire ship of sailors performed like a well-oiled machine. They were prepared to fight and defend. They would not stand down. The hair stood up on the tops of their heads. The veins in their arms pulsed. If fury could be measured in quantities, theirs would be off the charts. They smelled death. Fellow sailors lay dead, dying, and injured on the sister ship, and each and every one of them quietly, between clenched teeth, just dared the enemy to show his worthless self.

They waited, but no one came to their "take this and eat it" party. They all agreed that it was a good thing for the enemy that they backed off. They had a whole shipload of mad sailors ready to make mince meat out of anyone that came into their space. Mince meat! Some days were quiet, but at the end of others, before they would close their eyes to go to sleep, they would thank God above for letting them live another day and pray hard to not let them face another moment of battle like the one they had just witnessed. All in a day's work.

Pick and Earl had forged a brotherly bond. When it was time to play, they acted like they didn't have a care in the world. When the siren went off, they had each other's backs to the extent that they knew they would make the ultimate sacrifice for each other. Brotherly love.

Up until this time, Pick, Earl, and Johnny Prescott had been given three changes of ship assignments. Each time, they had been assigned to the same ship. Six months into their present duty, all three sailors were given notice that they would again change ships. Pick Watie and Johnny Prescott would be moving on together. Sadly for Pick and Earl, Earl Millette was going to another ship.

Pick had suffered loss so many times in his life, the death of his parents and his brother, the removal of his brothers and sisters; he felt sucker punched again. His friendship with Earl Millette, from Nawlins, Loozyanna, had been a light in his pretty dismal life. Earl was sad too. He was the only boy in a family of six children. Pick was the brother he never had. The ordeal was sad but inevitable. They exchanged addresses and promised to try to find each other after the war.

The small boat arrived at the port side of the ship. Earl and the others that were being transferred, hoisted their duffel bags over their shoulders and shinnied down and boarded, ready to be whisked away to the awaiting vessel in the distance. A glance back and a salute to each other, the friends bid each other adieu. Earl tightened his sailor cap down on his forehead and raised the collar on his jacket to cover his ears as the wind and choppy waves bounced the boat as it scurried through the waves.

"Goodbye my Cajun friend," Pick said as he tossed one last

salute to the sea.

Suddenly, Pick had an idea and scurried up the stairs to the signalman's area. The signalman was another one of his buddies, and when he heard his friend's request a smile beamed from ear to ear, and he told Pick "Hold tight, Sailor!" as he twirled around to his signal light.

From a distance, Pick could see Earl climbing onto the ship. The signalman began his message to the other ship's signalman. Pick could see other sailors tapping Earl on the shoulder and pointing toward his former ship's incoming signal message.

"Goodbye my Cajun friend. Have a good life."
Pick could see Earl running up the stairs to the other ship's signalman, and quickly came the return message.

"I will never forget you my Okie friend. I wish you a happy life."

They each removed their sailor caps and waved until Earl's ship became a dot on the ocean. The kindred spirits knew it was highly unlikely that their paths would ever cross again. It was not "goodbye"; it was "live the life you deserve."

Chapter 46

Letters from Home

Pick hoisted the mailbag up onto the counter. When his turn for mail duty came, there was a certain skip to his steps as he scurried down to the mailroom to collect the bulging duffel bag. An honorable duty as far as he was concerned was to make sure these precious pieces of mail, letters from home, reached their intended addressees. It could almost be labeled a sacred honor. He, as much as all of the other sailors aboard the battleship, looked forward to mail day just like a kid at Christmas. Was there ever bad news lurking inside those envelopes? Yes, quite often there was sad and disturbing news from the home front, but that never really dulled the enthusiasm for the piece of home in the form of a letter that would find its way into the clutches of a waiting seaman.

Each sailor's mail would be bundled together. As the bundles were pulled out of the bag, a name would be shouted, and a relieved sailor would make his way through the crowd to claim his letters. Letters from home.

Maybe it was a line by line offering of the daily activities on the family farm back home in Kansas: "Well, son, I don't know if you are even aware of the seasons or not, being as you are all the way over into the Orient, but Pa, your brothers, and I have spent the last 13 days plowing and seeding for the spring harvest." Or it was an admonition from an accountant father sitting at his desk in Philadelphia, lamenting over the son's choice of serving his country over sticking with the father's well intentioned plans for a solid career path, which included college and bean counting: "Henry, I am hearing such dreadful news from the battlefront, as I sit here today, and I am so concerned for your safety. Oh how I wish you had reconsidered your decision to join the Navy! Your mother and I pray daily that God will bring you home to us safe and sound. A saving grace will be your GI Bill. The university has an excellent accounting program, and Mr. Phillips has assured me that when you have completed your studies, he will find a place for you with the firm." Line by line, stories from home from mothers, fathers, kid sisters, pastors, and teachers. Every jot and tittle of every word was read and re-read.

The most coveted, however, was a neatly bound bundle with bright red kisses on the back of every single piece of mail tied together by a string. With the bundle held high and rotated for all to see, a name would be called out "Miller! Joseph Miller!"

The smug sailor would move his hat farther forward on his brow and walk pompously toward the mail clerk. "Ooh, la la!" Catcalls and whistles erupted from the crowd. With one hand, the sailor would gently collect his letters, and in his best impersonation of Errol Flynn, he would raise his bundle in the air and bring it down to his nose for a grandiose sniff of the flowery droplets of perfume that permeated each awaiting page. Wolf whistles would erupt as the next scented bundle was pulled from the mailbag. Letters from home.

Letters from dames. The skip in Pick's step was for the letters from dames. Not just any dame though, one particular scent rose above the all. He knew when the mailbag landed with a thud it would stir up the aromas circulating throughout the pages and pages of sweet things from sweet things. His keen sense of smell zeroed in on one particular scent that permeated his olfactory lobes. The scent that often came to him in the middle of the night as he lay in his rack gently swaying to the motion of the battleship as it cut its way through the ocean waves.

His mind wandered as he fought sleepless nights. He might start thinking about his brothers and sisters who were all serving their country in different branches of the armed forces. He often tried to think where they might be as he lay missing them all. Augie was in the Army, and last Pick heard, he was marching with the forces in France. Iris and Alice were WACs, and by way of their steady stream of mail, they informed him they were with 7,600 WACs throughout the European theater stationed somewhere across England, France, and the German cities of Berlin, Frankfurt, Wiesbaden, and Heidelberg. His little brother Cubbie, anxious to follow his brother Pick's footsteps was a proud sailor aboard a destroyer somewhere in the Pacific. He spent more time worrying about Cubbie than he did counting sheep.

Cubbie couldn't wait to sign his name and join the Navy, just like his brother. It was a proud moment for Pick, but he couldn't help but remember so many years ago that he swore to always be around to take care of his little brother. He was pretty helpless in that regard as he lay in the darkness of a battleship miles and miles from nowhere keeping a prayer vigil for his siblings—wherever they were. Praying and swaying and thinking.

Then, like sand in the hourglass, the wonderful aroma would come to him, and every effort he made to try to not think about her, every feeble attempt to try to focus on something besides the beautiful woman that was back home in Dustin, Oklahoma, sitting on a blanket on the soft grass picking little lilac flowers off her mother's bush at the side of the house. The visual was embedded in his imagination.

Every night he would reenact the little movie he had concocted for his own entertainment. The blanket would be spread neatly on the ground. She was wearing a cotton print dress, nothing fancy, but showing plenty of those long lithe legs. The letter was written, folded, and placed with care into the small white envelope. She would lay the envelope into her lap and have a starry eyed look as she dreamed of her sailor boy so very far away. Over and over in his mind he would see her reach for the lilac flowers, pluck a few and bring them to her nose. Her eyes would close, and he knew that she was wondering to herself, Will this remind him of home? Will he think of me? She would then take the small flowers and press them with her fingers to release the aroma and gently place them inside the envelope. She would bring the letter to her heart and hold it there for a few seconds. Then she would reach into her pocket and retrieve her tube of bright red lipstick. After a generous swipe of the creamy redness met her lips, she would transfer it to the back of the envelope with a big pucker and a smack! She would lie back on the blanket with her arm over her eyes, holding the letter with line after line of undying love scribbled over and over page after page, holding it to her heart and thinking of him. With a long sigh she would say his name. "Oh, Johnny..."

The pain cut like a knife into his heart. Julia Rose was writing the letters to her man—to Johnny Prescott, Pick's home town friend and shipmate. The lilacs, the lips, the sighs, and starry eyes were for Johnny. She barely knew Pick Watie existed. To Julia, Pick was just "Johnny's friend and that sweet, nice guy from Dustin that she vaguely remembered from grade school. The little poor child that always came to school in dirty overalls." Fact from fiction, Julia was in love with Johnny.

Johnny. Strikingly handsome, suave, and debonaire, that was Johnny Prescott. He was an out and out lady's man. Lots of ladies. Lots and lots of ladies. One thing Pick knew was that Julia Rose was head over heels in love with Johnny Prescott, and Johnny Prescott was head over heels in love with... himself. Many bundles of perfumed letters came Johnny Prescott's way each mail day. The return addresses would

read like a phone book. Jane, Helen, Prudence, Esther, Carolina, Louise, Shirley, Margaret, on and on. Oh and Julia Rose.

"Hey, Pick! Would ya mind helpin' a buddy out with some of these letters?" a grinning Johnny Prescott would say to his hometown friend as the stack got bigger and bigger. A girl in every port, that saying fit Johnny to a tee.

Pick knew that Johnny was teasing about the plea for help with the letters. For months, Pick had watched Johnny answer most of the letters that came his way in a style all his own.

"Gotta give the ladies what they want, Watie! Keep 'em coming back for more!"

The answered mail was sent back quickly in great anticipation of what Johnny regarded as the "good mail." Erotic and suggestive. It was like a production line. Send one out, and three came back.

The letters from Julia Rose had a tendency to stack up higher and higher. When Johnny pulled a duty and Pick's shift was over, Pick would saunter over to the letters. The "good mail" didn't interest him. He went straight for the stack from Julia. One by one he would read the letters, some over and over.

"Momma and Daddy send their love. Well, Momma said to tell you hello, and Daddy, well, darling, I know when he really gets to know you, he will love you as I do. He will discover the wonderful and gallant man that I know is in you. For now, Daddy just keeps busy fixing shoes and working for the railroad. He must have a lot on his mind. I'm sure you understand."

It didn't take too many letters for Pick Watie to really like Mr. Porter Devon. Julia Rose's father wasn't a dummy. He had Johnny Prescott pegged. Not a hard thing to do for a man with common sense, and Pick could tell that Porter Devon was loaded with it. Johnny Prescott pretty much ignored Julia's letters but kept her stringing along like he always did. All it took was one letter filled with "you're my one and only, and I can't wait to make you my wife," spread a few weeks apart and sprinkled with the usual Johnny Prescott self centered pat excuse, "Honey, I am fighting this war for you, and you know that I wish I could write more often, but being the captain's right hand man has me up all night and day defending this ship from the constant threat of torpedo fire. Think of me often, as I know you do. Your loving sailor, Johnny."

Pick knew that Johnny did not love Julia Rose Devon. Well, he knew that Johnny did not love Julia Rose like Julia Rose deserved to be loved. Johnny talked a great game of going back to Dustin and marrying Julia someday, but Pick knew that the girl in every port kept Johnny Prescott very busy and that ever-growing stack of letters from Julia was not what Johnny Prescott's lonely nights were centered around.

Pick's decades long crush on Julia grew with an intensity that he could not and did not want to control. He had read those letters over and over. He knew her; he knew her family. He knew every room in her parent's house and the smells coming from Fannie's kitchen. He knew that when Porter had to go on night watchman duty for the railroad that Fannie and her daughters, Julia Rose, Carlene, and Jennie Lou were afraid and would all sleep together in Porter and Fannie's bed with a shotgun resting beside Fannie "just in case."

He laughed harder and harder each time he would read the letter where Julia described the night after she had tucked little Violet in her crib, and her mother and she and her sisters were lying in bed. Fannie had turned down the coal oil lamp, joined the girls in saying the Lord's Prayer and settled down for the night when they heard the back door creak and with wide-eyed terror saw a hand come through the crack in the door. Momma Fannie had jumped straight out of bed, grabbed the shotgun, and shouted "Get away or I'll shoot!" With her finger on the trigger, she accidentally pulled it as it was pointing straight upwards and with a boom a hole as big as a watermelon was gaping in the roof above the bed! The intruder took off running, and from the window, Julia Rose saw it was Pete, the hired hand. And they were sure that he didn't stop running until he reached the Kansas line! Pick loved Julia's stories and delighted in each word that was written in beautiful cursive on every single page.

He passed over the mushy stuff. He couldn't bear to read it and just pretended that it wasn't there. With every letter, he loved her more and more. He wanted Julia like nothing he had every wanted in his life and dreamed of what his life would be like if he could just scoop her up and take her into his arms and plant sweet kisses all over her lips. Before he would fall asleep he would tell himself, "Pick Watie, fact from fiction... She loves Johnny."

Chapter 47

Shore Leave

News from the captain made Pick and Johnny Prescott do a double take. They read and reread the note they each held in their hands.

"You will be reporting to a new ship in 45 days. You have been granted 30 days of shore leave before commencing your service aboard your newly assigned ship. This vessel will be docking in San Diego in 15 days."

Glory be! Shore leave! Pick and Johnny didn't waste a moment until they solidified plans with their fellow shipmate, Ken Stanley, from Heber Springs, Arkansas, to split the costs and driving duties from San Diego eastward in Ken's jalopy that was stored on base in San Diego. Letters home were scribbled and stuffed into the outgoing mailbags as the seamen steadily marked the days off the calendar, until 15 days had inched by at a snail's pace.

The three sailors tossed their duffel bags into Ken's trunk at 2:30 that Monday morning and jumped into the old beater. It started right up, and they left the palm trees that lined the shores of the Pacific Ocean in the rear view mirror in San Diego and headed home. They hit Oklahoma City in record time. With 19 hours and 47 minutes of asphalt behind them, they wheeled into the designated drop off point. Pick and Johnny's friend, Jenkins Macfarlane, was waiting as promised. They tipped their hats to Ken as he sped off toward Arkansas. Home sweet home!

The air in the midwest smelled of newly mowed grass as the salty smell of the ocean, which had permeated their nostrils, slowly faded away.

"Get us home, Jenkins!" was their rallying cry as their buddy turned the key and revved up the engine for the comparatively short drive to Dustin, Oklahoma.

Pick had Jenkins drop him off at Momma and Poppa's. He was so glad to be home that even the thought of Momma's cooking didn't put a damper on his spirits! Jenkins promised to be back early the next morning for a trip to the old pond to plunk for fish. Pick had an enormous hankering for fried catfish. He had been dreaming of tasting a mess of crispy filets since he saw the last of San Diego far off in the horizon. He couldn't wait to try out one of the recipes that he had methodically written down word for word from Earl Millette. It was going to be Cajun catfish for supper!

Momma mustered up a hello for her grandson, and Poppa hobbled to the door to wrap his arms around the neck of his daughter's son. Poppa's body was fully engulfed with the debilitating effects of sugar diabetes. The neuropathy in his feet left him practically crippled, let alone the wear and tear of years of eating Momma's cooking.

Nonetheless, it was good to be home. The long and lonely nights, the stress related to being on a battle ship waiting for the next bombardment had taken its toll on Pick. He cherished every second of being back in his hometown. Familiar places and faces. Simple pleasures with no fear of a torpedo attack. He didn't want to go back to the war, but his pride would never let him admit that out loud.

Pick politely refused Poppa's offer of asking Momma to make him a home cooked breakfast. Home was nice, but he could honestly think of nothing worse than having his gullet clogged with those hard as rock biscuits. He told Poppa that the long trip left him with no appetite that morning. He reckoned that telling a little white lie was much more beneficial than ruining the start of his day with Momma's cooking. A handful of blackberries from a bush beside the fishing hole sounding far more appetizing.

A slow walk across the yard toward the old shed brought a flood of memories. Pick and Cubbie had made this walk many times.

Chapter 48

The Plow Goose

Pick laughed out loud as he made his way toward the shed. A long lost childhood memory came to mind. He would never forget that day. It had been a particularly long and hot summer day. A storm was brewing in the west, and Poppa had a limited amount of time to get the rest of the field plowed before the torrents of rain moved in to stall his efforts.

Pick and Cubbie were helping the best that they could. Pick was twelve, and Cubbie was ten. They were scurrying behind Poppa and the old mule. If a huge clod of dirt was left behind, the two youngsters would take their shovels and break them up as fast as they could. Old Tobe was pulling the plow at the only speed he knew in spite of the "hees and haws" that Poppa bellowed. The black clouds were approaching closer when all of a sudden there was a loud "ping."

Poppa muttered an inaudible curse word as the plow buckled and fell to the ground. The wind was whipping as Poppa shouted, "Pick! Hurry to the shed and get me a plow goose! Run fast, boy, and get back here so I can get this row turned up!"

Pick took off like a bolt of lightening was after his britches!

Barefooted and surefooted, he laid tracks like a racehorse as he arrived at the shed with breakneck speed. He opened the latch and flung open the door. Stopping just long enough to catch his breath, Pick began the hunt for the plow goose. The shelves were lined with all kinds of tools. Some had been purchased from the Gray's Mercantile, and more had been whittled or jerry-rigged by Poppa. Pick had never heard of the plow goose, but that didn't make a difference. He knew Poppa needed it in the worst way, and he was not going to stop looking until he found it.

In a few minutes, in walked Momma. "What are you lookin' fer?" Momma was having one of her more lucid days. She was fully aware of the urgency. The storm was coming, and Poppa and Cubbie were still out in the field.

"Momma, the plow broke, and Poppa wants me to hurry and find his plow goose!" Momma had a puzzled look on her face. In all the years of farming this patch of earth, she had never heard Angus mention a plow goose. Never mind that though, they needed to find it in a hurry.

"Is this it, Pick?" she said as she held up tool after tool that lined the shelves. "No, Momma, that ain't it. Keep looking!"

Their efforts seemed futile as they dug through old bushel baskets and wooden boxes looking for the elusive plow goose. The first crack of lightening stopped them dead in their tracks. Rain on the tin roof of the shed sounded like a battalion of soldiers marching to war. Big, fat, pelting, rain drops.

Pick's face fell flat to the ground as Poppa came storming into the shed.

"Pick Watie! I needed that tool! What have you been doing, boy?"

Tears began to run straight down Pick's freckled cheeks. "Poppa. We've searched high an low, and I swear we can't find your plow goose anywhere!"

Poppa's face changed from anger to quizzical. "What did you just say you were looking for, Pick?"

"Poppa, I was looking for your plow goose. Momma and I have looked high and low and we can't find it anywhere."

Poppa slumped to the nearest box and sat right down on it. He hung his head and slowly began to chuckle. His face became redder and redder and his chuckle became louder and louder. His big belly shook harder and harder as he took his straw hat off his head and looked at

Pick and Ella.

The two tool sleuths stood motionless as they faced Poppa as wide-eyed as a couple of hoot owls.

"Pick. I said go get me some pliers. My plow is loose."

Chapter 49

Home Ain't All Good

Pick loved those old memories. They brought back simpler times that weren't any part of war or trips to foreign countries. Just simple times before the war. Puffs of dust stirred as Pick pulled the stick from the latch and pushed open the door. The early morning sunlight caught the cobwebs that hung from the ceiling of the old shed. A smile crossed Pick's face as he saw the fishing gear in the corner just as he and Cubbie had left it several years ago. Jenkins would be driving up soon, so Pick took his hand and brushed the cobwebs from the area as he reached down to pick up his fishing pole and tackle box. Just as he had his hand on the handle, a small gray mouse darted across his knuckles and scared the liver out of him!

Pick grabbed the nearest thing he could get his hands on to throw at the mouse, but the little varmint had scurried through a crack in the wall of the shed and was long gone. Even more than he hated mice, Pick Watie hated the object that he held in his hand. A very painful memory poured over him as he realized what he had just picked up to kill the mouse.

Why hadn't he thrown this old thing away years ago? Why

hadn't it found its way into a brush burning pile so it could have been reduced to smoldering ashes?

A terrible pain grabbed him from the past and dragged him right to this spot in the barn. Right smack dab to the present. He hated this more than he hated mice.   The ax handle.

He would never forget that day as long as he lived. It had pretty much started off as any other summer day around the farm. He and Cubbie had been living with Poppa and Momma about three years and had begun to learn how to do the daily chores. They fetched water, fed the animals, weeded the garden, and chopped firewood.

With the ax.

Poppa had felled an old sycamore tree that had been struck by lightening the day before. The boys were to chop the tree up into firewood and stack it by the barn so it could season before winter.
Pick would do the chopping and splitting, as he was the oldest and strongest, and Cubbie would do the stacking and the fetching of a drink of cool well water for his sweaty brother upon request.

By midday, they had just about accomplished their job when Pick spotted one last limb that needed chopped. He and Cubbie dragged it over to the stump that Pick was using to steady the limbs. Pick raised the ax in the air to give the limb a good whack.

He would never forget that moment as long as he lived.

It didn't take but a split second for Pic to realize that the ax head had flown off the handle. He knew Cubbie was close behind him, and before he could twirl around, he heard it.

A blood-curdling scream came from his little brother!

Nothing could have prepared Pick for what happened next. His little brother had been struck right in the face by the ax head. As blood spurted and Cubbie screamed, Pick could see that most of Cubbie's nose was dangling by just a thread of skin.

Without wasting a second of time, Pick jerked off his shirt and placed it on Cubbie's nose, picked up his little brother, and went running toward the house, remembering as he ran to keep adequate pressure on the center of Cubbie's face. Thank God they were in the Boy Scouts. They had just had a class on first aid.

"Poppa! Poppa! Poppa! Help us please, Poppa!" Pick's frantic cries echoed into the house. Angus Scott bounded out of the door onto the porch. Pick was running toward him with Cubbie in his arms. All he could see of Cubbie was a blood soaked shirt covering his face.

Without hesitation, Angus shouted to Pick to get on the wagon with his brother. Angus didn't even remember slipping on his boots, running to the barn, grabbing Tobe the mule, hooking him up to the wagon, and going at breakneck speed to Old Doc Lett's office in town. The focus was speed and being ever mindful of the steady pulse of blood oozing from Cubbie's face as it defied the pressure being applied by his brother. Pick held his little brother tight, telling him along the way that he was safe in his older brother's arms.

Doc Lett was a masterful artist when it came to sewing and stitching body parts back together. He had gotten a lot of practice when the railroad was being constructed, and it's just a given that in a farming

315

community there are going to be accidents and detached body parts. He had Cubbie's nose nicely repositioned in no time. It had been a clean cut and as Doc Lett put it, "Son, that little nose of yours will never know a thing if you don't tell it!"

Cubbie could have died. Pick had almost killed his baby brother. Chills went up and down Pick's spine at the very thought of what could have happened that day. He knew deep down inside that it wasn't his fault that the ax handle was loose, but his vow to always protect his little brother was always first and foremost in his heart.

All of that was many years ago. Cubbie had gone out of his way to tell Pick that he knew that it was an accident. In fact, Cubbie often jokingly used it to his advantage. If he wanted something from his brother, he would grab his nose and pretend that it was hurting. They would laugh and often Cubbie would get his way. The memories came flooding in, some good, some bad. Pick took the old ax handle and stuffed it in an old barrel that Poppa used to burn trash. Good riddance!

After piddling with his lures and fishing line, Pick sat on the front porch until Jenkins Macfarlane drove up in his old jalopy. Following a brief discussion, the two agreed to stop by Gray's for something to eat before heading to the pond. A cloud of dust followed them as they headed south toward Dustin and a leisurely day of fishing and catching up on lost time.

Jenkins found a place to park smack dab in front of the store and jumped up and over the door to exit the vehicle. Pick watched from the passenger seat as his friend sauntered in and tipped his hat to old

Miss Winters as she sidled her plump little body past him in the door way.

It was surely fate that Pick decided to sit in the car while Jenks ran in to the store. Not more than an instant passed after he had run the match head against his zipper to light up the Lucky Strike dangling from his lips when he glanced up and saw a sight that felt like a fist landed a blow directly into his gut. Johnny Prescott and Julia Rose Devon were heading down the sidewalk hand in hand.

A fire lit in Pick like no other time that he could recollect. The green eyed monster crept onto him like a rash! The flush in his face burned slowly and had a pulsing beat to it like the rhythm of a bongo drum. He had a flashback of those times aboard the ship watching Johnny tossing Julia's unopened letters aside in favor of the salacious invitations from all of those other women. Pick turned his head but not before seeing the adoring look in Julia's eyes as she focused her entire being into the gaze of that scoundrel.

By the time Jenkins jumped back into the vehicle and saw the change in his friend's face, the two lovebirds had already strolled down the street.

"You look like you jest ate somethin' rotten, Pick."

"Jenkins, jest start this beater up and get me to the pond. I'm gonna catch Moby Dick today."

Chapter 50

Come on, Carlene!
Bob Wills Is Playin' at the Cain's Dance Academy!

Julia Rose loved to dance. She and her best friend, Julia Lorene Mason, were always the belles of the ball at every social function. They could jitterbug and cut a rug like nobody's business! As soon as Julia Rose Devon saw the poster hanging on the window of Gray's Mercantile announcing that the King of Western Swing, Bob Wills and his band, The Texas Playboys, were coming to the Cain's Dance Academy in Tulsa, it was a no brainer that Julia Rose and her friends would make the hour drive north!

The Cain's Dance Academy was the site of the The Texas Playboys' first regular radio broadcast, and Bob Wills and his band would play there on a regular basis. Their popularity continued to soar even more when they added the popular and talented local musician, Leon McAuliffe, on steel guitar. Julia Rose had not mentioned to her beau, Johnny Prescott, that she was going to the Cain's that night. He had already told her earlier that he had business to take care of and wouldn't be able to see her. She was glad that he was home on leave, but they really hadn't been able to spend a lot of time together. He told her that he was busy working on some deals for their future.

On that Friday afternoon, Julia Rose, her sister Carlene, their friend Julia Mason, and little Violet, Julia's daughter, all piled into Julia's car and headed up the road to Tulsa. The Cain's Dance Academy was a family oriented venue, and children of all ages were welcomed. Violet loved traveling along with the fun group of women as they drove along the road to see Bob Wills. Their plan was to get there early enough to get a table close to the stage and the dance floor. The doors opened at 5:00 p.m., and they found themselves in a great position in the long and winding line forming outside of the dance academy. As soon as they flew through the doorway, they garnered a table in a perfect spot. Bob Wills and The Texas Playboys would be tuning up in no time, and the girls from Dustin could not be any more thrilled!

Chapter 51

War Is Hell, Baby

When Julia Rose was in the presence of her boyfriend, Johnny, she felt as if she was the apple of his eye. He was gallant and the words that put a skip in her step rolled off his tongue like a fairy tale in motion. She loved Johnny Prescott, she would tell herself. She had missed him something fierce the whole time he was at sea. Didn't she?

Even though she didn't get very many responses to her daily love letters, he was her man. Each intermittent letter she received from her brave sailor filled her with... filled her with what? Julia had a nagging feeling in her spirit. Something just didn't feel right. Was God sending her a message? She had prayed nightly for a Godly man. A decent and loving man that would scoop her and her baby, Violet, up in his strong arms and protect them from the harshness of the world.

Something was wrong, and she had been having a sick feeling in the pit of her stomach.

The night at The Cain's in Tulsa, as she and her friends listened to Bob Wills and The Texas Playboys, Julia could have sworn that she had caught a glimpse of a man and woman wrapped arm in arm leaving the dance floor and heading toward the exit. In the split second that she looked their direction, she thought that the man looked just like Johnny Prescott. Her Johnny.

She also could have sworn that right behind the couple was another sailor. Was that Pick Watie? Did she also catch a glimpse of Sarah Wainwright, Naomi and Nelva Jones, and Jenkins Macfarlane? Johnny's friends. Her eyes must certainly be playing tricks on her. Her Johnny wouldn't lie to her, and he certainly wouldn't be with another woman!

As Julia Rose did a double take, the faces blended in the crowd, and they were already out the door. It couldn't have been Johnny. He told her specifically that he was going to be meeting with someone regarding a possible business venture when the war was over. Johnny was a good man and would never lie to her. Would he?

Several days later, her brow was furrowed as she flipped though the dresses in her closet. Johnny was coming soon to take her to a movie. This was to be their last night together before he was to head back to San Diego to report for duty. He had always been the perfect gentleman. They had exchanged sweet kisses, but that was the extent of it. She was more than happy to be courted in such a respectable manner.

Maybe she was just blue because he was leaving the next day. They hadn't gotten to spend much time together. He had come by her house a few nights here and there to sit on her parents' front porch and whisper sweet nothings into her ear as they snuggled on the porch swing.

There was just the undeniable nagging feeling that something was wrong. Her gut was aching for her to know the truth. What was the truth? She knew that couldn't have been him at The Cain's all wrapped up with that woman. That was just not the actions of the man that she knew. Convincing herself to stop the silly notions bouncing around in her head, she chose a pretty skirt and sweater just in time for the knock of her suitor on her parents' door. He looked so handsome standing in the doorway. His smile was a mile wide, and his blonde curl swooped down the middle of his forehead just outside of his bright, white sailor hat. He had a single red rose in his hand and thrust it toward her as she pushed open the screen door.

"Johnny, what a sweet gesture! A rose for me? Why thank you, darling!"

"Julia, I can't think of anything more fitting to place into your precious hand. A beautiful red rose for my beautiful Julia Rose!"
The night had started off with a bang. Johnny had a way of speaking and acting that could melt Julia into a puddle. The compliments and gestures rolled along like the third act of a one act play.

War was hell. That was a certainty. So many Americans never made it home from across the oceans. Bullets, bombs, grenades, and bayonets. Their lives could be taken from them in an instant, as they battled in the foreign lands to stop the opposing forces from victory.

Quick marriages were taking place in judge's homes just before the soldiers and sailors stole one last kiss from their sweethearts. It was a way of showing them that they would leave a light burning in the window for them. They would have someone to come home to, and life would start anew after the hellish war was over. Promises and rings and hopes and dreams were exchanged as they waved goodbye.

323

Even through the smiles and waves each couple knew the looming fear. What if he didn't come home? There was that black cloud hanging over them as they stood in train stations and bus depots all around the country and held each other tight. Many of the men had hopes and dreams that perhaps their wives were carrying a child that would greet them as a family when they returned. Therein the rub.

Sometimes, in the heat of the moment, the words would come tumbling out of their mouths. Maybe they weren't so much in love, but in that moment there was the fear that perhaps this could be their last opportunity, their last fleeting chance to feel a woman in their arms. What if they were never coming home? The words just came out. The words.

Johnny Prescott had escorted Julia to his car after the movie. The scent of her perfume as she jumped into the seat sent waves of pleasure into his senses. She was such a beautiful woman. He couldn't help but notice her cascading auburn hair as it fell on her shoulders. Her tiny waist.

"Where are we going, Johnny? This isn't the way to my house." Julia said with a puzzled look on her face.

"I want to take you somewhere so we can talk just a little bit. I don't want this night to end. I'm going to miss you so much." A sick feeling hit Julia's gut like a fist. Something about the tone of his voice gave her a chill. He sounded... different.

"We can talk on the front porch. The moon is so bright and shiny. The harvest moon. I love the way the harvest moon lights up the sky."

She seemed to be rattling on trying to focus her thoughts on why she was feeling so strange here in Johnny's car heading away from her parents' house. Heading down a dirt pathway. Nausea. Then a tinge of fear started creeping up inside of her.

He brought the car to a stop and reached into the back seat and felt around in the dark for a blanket. Before she could speak, he had exited the vehicle and was strolling around to her side of the car. "Johnny, I really don't know about this. It's a little chilly out there, and I had told mother and daddy that I would be home directly after the movie. I don't want them to get worried. Please. Let's just go talk on the porch."

Johnny was smiling that crooked smile that had her swooning in the past.

"Dear Julia, we will just be here for a few minutes. I just want to be alone and talk one last time before I leave."

Telling herself that Johnny was just wanting to tell her goodbye in a sweet manner, Julia slowly got out of the car and sat on the blanket that he had spread out on the ground. The moon was filtering through the trees and cast a jagged pattern of moonlight on them as they faced each other. Johnny put his arms around her and pulled her tight to his chest.

There in the dark, Johnny broke the silence. "Julia, I'm afraid. I have never admitted it out loud to anyone, but I have a fear inside of me that I'm not going to survive this war. I'm a proud man and would never even give a thought to running from my duties, but I'm telling you that the last thing on earth I want to be doing in the morning is leaving you and this town for more of the same awful things that I have seen. I've seen death, Julia. Lots of it. Men too young to die being blown to bits right in front of my eyes. I love my country, and I will fight to my death to protect it. But I don't relish the thought that this may be the very last time I ever hold you in my arms."

Before she could say a word, he gently pushed her backwards onto the blanket and began to pull himself on top of her.

"No,wait. Johnny. Please no! Please not like this. I will wait for you. I promise. Please don't. You will come home. I just know you will. No! Don't!!"

He forced himself on her, and when he was finished, he began to cry. She began to cry.

"I'm sorry. I couldn't help myself. It's this war. This ugly rotten war."

Not once had he told her he loved her. She wanted to vomit.

They rode home in silence.

Chapter 52

John Wainwright and Uncle Logan

The Dustin, Oklahoma sailors reported for duty upon their new ship, and it steadfastly headed toward the Ivory Coast of Africa. The war was raging around the world. Hitler's forces were on the run and the Japanese dive-bombers were decreasing in numbers.

They quickly resumed their duties aboard their newly assigned battleship, and it was full speed ahead. Days turned into weeks and weeks into months. News poured in that the allied forces were giving the enemy the "what for" at every turn, but the battle was far from over.

It just so happened that it was Pick's turn for the mail duty that day. After he made sure that all of the sailors had every piece of precious mail delivered, Pick settled down and began to sort through his own small bundle of letters. He smiled as he held a letter from his sisters. He knew he would be brought up to date on their adventures. He was anxious to see where they were stationed, and receiving a letter with both of their names in the senders' corner, he was relieved to know that they were together and safe. However, the next letter in the stack made him have a sinking feeling in his stomach. It was from Poppa.

Poppa hated writing letters, and when Pick saw his grandfather's name scrawled in the left hand corner, he knew it just couldn't be good news. He took a deep breath and began to read the letter.

Dear Grandson, Pick. Well, son, I have some really bad news for you. I hope you are sitting down before you get the story. It ain't good. I have to tell you that my blood is boiling as I write, so I hope this makes sense and that I don't stumble around with my words. You are well aware that Lena Wainwright's son, John Wainwright, ain't now or never was good for anything. Not now or never. I am so grieved to tell you that he has done shot your Uncle Logan dead. My hand is trembling with fury as I tell you, so please hold on.

You know your Uncle Logan was the city marshal here in Dustin. A fine one at that. God rest his soul. It seems as though John Wainwright had gone and deserted the Army and showed up back here in Dustin. As was his rightful duty, your Uncle Logan went after him to arrest him for being a deserter and was going to have him sent back to his unit. I guess John Wainwright didn't want any part of the Army any more and right in Main Street here in Dustin, he pulled a gun and put a bullet right through your Uncle Logan's temple. Killed him on the spot.

I am filled with grief to have to tell you that I just buried another one of my children. To rub salt into our wounded hearts, I have to tell you that there will be no justice for his death, Pick. Old Lena Wainwright has so many high con-

nections with every judge and politician in these parts that showed up at her door in the middle of the night to get a snoot full of her hootch, that she fixed it to where her son John was just gathered up and sent right back to the Army. He will not be prosecuted for your Uncle's death. It's a sad day in our family. I can tell you that. I am so sorry for this painful news son. I know you are serving our country proud, and I know that you loved your Uncle Logan.

    Poppa

Pick hung his head and began to weep. He couldn't believe that John Wainwright had murdered his uncle in cold blood. Logan was a good man. He had been a wonderful uncle and friend to Pick and Cubbie, and he couldn't wrap his mind around the fact that Logan's life had been taken in such a senseless crime. John Wainwright was nothing but a piece of worthless garbage, and now he had murdered Uncle Logan.

He instantly thought of Sarah. He knew that Sarah was devastated over what her no account brother had done. He knew that she too would be grieving over his Uncle Logan's death. Sarah was not like her bootlegger mother, Lena, and certainly, was not like her heartless brother John. They were lowlife criminals, and Sarah had moved as far away from them as possible, as soon as she was old enough to drive. Pick held no anger toward Sarah at all. He knew that she had no control over what her family did. Sarah would be grieved over the senseless crime committed by her brother, and Pick felt pity and sadness for her, along with grief for the death of his beloved uncle. The belly of the battleship seemed cold and lonely as he sat silently on his bed, holding the letter from Poppa in his hands.

A silent tear streaked down his face, slipping from his chin and landing in the middle of his grandfather's handwritten letter, smearing an entire sentence as it made its way across the page. Logan was dead and buried, and Pick was thousands of miles away. An intense longing for home and family overtook him. The tears welled up again, and he had no desire to stop them. Somehow at his moment, in this ship, it felt good to cry.

Chapter 53

More News from the Homefront

Pick knew something strange was going on within the "Johnny and Julia Rose" saga. Johnny Prescott hadn't seemed to skip a beat when he returned from leave. He got right back into his old habits and the "good letters" continued to arrive, lipstick and cologne in abundance, at a breakneck speed. The biggest difference was the letters from Julia Rose addressed to Johnny Prescott were at a standstill. That is after the last one Johnny received. A letter from Julia had been delivered to Johnny about three months after they boarded their ship to head to Africa. Pick noticed immediately when he dug it out of the mailbag, before he placed it in Johnny's hands, that there was not a hint of the aroma of lilac bush. It was just a plain and unscented letter with no trace of a lipstick kiss adorning the backside. He saw Johnny open the letter and read it slowly. He saw him put it down and pick it back up and read it again. After he seemed to read the one page letter several times, Johnny Prescott arose from his rack and proceeded to open his duffle bag and stuff it as far down into the darkness of that bag as it would go.

It wasn't three days later that curiosity got the best of Pick Watie. The first opportunity whereby Johnny was assigned a duty and Pick had the night off, it happened. Pick couldn't sleep. He just wasn't able to get his mind off that letter from Julia Rose stuffed in the bottom of Johnny Prescott's duffel bag. Sailors were snoring in their racks as Pick stood in the hull of the ship staring at the shadow of Johnny Prescott's duffel bag. Pick knew that Johnny was manning the guns on the deck, and there was no possibility that he would be caught digging around in his friend's bag. He knew he wouldn't be caught, but he couldn't help but feel a sense of guilt for his intrusion into a personal matter that had nothing to do with him as he slowly advanced toward Johnny's bag. The fact of the matter was that the guilt was fleeting, and he continued to make a beeline straight toward that duffel bag.

As Pick sat on the side of Johnny's bed and dragged the bag between his legs, he felt an urgency to feel that letter from Julia to Johnny. He rammed his hand as far as it would go into the belly of the canvas bag.

His fingers wrapped themselves around the crumpled envelope and pulled it swiftly up and out. With his foot, he pushed the duffel bag back to its resting spot, stuffed the letter under his shirt, and headed back to his bed.

Pick grabbed his flashlight as he pulled the covers over his head. With a click of the switch, the envelope with Julia's dainty handwriting was illuminated enough for him to read every word. Trickles of sweat ran down his spine and into his skivvies as his mind absorbed the contents of the enclosed letter.

Johnny, I truly hope this finds you safe and out of harm's way. The news coming by cable to our shores is a constant barrage of battle inflicted death and mutilation. I pray for you, and all of the men and women that are across the waters protecting us as we sleep.

I find myself with pen in hand and do not have a clue how to finish this letter. I am so confused. I am hurt. I am angry. I am sad. My confusion is from the realization that I do not think I know the real you. I honestly think I fell in love with a figment of my imagination. I have so many unanswered questions.

You know that I was not a willing participant in what happened on our last night together. That is in no way how I wanted our evening to end. I do not hate you, but I am angry with you just the same. I know that you were battle scarred and fearful, but it was not right that you took advantage of me in that manner.

With that said, I must inform you that I am carrying your child. I do not know what else to say at this time. I just thought you should know.

Julia

He saw red. Pick Watie sat cross-legged under a blanket with the crumpled letter dangling from his hand. If Johnny Prescott was standing there at that moment, Pick would have decked him. He even thought that he would have decked him, stood him up, and decked him again.

It all came tumbling down upon him. He had an unrequited love for the pretty girl from Dustin, Oklahoma since they were children. From a distance, he had seen her heart broken so many times, and there was nothing he could have done to protect her from the pain. She had such a beautiful spirit. He loved her, and she barely knew he existed. Johnny Prescott had done her wrong. She didn't deserve what he had done to her. He had sold her a bill of goods, and in her naivety, she had bought it hook, line, and sinker. Now she was carrying Johnny's child, and Pick knew as he sat in the dark hull of the battleship that there was no place for Julia and an innocent baby in the mess that was Johnny Prescott's life.

As he threw himself back on his bed, Pick realized that this was none of his business. Who was he to stick his nose in other peoples' business like this? It was such a pipe dream that Julia would ever even look at a man like him. He came from a poor family. A family that had barely scratched out a living.

She was Porter and Fannie Devon's daughter. Such a fine family. He would never forget that day at school when he first got a glimpse of Julia Rose Devon. She was so clean and pretty. Her eyes lit up like the moon in the sky. He was in tattered and dirty overalls. An orphan. A poor little orphan.

She would never give him a second look.

Chapter 54

Victory Across the Distant Shores!

The news came in bits and pieces to the sailors aboard the battleships strewn across the world. The allied forces were winning. Victory was in sight, but the battles weren't over. Gunners and their mates were steadfast. They manned their guns and continued to have skirmishes here and there with the enemy.

On May 8th, 1945, Germany's surrender took effect. VE (Victory in Europe Day) was announced. August 14th, the Japanese Emperor accepted the terms of the Potsdam Declaration, and on August 15th, the Japanese Emperor declared Japan's surrender on the radio. That was VJ Day (Victory in Japan Day).

The sailors aboard Pick's battleship had been brought up to speed that VJ Day had occurred, but until an official surrender had been announced, the war was not over. Orders from their commander had been given that they were to proceed full speed ahead to bomb a Japanese island in the Pacific.

On September 2, 1945, Pick Watie's ship, the George Washington, was passing by the islands of Hawaii on its way to bomb the Japanese island. It was dusk. They had been preparing for battle all day and the guns were ready. Ammunition was stacked and waiting to be loaded upon the captain's orders. Accompanying submarines were well stocked with torpedoes as the fleet made their way to Japan. They were antsy, edgy, and ready for battle. All hands were on deck.

Little did Pick know that his brother Cubbie was aboard the USS Nelson, a destroyer, that was anchored in Pearl Harbor at the exact same time that the George Washington was passing by the islands.

Suddenly, without even a moment's warning, they saw what looked like bombs going off on the island of Hawaii!

"Man your stations! Man your stations! Hawaii is under attack! Man your stations!"

At first thought, every sailor on every ship in that fleet supposed that Japan had decided to not go down without a fight! Sirens and horns began blasting. Every man was in his place, ready to fire when ordered.

Adrenaline and perspiration. Ready to defend their nation and the nations of their allies.

Armed, ready, and waiting, the news began to filter in by dribs and drabs.

"Stand down! Stand down! Stand down!" The orders were blared over the speaker.

Every man stood up and fell silent. Mouths opened wide as they realized what they were witnessing. History was in the making. At the very spot that the war had begun, Pickford Watie and his fellow ship-mates, looked out across the water at Pearl Harbor. The news had been spread that the Emperor of Japan had officially surrendered. The war was over. Fireworks were blasting in the sky. Pick later learned that aboard Cubbie's ship, there in Pearl Harbor, sailors celebrated the victory by shooting their guns and shouting to the heavens! "God Bless America!!"

The war was over and the allied forces had been victorious!

Chapter 55

Ruidoso, New Mexico

Pick's Uncle Jubal and Aunt Maisie had cotton fields and a horse ranching operation in Ruidoso, New Mexico. After the war was declared over, Pick just didn't have the stomach to go back to Dustin, Oklahoma. He didn't think he could stand the thought of seeing Julia Rose, especially if she continued to be under the spell of Johnny Prescott. His heart just couldn't take it any more.

Therefore he decided to take Uncle Jubal and his mother's sister, Aunt Maisie, up on their offer to come stay with them, pick cotton, and break wild horses for a while. The New Mexico sky was almost magical. Pick could almost swear that he saw every color in the rainbow streak across the horizon in zigs and zags and splashes. He had never seen anything like it in his life. Oklahoma could boast of some glorious sunrises and sunsets, but there was no comparison to the spectacle he beheld at that moment.

He was in "Billy The Kid Country," and the history was not lost on him as he bent over to grab a handful of cotton bolls. His imagination ran wild as he pictured the notorious outlaw streaking by on his palomino, guns a' blazin, with a posse on his trail. The more cotton he stuffed in his cotton sack, the more elaborate his portrayal of Billy The Kid came to life.

He had to keep his mind busy.

The war had taken a lot of starch out of him. He had witnessed death and destruction, and those years of his life, he knew he would never get back. He had to place the painful memories in a special compartment in his soul. Pick knew he could never forget the sacrifice of the American troops as they lay dead, maimed, and broken on the shores, in the bombed out cities, along the roads, and in the hulls of torpedoed battleships, all throughout the world. It had been a World War spanning other continents and other oceans all over the globe. He hadn't really had the wanderlust to see other countries, but if he had, he certainly wouldn't have wished for a cruise aboard a battleship in the middle of the ocean.

He had to keep his mind busy, or he would start to think about Julia. Pick had spent most of the day before in a sunny corral chasing, roping, and riding—sort of—wild stallions. His uncle Jubal had a thriving business of breaking and selling wild horses that he bought from the locals. Pick had certainly ridden a lot of horses in his time, but he had never before sat his rear end on the bare back of an angry, snorting, bucking bronco. He did have a knack for interacting with animals, and he didn't get thrown as many times as he should have (Thank God for the wad of mane that he held on to for dear life.), and he headed back to the house many evenings limping and sore. But it was actually fun, and it kept his mind occupied.

On this day, after he emptied his last sack of cotton for the day on the back of the wagon, Pick had been somewhat "ordered" by Aunt Maisie that he was to come home and clean up in his best clothes. It was a crisp, fall Friday, and the families in Ruidoso were gathering in town for the annual Harvest Festival. Aunt Maisie had hinted that they were going to introduce him to someone "special."

Pick was very nervous about meeting another woman. He had gone to pie suppers and the like over the years with several hometown girls, but never felt a spark with any of them. He knew that it was because he was carrying a secret torch for Julia, and he just hadn't ever been able to get over her. Ever.

Aunt Maisie had put a hot iron to his best shirt and had made sure that his dungarees were clean and fresh. He had splurged a bit and bought a nice leather belt in France on one of his shore leaves during the war. It was very rare for him to spend money on himself like that, but he couldn't seem turn down the little boy that was beckoning him to his father's shop. France had been bombed unmercifully. A few of the shopkeepers were doing their best to ignore the devastation and try to eek out a living for their families. Pick felt like he had done a good deed by spending his money in that way. The shopkeeper and his family kept thanking him and all the Americans for their help in the war. It made him proud to be an American. Even if he did a lot of dickering on the price, he left there feeling good.

There he was, standing in the bedroom that had been so graciously offered to him by his aunt and uncle, dressing in his finest. Pick Watie was feeling pretty dapper as he pushed the pointed end of the belt under each belt loop. He was beginning to have a sense of relief from the nervous jitters as he placed his straw cowboy hat on top of his ample waves of dark brown hair. The pearl snap buttons on his shirt pressed together with a familiar click. He was clean-shaven and had scrubbed himself with Aunt Maisie's lye soap so well that he knew there couldn't be a trace of sweat from those long hours in the cotton fields. He had to admit it, he was almost anticipating this evening. Almost.

Aunt Maisie hailed to a man and woman across the way. "Pierre and Albertine, this is our nephew, Pickford Watie. He goes by the name Pick. He is from Dustin, Oklahoma. That's the area that Jubal and I are from. Pick was a sailor in the war and has come to spend some time here in New Mexico with us. Step over here, Pick, and meet our friends, the Archambeaus."

Pick removed his hat and stuck his hand out to Mr. Archambeau for a manly handshake then turned to his wife, Albertine, and took her hand in his, slightly bowing his head toward the strikingly beautiful woman.

"My pleasure, Ma'am."

The Archambeaus looked at each other with a smile and spoke a smattering of French to each other.

"Oh, pardon us, Mr. Watie. We didn't mean to be rude," she spoke with an accent that Pick immediately recognized. "We were both so excited to meet an American that risked his life to free our former countrymen from the clutches of the German forces. We honor you and thank you."

"Aw, shucks, Ma'am. There's no need to honor me. I'm just glad I could help and extra glad that I made it home, seein' as how so many of our troops didn't." The Archambeaus had a cattle ranch a few miles down the road from Uncle Jubal and Aunt Maisie. The two families had become dear friends over the years and were always ready to help each other out.

Therefore it seemed almost a no-brainer that Aunt Maisie and Albertine Archambeau would feel the need to put their heads together and be potential matchmakers between Pick Watie and the Archambeau's daughter, Aline.

At that moment, the Archambeaus parted, similar to the parting of the Red Sea, and there behind Albertine stood their breathtakingly beautiful daughter.

Aline Archambeau had her head turned away from the conversation. She had been watching a group of young children playing in the piles of corn shocks in the distance. Aline Archambeau was oblivious to the fact that her mother and her mother's dear friend had orchestrated this setting down to the smallest detail.

"Aline! Aline! Ma cherie!"

After hearing her mother call her name, Aline turned her face toward the small gathering.

"Aline, we have someone here that we think you would like to meet! This handsome fellow is our friends' nephew, Pickford Watie. Pick, this is our daughter, Aline."

Pick could not hide his surprise. Aline Archambeau was very

343

pretty and her eyes sparkled, the kind of sparkle like the sun bouncing off the waves in the ocean. He remembered thinking about Julia's eyes as his battleship cut through the waves on a bright and sunny day.

He could tell that Aline was somewhat enamored herself.

Eventually Pick and Aline found their way to an available hay bale where they sat and talked the rest of the evening. Pick made her laugh until her eyes crinkled. She even slapped her knees a couple of times too. She was very feminine but didn't hide the fact that she had a tomboy side to her. Annie Oakley. That's who she resembled. Pretty, sassy, and comical.

Pick could not stop taking in Aline's beauty. From what he gathered in their conversation, Aline could ride and rope as well as any of the cattle hands, and that was a big plus in Pick's eyes. However, the scattering of freckles on her rosy cheeks and the way her hair was pulled back and tied with a satin scarf was very alluring. Pick was having a different kind of fun for the first time in a very long time. Actually for the first time ever. The few women he had dated over the years were very sweet, nice looking, and good company. He just hadn't ever been attracted to any of them for anything beyond a friendship. The torch that he carried for Julia hampered any connection that might have been out there.

Julia... His mind wandered to Julia. A wave of sadness enveloped him at that very moment. He would never have her, and he knew it. Aline was so pretty and funny… and available. The bird in the hand. He realized then and there that the night needed to come to an end for him so he could go back to his room and do some serious pondering. From all indications, it looked like his life was getting ready to take some interesting twists and turns, and he knew it was necessary to have a level head on his shoulders to be able to decipher any flags (red "danger" or green "go"), mainly because whatever happened next in his life, he didn't want to botch it up.

As Pick rose to leave the festival, he told everyone goodnight and that it was such a pleasure meeting them. He agreed to join Aline the following Tuesday evening for horseback riding along the mountain trail. She seemed elated at the prospect of that scenario and gave Pick a quick hug before he turned to stroll away into the night.

He decided to walk home that evening. There were plenty of horses he could borrow, but he couldn't help but notice that the stars in the New Mexico sky were on full display and a slow walk home would allow him to be able to fully enjoy their splendor.

The air was crisp, and there wasn't a lick of a breeze. A nosy old hoot owl seemed to be asking a lot of questions. He chuckled to himself as he strode up on his aunt and uncle's wooden porch. He momentarily occupied himself by scraping off imaginary dirt from the bottom of his boots. Instead of going on into the house, Pick plopped down upon the old porch swing.

The night was alive with noises.

He had seen this same sky on many evenings as he was on his night watch aboard the navy vessels during the war. Whether he was heading toward Africa, the Mediterranean Sea, or sitting on his family's porch in the middle of nowhere in New Mexico, they were the same stars. A clear night anywhere in the world, and it was always the same stars.

But they weren't the same women.

No amount of beauty, personality, wit or charm could change the way he felt. He had prayed on many occasions for the good Lord to send His great wisdom down from heaven and heap it on his heart. If loving Julia Rose was a futile effort, he prayed that God would send him a sign.

Was Aline a sign from God that Pick needed to move on and forget about the pipe dream of ever holding Julia in his arms the way he had longed to do for years? Had this woman here in New Mexico been placed before him at this moment in time to show him that there were other women out there that could love him as he deserved?

He drummed his fingers slowly and purposefully on the back of the seat of the swing, pondering and pondering. Pick leaned forward, placing his hands in his lap as he hung his head down to look at a doodlebug pushing something across the porch. It would seem that he was fixated on the toiling of the ambitious bug, but that was nowhere near the truth.

He was fixated on his plan.

At the end of the war, Pick and a shipload of other sailors had been deposited at the Boston harbor with papers releasing them from their obligation to the United States Navy. Thanks, boys. Now find a way home.

A very long bus ride to Oklahoma from Boston, cash to a local car dealer for a beater jalopy, and a long drive to New Mexico, then fast forward a few months, and here he was sitting on that porch, on that night with a plan.

In the moonlight, beside Uncle Jubal and Aunt Maisie's house, Pick's jalopy sat full of his belongings. A heartfelt letter had been penned, thanking his relatives for their hospitality, kindness, and love. He gave a brief explanation for his sudden departure, left some money on the kitchen table for the gasoline he poured into his car from the can in Uncle Jubal's barn and headed northeast to Oklahoma at breakneck speed. (Well, whatever breakneck speed would be for an old jalopy.)

After a few stops to stretch his legs, a couple of catnaps, and refueling, Pick made it to Dustin, Oklahoma around ten o'clock the next evening.

Momma and Poppa had both passed away during Pick's stint with the Navy. Poppa from the debilitating effects of sugar diabetes and Momma... from extreme meanness. With their passing, Pick did not have a home to go back to, therefore late that night, he decided to pull quietly into Uncle Carter and Aunt Esme's front yard, turn off his lights, and sleep until morning. Uncle Carter had been with him when he purchased the car, so he knew if they peeked out their bedroom window, they would recognize that it was him. He had hoped that they slept through the night because he didn't want to disturb them until morning.

They were apparently very sound sleepers because when he woke up early the next morning, he could see Aunt Esme coming out of the front door and down the steps to head toward his car. She opened the door for him and insisted that he come right in for a good hearty breakfast and a cup of steaming black coffee.

Aunt Esme was happy to hear that her sister Maisie was doing well in New Mexico, and my oh my, did her ears perk up after she asked Pick what brought him back to Oklahoma before the frost ended the cotton harvest.

The story that came from her nephew's lips was like an avalanche. Pick Watie had never shared his personal life with anyone, except his brother Cubbie, and Aunt Esme couldn't believe her ears as he filled her in on his reason for showing up like he did and his plan of action for carrying it out to the finish line. Aunt Esme peered at her nephew Pick over her glasses. Was he nuts?

Chapter 56

Perplexities and the War

Julia Rose had given birth to her son at her parents' house in Dustin, Oklahoma. It was a difficult birth, and Old Doc Lett had his work set out for him upon his arrival at Porter and Fannie Devon's home. There was no hospital in their small town; therefore welcoming a ten-pound, bouncing baby boy being carried by a one hundred and ten pound woman in a home setting was no small feat, but all went well and the baby and his mother were fine and healthy.

Johnny Prescott had pretty much dropped off the map during the final years of the war. Upon hearing the news of the impending birth of a child with Julia Rose, he pretty much stuffed his responsibility in the same manner as he had stuffed the letter. Out of sight, out of mind.

The blonde haired child was named Porter Edward, after her father, and he, his older sister Violet, and their mother, Julia Rose proceeded to live with her parents, Porter and Fannie Devon for the next three years.

During that time, there was not a peep from Johnny Prescott. Julia Rose didn't peep his way either for that matter. Out of sight, out of mind.

Julia worked in a beauty parlor over in Weleetka, giving permanent hair waves and hair cuts to the local ladies of that and the surrounding towns while her parents helped by watching her two children.

Life was pretty uneventful around Dustin during that time. Julia's children were thriving, and they were living in a loving and peaceful environment with their mother, and grandparents, Porter and Fannie.

However, when the news that the war was over was broadcasted over the airwaves all around the nation, Julia Devon was overcome with a sense of dread. She knew that the local soldiers and sailors would be coming home, and the thought of the arrival of one particular sailor put a wrinkle in her pretty brow.

Johnny Prescott would be coming home from the war, and he had a three-year-old son that he had never met.   Julia was so conflicted in her heart. She had loved Johnny once. At least she had thought that she loved him. She reasoned that she had loved the Johnny Prescott she had been exposed to but had anxieties with regards to the other Johnny Prescott that she was sure existed on the other side.

Julia had already made up her mind that she would just take each day as it came. If Johnny wanted to meet his son, she would not stand in the way. If he tried to reconcile with her, she knew it would be pretty hard to penetrate the wall that she had built around her heart. Time would tell, and just like Scarlett O'Hara, she would worry about that tomorrow.

Chapter 57

He's Home and He Has Flowers

It was a sunny Saturday around the Devon home. Porter Devon was in his shed in the back of the house catching up on cobbling the pile of his customers' shoes that had built up when he was working extra hours in his railroad night watchman job.

Tap, tap, tap went his hammer as he took another nail out of his mouth to place it in the leather sole of the shoe resting in the stand. Fannie was in her kitchen trickling the last of the fresh coconut on the cake that she had just baked for her husband Porter's birthday.

Five-year-old Violet was teaching her three-year-old brother, "Eddy" as he was now called, how to put dresses on her baby doll. They played very well together, even if Violet always got to pick the games they would play.

Julia had the rare Saturday off from her job at the beauty parlor, so she was spending her afternoon helping her mother with housework. She was hoisting the broom up by its handle to the ceiling of the front porch knocking down cobwebs. She didn't want to get any of the debris in her eyes, so they were closed tightly as she poked the crevices and cracks with the long broom. Therefore she wasn't aware that someone had tiptoed up the steps to the front porch and was standing quietly behind her. When she least expected it, a pair of hands came from nowhere and covered her eyes.

"Guess who?"

She was caught so totally off guard that she almost choked on the song that she had been humming under her breath. A startled Julia, dropped the broom and proceeded to grab the two mystery hands, pulling them off her face, immediately turning to look directly into their holder's eyes.

"Johnny! Umm, hello."

Her face was flushed with a bright red glow. Heat rose to her temple as she tried to regain her composure. Turning her back to him, she reached down, picked up the broom, and propped it against the house. She paused before spinning back around, looked up at the sky and mouthed, "Jesus, help me here."

Upon slowly turning to face the errant sailor, Julia Devon was overtaken by the vision standing before her. He looked so handsome. Even better than she had remembered. In his hand, he had a fresh picked bouquet of flowers. Flowers.

What in the world was she going to do?

Chapter 58

It's a Date

Julia opened the screen door to her parents' home and invited Johnny Prescott to follow her inside. The door shut with the familiar smacking sound, bringing Fannie out of the kitchen, dusting the flour and coconut from her apron, to see what was happening.

It was a darn good thing that Julia's father, Porter, was oblivious to the goings on inside his living room at that moment. It was a darn good thing for Johnny Prescott that the tap, tap, tapping was drowning out any other sounds. Porter's hands were occupied, and his mouth was occupied, and that was a darn good thing for Johnny Prescott. No doubt about that.

The three exchanged formalities as Fannie rightly refrained from inviting Johnny Prescott to Porter's birthday dinner. She knew better than to even think such a thing. Her husband Porter was not a fan of Johnny Prescott. Not by any stretch of the imagination. She excused herself to go back into the kitchen leaving Johnny and Julia standing awkwardly in the living room.

The silence was deafening until Julia spoke up and asked Johnny if he wanted to meet his son, Eddy. Johnny removed his hat, lowered his head, and with an unusual softness to his voice, expressed to Julia that not only had he come to see her, he also wanted to meet his son.

Julia went into the bedroom, bent down and picked up the toddler and carried him to the living room. It was by no means an emotional meeting. Little Eddy had no clue who this stranger was and was really not very happy about being taken away from playing with his sister, even if it was baby dolls.

Johnny didn't ask to hold the boy. He kept a comfortable distance between them, as he seemed to be looking the child up and down, somewhat like surveying an expected purchase in the market.

The resemblance was uncanny. Eddy was the spitting image of his father, and Johnny Prescott couldn't deny that this boy was his son. He reached toward the squirming child, tousled his hair for a brief second, and turned to Julia.

"Julia, I know we have a lot to talk about. That fact is not lost on me for one second. I'm a changed man. The war changed me, and I am back home wanting to right the wrongs and make a good life for myself. Please go with me tomorrow night to the pie supper and school play. We can talk. I promise you we will just talk. You don't have to worry about anything else." His face turned beet red as he looked away from Julia's eyes.

Julia had mixed emotions about making a date with Johnny Prescott, but she agreed that she would accompany him the next night to the school, as she walked him toward the door.

He gave her a tender hug and left.

354

She went back to sweeping cobwebs with a new fervor. Jabbing and poking and sweeping. What in the world was she going to do?

All she had ever wanted was to find true love. She just wanted someone to love her the way she felt that she deserved. That's all she wanted. That's all she had ever wanted. With a jab of the broom, Julia reflected upon how she had been so duped by Lon Holcomb (and his mother). He seemed to be the perfect man, she told herself. Why had she been so blind to the obvious? Frankly, he had marketed himself as such. Whether on purpose or not, Julia had been taken in by the façade—the false and artificial appearance that Lon Holcomb could love anyone, not even his precious little daughter, more than he loved himself or his mother. She had been duped, and she knew it.

Was she setting herself up for another huge disappointment by giving Johnny Prescott a second chance? When she had cleared the ceiling of all of the cobwebs and had used a piece of old tin as a dust pan to scoop up all of the debris, Julia propped the broom against the house and found herself plopped down on the porch swing.

Gently swinging back and forth, she let her head tilt backward as the calming ray of sunshine patted her face with its warmth. Time stood still for her at that moment. It was heart time. Julia's heart was talking to her louder than it had ever spoken in the past.

Before this day, Julia had always gone with her head. She had let her head see the checklist. Did Lon meet the checklist points? On the surface he surpassed them! Check, check, check!

Unfortunately, she forgot to put love on the checklist. She just assumed it was tucked in there somewhere among the perfection. Johnny Prescott. Her heart was waving huge red flags in her face every time she let herself think about him.

Inside her parents' house were two young children. Each child had a different father. She hadn't wanted it to go this way at all. She never for one minute dreamed that her life would ever get so complicated. She just wanted to feel safe. Safe in the arms of love.

Lord, what was she going to do?

Chapter 59

The Little Black Sweater

Julia Rose knew that choosing the little black sweater was taking a chance. It was her favorite article of clothing that she owned. She always felt very confident that it looked very nice on her. Maybe she looked too nice. The little black sweater and the box pleated skirt. She twirled in front of her mirror. Julia felt very pretty, pretty on the outside but apprehensive on the inside.

Julia had been trying to convince herself that she needed to give Johnny Prescott the benefit of the doubt. He was the father of her child. It made her uneasy to think that she might be denying her son the chance to have his father in his life.

"One day at a time. Lots of prayers and keep a level head." Julia kept giving herself a pep talk up until the moment that Johnny showed up for their date. Porter and Fannie Devon lived within walking distance of the Dustin High School, so Julia and Johnny were going to take advantage of the lovely evening and walk to the event.

Johnny Prescott was dressed to the nines. His blonde hair was slicked back and sat like ocean waves on top of his head. Julia couldn't help but feel a bit of a flutter as they walked hand in hand to the school. It was an undeniable fact that he was definitely a handsome man. Undeniable.

As they approached the schoolhouse, Julia felt exhilarated. The crowd was gathering outside waiting to be allowed to enter into the building. It was the first local event in the months following the end of the war. It was somewhat of a homecoming welcome to the soldiers and sailors that had put their lives on the line for their country. She immediately started to recognize her friends and fellow townspeople. It was such a good feeling to see many of the men that she knew that had just gotten home from the war. This was going to be a good night. She just knew it!

She and Johnny found their seats and proceeded to enjoy the play. It was fun to laugh and have a good time with Johnny. She still had a lot of mixed emotions about the whole thing, but for the moment, she was enjoying the company.

The curtain came down to thunderous applause. Johnny told Julia that he would be right back. He was going to go over to the back of the gymnasium to the concession table and get them both a piece of pie and a cup of coffee.

Julia had turned to a lady that she knew that was seated next to her, and the two women began a friendly conversation. In the middle of their conversation Julia felt a presence in the seat next to her. Johnny must have returned with our pie and coffee, she thought to herself.

"What kind did you get me?" Julia said as she twirled back around in her seat.

To her surprise, there was someone sitting in the chair, but it definitely wasn't Johnny Prescott. "Why, Pick Watie! What a pleasant surprise! How in the world are you?"

Julia was speaking directly to Pick, but he noticed that she kept looking around as if she was trying to find someone.

"Hello, Julia Rose." As he spoke the greeting, he turned his head in the direction that Julia was looking.

"Are you trying to find someone?" Pick asked her.

"Oh, I was actually looking for Sarah Wainwright. Your Sarah." Julia said.

"My Sarah Wainwright? What do you mean by saying she is my Sarah, Julia?"

"I guess I thought she was your girlfriend. Isn't she your girl-friend?"

Pick laughed a hearty laugh. "Oh, no Sarah isn't my girlfriend. She is just a good friend of mine. That's all. Just a very good friend." Julia looked at Pick in a quizzical manner. "Really? I guess I always thought you and Sarah were an item. Every time I would see you, I would see Sarah. Just friends, huh? Well, interesting."

Pick leaned in toward Julia and whispered in her ear. "You were wearing that little black sweater the last time I saw you. I guess it's been a little over three years. I have never forgotten how you looked in that sweater." Pick blushed as he went for it. No holds barred.

"When did you see me in this sweater, Pick?" Julia cocked her head and grinned ear to ear. "Well, as I recollect, you were at the Cain's, out on the dance floor. Bob Wills and his boys were playing. It was just after I got home on leave..."

"The Cain's! That was you! It was you and Sarah, and did I see Naomi and Nelva Jones and Jenkins Macfarlane too? The Cains! So that was also Johnny Prescott moseying through the crowd too, wasn't it? What a rascal!" Julia jumped up from her seat and began to search through the crowd gathered at the back of the gymnasium. She was livid. "Where is he? Do I ever have words for him!" Julia blurted out as she folded her arms and began to tap her foot.

Pick just smiled and stood up and faced Julia, blocking her view of the back of the room.

"I came here tonight to walk you home, Julia. Plain and simple. I'm not taking no for an answer either."

"You did what? Are you telling me you came here specifically to find me and walk me home? I don't understand, Pick. I, uh, I came here with someone else. I can't just leave with you. I am... well, I am on a date. I'm here with Johnny." Julia stepped to the left of Pick and continued to look for Johnny Prescott in the crowd. "Where is he anyway?" she meant to say it to herself but the words trickled off her lips in an audible fashion.

Pick knew exactly where Johnny Prescott was to be found. He had seen him out of the corner of his eye when he walked into the gym. He saw Johnny Prescott being Johnny Prescott.

Right about then, Julia spotted him also. Johnny Prescott was over in a corner behind a bin of basketballs talking. Oh whatever. He was smooching Helen Brown. Right on the lips.

Julia had her answer.

"Come on, Pick. I will let you walk me home. Yes, that's exactly what I am going to do! I am going to walk home to my house with you! Let me grab my jacket, and let's go!"

So there. Just like that Julia Rose Devon grabbed Pick Watie's arm and practically pulled him out of the door of the gymnasium. She didn't even look back to see Johnny Prescott making his moves. She had her answer.

Oddly, the anger that Julia had been feeling when she spotted that worthless Johnny Prescott canoodling with the likes of Helen Brown had been replaced very quickly by waves of relief. An ocean full of waves of relief. She was almost giddy!

An hour ago, she was sitting beside Johnny Prescott in the Dustin High School gymnasium, and now she was sitting on the porch swing at her parents' house with Pick Watie?

She had always assumed that he was in love with the pretty Sarah Wainwright. So much so that she had never really taken a good look at him. He was a very handsome man. She could tell he was Cherokee. Lon and Johnny had both been blondes. She had never dated anyone as dark and handsome as Pick Watie....

Dated? It suddenly struck her! He came to the school to find her? The walk home from the school took no more than 15 minutes. During that brief time, the conversation between Julia and Pick had been geared more toward small talk about the war and life in their small town of Dustin.

Upon arriving at her house, Julia stuck her head in the door and told her parents that she was home, and if they didn't mind, she was going to sit outside with her friend, Pick Watie.

Pick Watie? She left with Johnny Prescott, and now she was sitting on their front porch with Pick Watie? Kind, sweet Pick Watie? What in the world was going on? Porter Devon almost shouted out a resounding "hallelujah" at the news that just left his daughter's lips. Porter had never heard anything but good things about Pick Watie. If she was trading the likes of Johnny Prescott in for Pick Watie, Porter wanted to holler "yes!"

Porter immediately suggested to his wife, Fannie, that she go into the kitchen and fetch Pick a good-sized piece of his coconut cake. Fannie's mouth fell open wide.

"You want to share your birthday cake with Pick Watie, Porter?" She couldn't hold back the grin.

"Well, sure I do! Pick Watie served our country honorably. He d eserves a piece of cake! I will stick my head out there and ask him if he likes his coffee black."

Fannie walked into the kitchen laughing to herself and shaking her head. Who was this new man inhabiting her husband's body?

Chapter 60

The Courtship

Pick came clean about it all. He didn't mince his words as he told Julia the whole thing. He had been carrying a torch for her since they were young, and he didn't care if she knew every detail.

She sat on the porch listening intently as the light of the silvery moon cast a glow across the face of the tall, lanky, dark, and handsome man, slowly rocking the porch swing with her beside him spilling his guts right out there before God and anybody that wanted to listen.

And they did.

Porter and Fannie's curiosity had gotten the best of them, and they quietly hunkered down in their living room underneath the window to the front porch. They were a sight to behold, but they didn't care. This young man sitting out there with their daughter had a story to tell, and it was well worth any cramp they might get in their legs as they squatted down underneath that windowsill like a pair of jackrabbits. Silent and listening, they didn't want to miss a single detail. Pick poured his heart out to Julia. She was in shock. It was a good shock though.

The more he talked, the more he made her laugh. He was comical and sweet, and most of all, he was genuine. There wasn't a thing about this guy that wasn't authentic. He was the real deal, and she knew it.

Over the next two weeks, Pick and Julia Rose were inseparable. He came over every night, at Julia's request, but with the whole hearted blessings from her father. Porter thought the world of Pick Watie.

Fannie and her daughter Julia had put the finishing touches on the fried chicken supper that they had been working on that Sunday afternoon. Pick had eagerly accepted the invitation and had told them he would be arriving by four o'clock that afternoon.

There were rolling black clouds off in the distance, and Porter Devon knew just by the smell in the air and the electricity in his wool socks that he had just put on his feet that there was a pretty nasty storm brewing in the east.

"Fannie, I'm going to walk over to Gray's. I'm out of Prince Albert tobacky. You need anything?"

"Nothing from Gray's, Porter, but could you please check the mail at the post office?" Fannie said from the kitchen, "and hurry back before it starts to rain. You don't want to catch your death!"

Fannie was still yammering as Porter stepped off his porch and headed for the short walk to town. "Let her yammer," he giggled to himself. He loved his wife dearly, but sometimes, it was nice to have a bit of time to himself. Yammering-free time.

Unfortunately, Porter lost track of time after seeing several neighbors at the post office and swapping vegetable planting stories for longer than he realized. He bade them all a goodbye and with rain pelting the sidewalk, he ducked into Gray's Mercantile to purchase his tin of tobacco for his pipe.

It was a torrential rain.

He glanced at his pocket watch and saw that it was half past four. He was late for dinner. From the corner of his eyes, he saw Pick Watie standing in the rain talking to a young lady. He recognized the woman as Sarah Wainwright, the blind bootlegger's daughter. He saw Pick scoop her up and run with her in his arms, crossing the street, dodging mud puddles as he went. Porter witnessed Pick set her down and give her a hug.

It was a bit troubling. It was after four. Pick was supposed to be at his house sitting at his dinner table, eating food at his table with his daughter.

Something stopped him short of going out all angry at what he had just seen. He felt like he better sit on this one a bit as he pulled his fedora down tightly on his forehead, raised the collar on his shirt, and ducked and trotted toward home.

He sensed that things would not be pleasant when he got there. Porter didn't know that his youngest daughter, Jennie Lou, had been just ahead of him as he ran home. She had been visiting a friend and also got caught up in the storm. If Porter thought there was a storm outside, he would sure be convinced when he walked through the door that there was one happening inside too. It was a doozy!

Jennie Lou had bounded into the kitchen at breakneck speed. She couldn't wait to spill the beans on what she had just seen. As she ran down the sidewalk toward home, right across the street from Gray's, she had seen Pick running with Sarah Wainwright in his arms. She told Julia and Fannie that Pick even gave Sarah a big hug! Julia was seeing red! Pick was late for dinner because he was with Sarah? Sarah Wainwright? His "so called" friend? Fury. Unabated fury.

"Wait until he gets here! I'm going to get to the bottom of this!" And wait they did.

Pick Watie never showed up for dinner at the Devon home. Julia had gone to bed bawling her eyes out. Fannie had been pacing the floor. She knew that her daughter didn't need any more heartbreak in her life.

"What do you make of all of this, Porter? This is so unlike Pick to do this to her. I thought we knew him to be such a nice young man."

Porter took a long puff on his pipe. He blew a perfect smoke ring that encircled his balding head. "I say we don't jump to any conclusions, Fannie. We need to see what he has to say for himself."

At that time there was a knock on the door. It was just after ten o'clock.

"Who can it be showing up at our house so late in the evening, Porter?"

Porter Devon went to the front door and cracked it open. There on his stoop stood a very wet and muddy Pick Watie . He was standing in the rain with his hat held to his chest by both hands.

"I'm so sorry to be here so late, Mr. Devon. I feel awful about not showing up for dinner on time. I just couldn't wait until the morning to tell you why I couldn't get here. It's been quite a night. The Canadian River breached its banks about three o'clock today. I guess it had been raining buckets downstream all afternoon. The Graham School house went under about the same time that Lena Wainwright and her house got washed away. She's dead. They found her body wrapped around a tree about an hour ago. Jenkins Macfarlane and I jumped in his truck when we got the news about the flooding and headed over there as quick as we could. We were too late to save Lena. I had heard that Sarah had come in from Tulsa to visit her mother so we sure thought Sarah was gone too. We looked high and low for her. Come to find out she had swam to shore and Mr. Mason found her wandering on the road by where Lena's house had stood.

"By the time we got there, she was sitting in Mr. Mason's car, wrapped in a blanket that Mrs. Mason had in the back seat. Jenkins and I put her in his truck. She asked us to bring her to the bus stop so she could get back home to Tulsa. We dropped her off, and since then, we have been bailing water out of the Graham school all night to try to keep the damage down. Again, sir, I am so sorry to have caused any bad feelings this evening. Can I please speak to Julia? I hope she finds it in her heart to forgive me for missing dinner."

Chapter 61

Starting This Thing Off with a Bang

Pick proposed to Julia five weeks to the day that he came home from New Mexico, galloping in his jalopy, to decisively scoop her up at the school play. She almost said yes before he got the entire proposal out of his mouth. The wedding was planned for the following Saturday. It was to be held in the living room of Porter and Fannie Devon's home.

Bright and early that sunny Tuesday morning, Pick knocked on the screen door of the Devon's house. He was there to pick up his sweetheart. Today was the day they were going to Okmulgee to get their marriage license.

The process went off without a hitch, and after a nice lunch at a diner in Henryetta, Pick and Julia headed back to Dustin, marriage license in hand. The road from Henryetta to Dustin was carved into a mountainside. Some of the twists and turns could be a bit treacherous, and most of the locals were cautious and took their time in their maneuvers.

Little did Julia and Pick know there was a truck driver coming their way. He was lost and in a hurry to make his delivery so he could find his way back to the main road. He needed to hurry back to Tulsa to get his next load.

The truck failed to make the turn. Pick came around the corner and had no idea that there would be a big box truck sliding right at his car. With not a second to spare, Pick jerked on the steering wheel in time to avoid hitting the truck head on, but they were not yet out of danger.

With the force of the overcorrection, Pick's car careened off the road and started going straight down the side of the mountain. Fortunately for the two lovebirds, a boulder was jutting out of the ground and stopped the runaway car from continuing its course over the edge of the cliff. Pick's car met the boulder with a loud bang, and Pick and Julia went flying toward the windshield. They both had deep gashes in their foreheads, but after pulling themselves from the wreckage, they instantly realized that they could have easily been killed in the crash. They were just thankful to God to be alive. A friend of theirs from Dustin happened upon the wreck just after they went over the side of the mountain. The other driver was unhurt, so he declined a ride to the hospital. He gave them the phone number to the trucking company in Tulsa and asked them to kindly call his employer so they could send a wrecker. The doctor in the emergency room stitched up their foreheads, and they were on their way back to Dustin before dusk.

Chapter 62

Bandages and the Bride

Nothing was going to stop the wedding. The bride and groom both sported huge bandages on their foreheads, but they didn't mind it a bit. The excitement was in the air as family and friends started arriving at Porter and Fannie's.

Many of Pick's relatives were coming to the wedding, but sadly, both of his sisters and his younger brother Cubbie had decided to stay in the armed forces after the war. Pick was able to locate them with the help of the Red Cross in different places around the globe to tell them about his plans. They were delighted to hear the great news, and let him know how happy (and surprised) they were for their brother and his bride to be.

Pick had already met Julia's sister, Hilda Ruth's husband, Hulbert, and Pearl's husband, Thomas. However, her younger sister Carlene had been out of state for a few weeks while her husband went through training for his new job at the glass making plant over in Henryetta. Carlene and her husband were driving back to Dustin so they could be at Julia's wedding to Pick. Pick had known Carlene from grade school and was anxious to see her again after so many years. He had also heard that her husband's name was James and that he was from Henryetta.

Julia saw Carlene's car drive up in the yard, so she grabbed Pick by the hand to accompany him outside to greet her sister.

"Hi, Carlene!" Julia and Carlene ran and gave each other warm hugs. Pick saw that Carlene still looked like the Carlene he remembered from so many years ago, as he bent down to give her a hug also.

The sun was shining bright that day, and Pick had to shade his eyes as he looked toward the Oldsmobile parked in the Devon's yard. Carlene's husband was bent over getting the suitcases out of the back seat. Pick headed toward their car to help carry in the luggage when Carlene's husband James stood up. He found himself to be face to face with Pick Watie.

"Hello, Pick." The man shyly stuck out his hand for a handshake. You could have knocked Pick over with a feather.

"Jimmy Dyson. James. James Dyson, I guess, huh?" Pick stumbled over his words. It was Jimmy D. Jimmy D. had gone and married Carlene, Julia's sister. Pick was going to be Jimmy D.'s brother-in-law. It was awkward for a moment.

The two grown men were in somewhat of a standoff. Pick, being a forgiving man, went toward Jimmy D. with his hand outstretched. Next Pick went even further and turned the handshake into a bear hug. Jimmy D. was extremely humbled and looked Pick into the eyes and said, "Welcome to the family, brother." His four front teeth sparkled in the sunshine as he smiled.

Chapter 63

Pick and Julia Tie the Knot

The preacher motioned to Porter Devon that the time had come to start the wedding.

Before the ceremony, Pick knelt down and hugged and kissed Julia's two children, Violet and Eddy. He held their faces in his hands and told them that he was going to love them and take good care of them and their momma for the rest of his life.

It was time to marry the woman of his dreams. Pick stood up, straightened his pants and walked toward Julia. He took her dainty hands in his, and with his mile wide grin, tilted his head down toward her face and spoke:

"Julia Rose, I never stopped dreaming about you. God knew my heart, and in His infinite wisdom, He has answered my never ending prayer. I wouldn't be surprised one bit that the good Lord jest got tired of me and that same old prayer, day after day and long night after long, lonely night and jest said to go ahead. I will vow to you before the Lord that I will not stop praying and asking Him to guide me to do my best every single day for the rest of my life to protect you and love you and wrap my arms around you and keep you safe."

Pick couldn't help but think of Psalm 98:8 (ESV): "Let the rivers clap their hands, let the mountains sing together for joy."

Two rivers, joining together like two hands clapping, blending two different worlds to make one flowing stream. Each river carrying the droplets within their depths, the droplets that held the stories. The lives, the hearts, and the stamina of the ancestors that had fought the fight, wept the tears, and laughed until they cried.

When Pick Watie took Julia Rose Devon as his bride, the hills sang together for joy.

The English and the Cherokee joined together until death did they part.

Epilogue

July 15, 2004. The sweltering temperature soared. Six elderly men in VFW hats perched proudly on their balding heads, stood soberly preparing to perform military rites for a deceased local veteran. The trumpet player pursed his lips and slowly filled the air with "Taps."

Sitting under the small tent in the rickety and uncomfortable folding chair, Madelyn could feel the sweat trickle down her back. The dearly beloved were gathered in the cemetery surrounded by so many friends and family members to humbly pay their final respects to Daddy.

Pick Watie and his wife, Julia Rose, raised their family in Miami, Oklahoma. Fifty-four years had passed since the day they had exchanged wedding vows in Porter and Fannie Devon's living room. It was a blessed marriage, and their love for each other never waned. Earlier in the morning, they had held the funeral service in the Northwest Baptist Church. The funeral had been a great tribute to a wonderful man, and after the service concluded, the crowd stood outside the church as his six strong grandsons tenderly loaded the coffin into the waiting hearse.

"They are such a handsome bunch of guys! Daddy would be so proud! " Pick's daughter, Madelyn, thought to herself as she peered out of the window of the limousine as it began the solemn trek to the cemetery. It was a given that those boys would be the pallbearers.

Those six grandsons would never allow anyone else to carry their PaPa for the last time. They knew he was safe in their arms.

A tiny tear trickled down Madelyn's cheek and landed on her chin. She was too weary to wipe it away. After Julia Rose and Pick got married, they added three more daughters to the family. Joining their half siblings, Violet and Eddy, were Madelyn, Josie, and Evette.

"How will any of us go on without that precious man in our lives?" It was her sister, Josie that broke the silence with that question. Everyone was thinking it. It just so happened that Josie was the one that vocalized it. There was no reply. Simply put, no one had an answer to that raw question. No one. Evette, the youngest sister, Daddy's baby daughter, gently patted Josie on her leg and sadly turned her head away. The sound of car doors shutting and engines beginning to purr filtered into the limousine. It was time to go to the cemetery. It was time to take Pick Watie to his final resting place.   It was a very silent ride to the outskirts of town as the procession wound its way to the cemetery.

Madelyn could not take her eyes off of the flag draped coffin in the hearse that led the way.   Daddy was gone.   Madelyn knew it. Josie and Evette knew it.

The thought suddenly crossed her mind.

Did Momma know it?

Momma hadn't shed a tear. Daddy was gone, and Momma hadn't shed a single tear. Daddy's health failed so fast. The love of her life left so suddenly, that it was obvious that Julia Rose Watie was in major denial.

Daddy was Jimmy Stewart and Momma, Momma was Scarlett O'hara! How many times had she faced an insurmountable difficulty and after giving it a moment's thought cheerfully said, "Well, fiddle dee dee! We'll worry about that tomorrow!"

Yep. Julia Rose was in major denial.

Even as they helped Momma back into the limousine after the graveside services were completed, her daughters knew that their mother had been strangely unemotional throughout the entire ordeal.

Less than a week earlier, the doctors had given them a slight ray of hope that with massive doses of intravenous antibiotics, they could possibly win the battle with the life threatening complications of the infection that he had contracted while being hospitalized in Tulsa. Momma never lost that hope that he would be coming home to her.

He would be fine. They would be fine. She refused to accept that he would never be coming home again. That was not the love of her life being lowered into the cold ground as the long, black limousine crept onto the highway as they departed the cemetery.

Life would not go on without him. This was just a bad dream. Julia Rose kept telling herself that after she got back home, she would start supper, and Pick would come strolling through the front door. He would walk over to her and place big kisses all over her forehead. Just like he had always done. Fifty-four years of his kisses. It couldn't end here. That was not enough time. She wanted to wake up and know that the kisses were not over.

Sadly, Julia Rose had even forgotten that she would not be going back home. There would be no cooking happening in her kitchen. She had put it out of her mind that she and Pick had recently been moved to an assisted living facility, unable to care for themselves.

Where had the years gone? When did he get sick?

Poor Momma. Denial was a hard cross to bear.

Back at her home later on that evening, Madelyn's head sank slowly into her cool pillow. It felt so good to be in her own bed. So tired. So very exhausted. She and her husband, Matt, silently drifted off to sleep. Daddy was gone. He was in heaven now. It had been such a long, long day.

"Madelyn! Madelyn! The phone!"

It was her husband Matt. With several nudges of his elbow, she quickly jolted awake to the sound of the ringing of the telephone that was on a nightstand on her side of the bed.

Fumbling in the dark she finally had the receiver firmly in her grasp.

"Hello." She wasn't quite awake. "Hello," she said again. The voice over the phone did not sound at all familiar. As Madelyn sat up in bed, the phone planted against the side of her head, she heard the voice of an elderly woman on the other end.

"Hello, honey. Who is speaking please?"

Madelyn returned the question, "Who are you?"

It suddenly occurred to Madelyn that they had gone to Pick and Julia's house and programmed their parents' phone calls to be forwarded to Madelyn and Matt's house. Since no one was living in their parents' home now and with the word of her daddy's death traveling across the miles, she and Matt decided that it would be easy to transfer the calls to the phone at their house.

This must be someone that had dialed Momma and Daddy's number, Madelyn thought to herself.

"Why, honey, my name is Sarah. Sarah Bingham. Are you any relation to Pick Watie, honey?" The name Sarah sounded vaguely familiar to Madelyn in her sleepy state of mind.

"Sarah... Sarah..." she recirculated the name over and over in her mind.

"Yes, I am Madelyn. Pick Watie's daughter." Her voice trailed off as Madelyn was pensive yet curious.

"Oh, my goodness, Madelyn. Bless your heart. I just read in the Tulsa World that your father, Pick, passed away. I am calling to say how very sorry I am about your loss. He was such a fine and outstanding man. I am an old friend of your daddy's. You might know me by the fact that my brother, John Wainwright, shot your Great Uncle Logan."

"That Sarah? Oh my Lord!" Madelyn's jaw dropped all the way down to the blankets covering her bed.

Immediately, Madelyn lowered the receiver to her chest and looked at her husband Matt and whispered to him. "Matt, wait until I tell Momma who this is on the phone! She is gonna have a cow!"

Madelyn's prediction came true. Julia Rose Watie did have a cow. Possibly an entire herd. Julia had always carried a tinge of jealousy for Sarah Wainwright. Possibly more than a tinge.

To his credit, Pick never given her any reason to believe that Sarah was anything more to him than a old friend. In fact, Pick had spent fifty-four years telling Julia every day that he had carried a torch for his Julia Rose and never thought of any woman but her.

That was all well and fine, but Julia had always had the feeling that Sarah carried a torch for Pick. More like an inferno with an eternal shooting flame. How could she not? Pick Watie had rescued Sarah Wainwright from her dangerous and sad world and introduced her to a life free from the shame of being Lena Wainwright's daughter. Julia even conceded that Sarah had been married for many years to a successful man from Tulsa.

Wild horses could not shake Julia's feeling that Sarah Wainwright Bingham had always been in love with Pick Watie, her husband. In Julia's mind, the phone call from Sarah solidified her hunch. The plot thickened even more when two years later, Julia's daughters showed their mother Sarah Wainwright Bingham's obituary in the Tulsa World. Sarah was dead. She was in heaven now. God rest her soul.

Julia sat in her rocker with a furrowed brow as her daughter, Evette, folded the newspaper in half and began to read aloud from the published account of the life and death of Sarah Wainwright Bingham. With the morning sun washing her face with streaks of warmth, Julia closed her eyes and listened halfheartedly as her daughter ticked off the memorable accomplishments and vital statistics of the recently deceased Sarah Wainwright Bingham.

Sarah Wainwright Bingham. Word after word, line after line,

the obituary seemed to rattle on and on with a cadence that Julia wished would be said and done and over. Suddenly and without hesitation, Julia Rose Watie's hands flew up to her gaping mouth. Horror stricken she hunched forward, peering over her glasses at all three of her daughters and forced out the words, "My God girls, she's in heaven with your daddy."

It seemed as if Julia Rose Watie had given up the will to live. Her three daughters tried everything they could to cheer her up.

Gospel sings. Every song they could think of that usually put a smile on their mother's face fell flat. Even her all time favorite "I Want To Stroll Over Heaven With You," Alan Jackson's melodic and angelic country twang didn't put a dent in Julia's melancholy and overwhelming sadness.

They shook out the entire bag of tricks and lastly one whole Saturday afternoon, Madelyn, Josie, and Evette climbed in bed with their mother and turned the television station to the Dallas Cowboy Cheerleader tryouts. Julia absolutely hated football, but she had gotten hooked on the cheerleader tryouts. The girls and their mother watched and cheered their favorite contestants on with Julia usually solidly nailing the winning names. She had a very good eye for talent. Alas, when the episode was over, so was Julia.

"I'm ready to go. I don't want to be here anymore without Pick" Julia told her daughters as they gathered around her bed three weeks later. She was dying of congestive heart failure. (Her daughters called it "missing Daddy in her heart" failure.)

Josie patted her mother's frail hand and bent down to give her a soft kiss on her forehead. "Momma, the doctor is going to try a different type of heart medicine. We don't want you to go."

"Girls, please let me go. I don't want to try any more medicines. I miss your daddy. I've had a wonderful life here on earth, and I am ready to go to heaven. I will miss you so much, but I am ready to go. Besides that, Sarah is up there with your daddy, and I just can't stand it anymore. I need to be up there!"

Julia ached to be with Pick again. She knew she was being overly dramatic about Sarah, but it was unbearable to think Pick and Sarah were in heaven together. Of course she knew Pick would be the same sweet and gallant man as he was on earth, but did Jesus possibly orchestrate things whereby Sarah may have just passed by and waved and Pick was busy with his new heavenly duties and just returned her wave with a cursory smile? Julia searched her mind for the perfect scripture, any scripture that would assure her that Jesus had everything under control in heaven.

She fretted about it for a moment and felt a stabbing pain in her chest that took her breath away before a beautiful sense of peace overtook her mind. She knew she was dying, and she wasn't afraid at all. Julia couldn't think of anything more divine than to be able to take her last breath on earth and be instantly reunited with the man that showed her what true love looked like for 54 years. Pick was the best thing that had ever happened to her, and she missed him more than words could express.

Julia struggled to breathe even though she had an oxygen mask secured tightly to her face. She was comforted knowing that her family was in her room. She was unable to open her eyes to look at them, and that seemed to be exactly how it was supposed to be. Her family had said their goodbyes after the doctor came in and told them that Julia's organs were in the process of shutting down. It seemed to Julia that she was floating above her hospital bed. It was peaceful. The distant click of the monitors beside her lulled her to a place of stillness and reflection. She almost giggled to herself as the vision of life with Pick passed through her head like a movie on the screen at the Coleman Theatre. He was so comical. Even fights with Pick usually ended with the two of them bursting out in laughter.

"Julia!"

The light in the distance was blinding her as she strained her eyes to see who the figure was that was running toward her. She felt light as a feather as she began to run toward him.

It was Pick.